Hand-Manipulated Stitches
for Machine Knitters

Hand-Manipulated Stitches
for Machine Knitters

Susan Guagliumi

The Taunton Press

Library of Congress Cataloging-in-Publication Data

Guagliumi, Susan, 1948-
    Hand-manipulated stitches for machine knitters / Susan Guagliumi.
        p.   cm.
    "A Threads book."
    includes bibliographical references.
    ISBN 0-942391-03-9 $29.95
    1. Knitting, Machine.   2. Knitting, Machine—Patterns.   I. Title.
TT682.G83   1990
746.43'2--dc20   89-51219
                                                                   CIP

PHOTOS BY JOSEPH KUGIELSKY

© 1990 by The Taunton Press, Inc.
All rights reserved

First printing: May 1990
Second printing: October 1990
Printed in the United States of America

A *Threads* Book

Threads magazine® is a trademark of The Taunton Press, Inc.
registered in the U.S. Patent and Trademark Office.

The Taunton Press
63 South Main Street
Box 5506
Newtown, Conn. 06470-5506

To my mother, Frances Fletcher, who did what mothers do a bit better than most, especially for ten years of summer camp and for letting the dog sleep on the bed.

Contents

.

Acknowledgments

My sincere thanks to a number of friends in the knitting-machine, yarn and publishing industries for their assistance and support, especially Helen Deckelman, who introduced me to my first knitting machine; Susan Berke; Chris Cook; Yo Furuta; Vivianne Lavinskas; Rob Pulleyn; Dick and Anita Rollins; Gary Welden; the staff of *Threads* magazine; and Heirloom Yarns, which provided all the yarns used for the swatches shown in this book.

In my extensive job-related travels through the country in recent years, I've worked with many talented knitters and teachers who have been generous with their ideas. Their input and encouragement were important factors in getting this book written. I am grateful in particular to Gene Bailey, Denis Cook, Carolyn Dadisman, Chris Gibbons, Lynne Higgins, Susanna Lewis, Chrystina Sheldon and Bonnie Triola.

I would also like to thank all of the knitting-machine dealers whom I have trained over the last few years and who, in turn, managed to teach me a thing or two—most notably, Janet Austin, Barbara French, Eileen Cronin, Carlene Sage and Betty Wilkinson.

Without the help of two very patient friends, I would never have become computer literate or been physically able to sit at the knitting machine for more than an hour. Respective thanks to David Swift and Dr. Bill Ziedman.

I wish there were a more adequate phrase than "thank you" to express my gratitude to Chris Timmons for the energy and effort she put into editing this book. Her warmth, wit and gentle ways made it a unique pleasure working with her and the "ladies of the committee."

To Arthur and Jordan, who deserve medals for their patience and confidence in this project, I can only offer my love and my thanks.

*Susan Guagliumi
Cheshire, Connecticut
May 1990*

Introduction

When I encountered my first knitting machine, I had been a hand weaver for more than ten years. By then, I had also learned to hand knit, but the yield of my efforts was only a few hats and two Aran sweaters. These sweaters, however, were challenging enough for me to conclude that beautiful knits grow from a marriage of hands and time — lots of time. And, although I enjoyed the intricacy of forming all those ivory-colored stitches, the fact is, knitting those Arans was a slow, painful experience. But they did serve to define knitting for me as involving texture and considerable hand manipulation.

Although my first knitting machine offered all kinds of electronic possibilities for design and discovery, what I saw in it was a vehicle for merging intricate patterns with practicality. For the first time in my lifelong passion for textiles, I saw hope that my hands and my head would finally keep pace with each other.

My first machine-knit sweater was a simple rose-colored turtleneck with a pair of cables up the front, which I tried to split so they would continue on either side of the neck. I consulted every machine-knitting book I could find, but none of them offered much more than a basic cable or came close to addressing how to work a diagonal cable. So I decided it couldn't be done and settled for a cable that ended at the neckline. My quest for that diagonal cable, however, planted the seeds for this book.

A knitting machine, like a pair of hand-knitting needles, is a means to an end, a tool. It enables you to produce a variety of useful products, quickly explore inspirations, experiment with new ideas and make a very personal fashion statement. Yet, without you to call the shots, the machine is really worthless. Of course, it takes some time and effort to learn to knit on the machine, but as with any skill, the practice and effort yield rewards, and soon you're likely to grow interested in going beyond what's familiar, easy and controlled by the machine.

For all its practicality, though, the knitting machine is, above all, the ultimate textile toy. While we may be pleased with the useful things it produces, the truth of the matter is that most of us really think of machine knitting as fun — and for me, fun equates with play. What I mean by play is the freedom to define things to suit the needs at hand — that is, not being bound by someone else's expectations, rules or methods. And from the start, I've played with my knitting machines. I've explored every possibility that occurred to me and developed two simple rules that help me evaluate each new technique or method I try: [1] If it works (and I know what I did and can repeat it again), it's right. [2] If there's an order or rhythm to what I do with my hands, there must be a resulting order or pattern in the fabric.

This approach to machine knitting always leaves room for the "happy accident," which usually leads to more exploration and play. I do knit sweaters and I enjoy knitting them, but I'm more often challenged by the designing, planning and playing that lead up to the sweater than by actually producing the garment. Consequently, this is a book of fabric textures and techniques rather than sweater patterns. Yet once you start applying these techniques to standard garment shapes, I'm sure you'll have more sweater ideas than time to knit them.

One of the best things about hand-manipulated stitches is that they are basically generic in nature. They don't depend on having a particular model or brand of machine. Any machine can be used for these techniques — and used well — provided the knitter makes an effort to practice and master them. (Though all knitting machines produce knit, tuck and slip stitches, the way they produce these stitches in combination is what distinguishes one machine from another. In general, all Japanese machines function similarly, the Passap differs totally and Superba/White machines bear similarities to both.)

Hand-manipulated techniques enable you to override and/or enhance some functions that are otherwise automatically controlled by the machine. By hand manipulating yarn, stitches, needles or carriage cams, you can create rich, unpredictable fabrics that the machine alone cannot produce. Human intervention allows the machine to function at its most creative and you to achieve both designer looks and traditional classics on the same needle bed.

Most of the techniques in this book emphasize single-bed knitting because it's generally easier and less clumsy than maneuvering hands and tools in the space between two beds. However, some techniques are presented for double-bed work, and many others could be applied or adapted for two beds. With regard to the other specifics of this book, all samples were knitted on a chunky-gauge (9mm) machine for reasons of production speed and photographic clarity. For the same reasons, Heirloom's "Reflection" acrylic yarn was used for most of the samples and was knitted on stitch size 6.

How you use the techniques in this book depends largely on your knitting skills and experience as well as your taste. Whether you've ever hand knitted or crocheted is also likely to influence you when deciding if a particular method is worth the time it will take. Clearly some of these techniques are impractical for allover use and are intended for accent, and others are not suitable for beginners. I hope nonetheless that, even if you're new to the machine, you'll soon be working the more challenging methods and finding new uses for and variations on the techniques with which you're familiar. Perhaps, too, these chapters will remind you of maneuvers you may have forgotten or used differently in the past, and so provide further challenges, possibilities and inspiration.

The book itself is divided into two sections. The first two chapters are aimed at familiarizing you with the fundamentals of the machine and the basic maneuvers at the heart of all hand-manipulated techniques. The last six chapters present a glossary of hand-manipulated stitches, including twisted, wrapped and woven, lifted, rehung, transferred and crossed, or cabled, patterns. If you read the first section of the book before going on to the second, I think you'll find it easy to make your way through any pattern. The chapters in the second section of the book can be read in any order since each technique presented is independent of the others.

To help make the book easy to use, the first chapter contains a fully annotated glossary of symbols used in the charts throughout the book (an abbreviated symbol chart also accompanies each chapter). At the end of Chapter 1, you'll also find a list of the abbreviations used in the knitting directions and many of the photo captions.

With regard to the specifics of the knitting directions, many patterns call for beginning with the carriage on the left or right in order to simplify the instruction. If you're more comfortable starting from the opposite side of the bed, you can, of course, do so, substituting left for right (or vice versa) throughout the pattern directions. Also, I've often provided alternative methods for some of the techniques, which produce the same or similar results. The differences in method may involve the level of difficulty, various means of overcoming machine-imposed limitations or my continuing effort to reduce the number of yarn ends needing to be finished off (a task I dislike). Finally, any of the techniques presented in one color can always be varied by using two or more colors.

To help you use this book and the techniques it presents, the back matter, which begins on p. 209, contains additional reference tools. There, you'll find an appendix on planning garments with hand-manipulated stitches, a glossary of terms, a bibliography, a list of sources of supply, and an index.

If, as a machine knitter, you've begun to wonder, "How can I make the machine do this or that;" if you find the result more important than the time it takes to knit; if the eyelet tools have begun to feel like extensions of your fingers; if you find yourself measuring sweaters by the number of cables instead of by the clock; you've come to the right place! Turn the page, and get your transfer tools ready.

THE PRELIMINARIES

CHAPTER 1

Before You Begin

Knitting machines are wonderful tools. They can automatically knit in minutes what would take hours to knit by hand. Yet although these machines can effortlessly perform a host of knitting maneuvers, there are some stitches and effects that the machine alone cannot execute. For these stitches and effects, the human hand must override the machine, and it is these hand-manipulated techniques that are the subject of this book.

In order to understand the mechanics of manually overriding a knitting machine, you must first understand the basics of the machine and how it forms stitches. If you stripped away the dials, levers and knobs

on any knitting machine, you would be left with the machine's most essential parts: the bed and the carriage (see the drawing below). The bed holds the machine's needles, and the carriage simply moves the needles back and forth in their slots on the bed to form stitches.

If your machine is like most, when you look at the underside of the carriage, you'll see what are called cams as well as some brushes and/or wheels and some magnets. The cams are a series of movable metal or plastic parts that alter their configuration to form three distinct pathways through which the machine's needles can pass. There is a triangular (or, so-called, working) pathway in the midsection of the

KNITTING MACHINE.

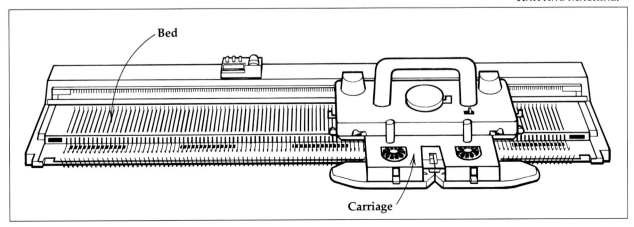

Bed

Carriage

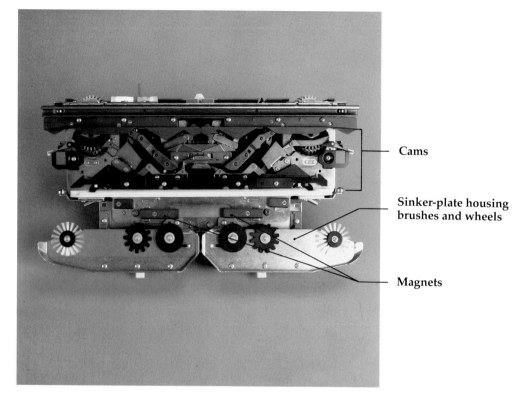

Cams

Sinker-plate housing
brushes and wheels

Magnets

*ELEMENTS OF
COMMON MACHINE
CARRIAGES.*

*On the underside of
this common
carriage, the brushes,
wheels and magnets
in the lower portion
assist the cams in
the upper portion to
form stitches.*

carriage and a straight channel across both
the top and bottom of the carriage. These
pathways accommodate the knitting and
nonknitting positions of the needles, which
determine where the needle butts enter the
pathways and whether the needles will
knit or perform some other function. On
most machines, the cams can be shifted by
a cam lever on the top of the carriage to
produce a variety of stitches and stitch
combinations. The photos above and on
the facing page show the parts of a
knitting-machine carriage.

The brushes and/or wheels on the
underside of the carriage help the machine
form stitches by keeping the fabric close to
the bed, where it belongs. The magnets
open the needle latches when the needles
are in one of the positions in which new
stitches can be formed.

As shown in the drawing on the facing
page, there are four needle positions on
the beds of most knitting machines

(Passap has two). Moving from the front
to the back of the bed, these positions are:
holding, upper working, working and
nonworking (see the chart on p. 235 for
the various brands' designation of these
needle positions). In order for needles to
form stitches, they must be in working or
upper working position. In either position,
as the carriage moves across the bed, the
needles' butts will be scooped up at the
entrance to the triangular pathway and
move the needles through the pathway to
form stitches. The needles that are pushed
all the way back to nonworking position
are too far back on the bed to connect with
the working pathway and form stitches.
Instead they will simply pass straight
through the lower channel on the
underside of the carriage. Similarly,
needles pushed all the way forward into
holding position will not connect with the
working pathway but instead pass straight
through the upper channel.

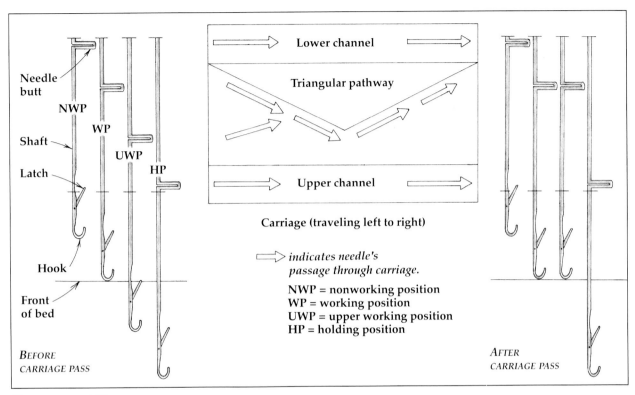

Carriage (traveling left to right)

⇨ *indicates needle's passage through carriage.*

NWP = nonworking position
WP = working position
UWP = upper working position
HP = holding position

BEFORE CARRIAGE PASS

AFTER CARRIAGE PASS

NEEDLE POSITIONS ON BED AND IN CARRIAGE.

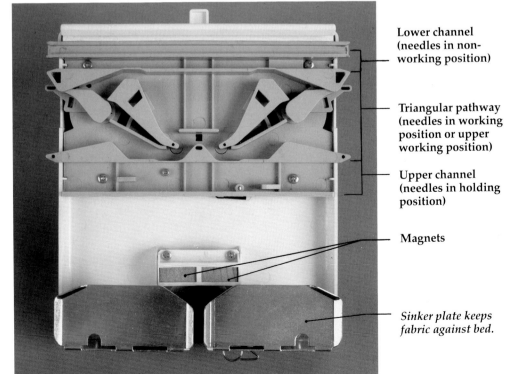

PATHWAYS ON A MACHINE CARRIAGE.
The underside of this very basic carriage clearly shows the three pathways found on all knitting machines, through which the machine needles can pass. The pathway traveled by the needles determines whether they form stitches and what type of stitches they will make.

Lower channel (needles in non-working position)

Triangular pathway (needles in working position or upper working position)

Upper channel (needles in holding position)

Magnets

Sinker plate keeps fabric against bed.

*FORMATION OF A
KNIT STITCH.*

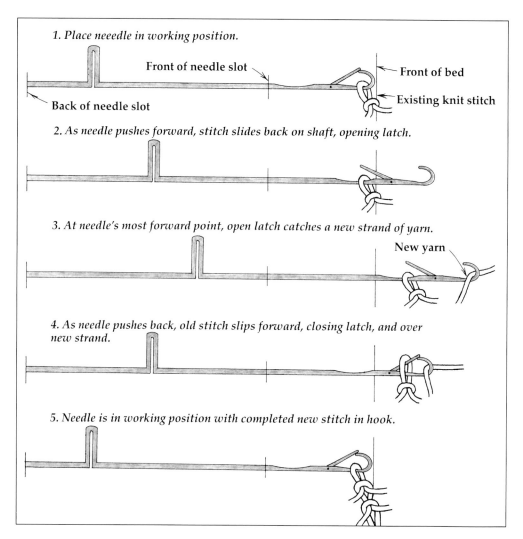

1. Place neeedle in working position.

Front of needle slot

Front of bed

Back of needle slot

Existing knit stitch

2. As needle pushes forward, stitch slides back on shaft, opening latch.

3. At needle's most forward point, open latch catches a new strand of yarn.

New yarn

4. As needle pushes back, old stitch slips forward, closing latch, and over new strand.

5. Needle is in working position with completed new stitch in hook.

*NEEDLE'S
MOVEMENT IN
CARRIAGE TO FORM
KNIT STITCH.*

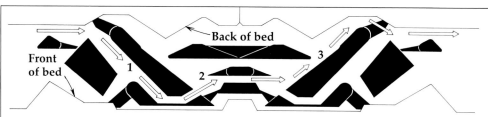

Back of bed

Front
of bed

1

2

3

Knit stitches are formed in five distinct steps (see the drawings on the facing page). First, with the needle in working position, the needle butt enters the triangular pathway, where the entire needle is then pushed forward, causing the existing stitch on the needle to open the latch and slide back on the needle's shaft. Next, at the needle's most forward point, its open hook catches the yarn from the carriage feeder. Finally, as the butt travels back in the pathway, the needle pulls back in its slot. The old stitch slips over the closed latch and off the needle, leaving a new stitch in the hook. This series of movements is mimicked when a needle is manually manipulated to "hand knit" a stitch on the machine.

If your carriage has additional cams, as many do, it can automatically produce not only knit stitches but also tuck and slip stitches when the cam levers or the carriage dial are set to tuck or slip. A tuck stitch is formed by the same three movements that produce a knit stitch, but with the carriage set to tuck, the triangular pathway is shortened (see the drawings at right and below). As a result, the needle passing through the pathway never comes far enough forward for the stitch to slide behind the latch. Instead it comes forward only enough to open the latch and allow the needle hook to grab another length of yarn from the carriage before the needle returns to working position upon leaving the carriage. The loops thus accumulate on the needle until the knitter manually changes the needle's position or function, or adjusts the carriage settings to enable the needle to form another knit stitch. As the knit stitch forms, all the loops on the needle slide over the closed latch and appear as texture on the fabric's purl side.

The number of loops, or tuck stitches, a needle can collect depends on the size of the yarn, the size of the stitch and how much weight has been used to hold the fabric firmly on the machine. This number varies greatly from one machine to another, but most machines can collect six to eight tucks on a needle before the needle has difficulty knitting them off. The Passap is an exception to this rule. Its carriage, or lock, as it is called, has stripper blades that push the fabric down and enable the machine to pile numerous tucks on a needle without jamming.

FORMATION OF A TUCK STITCH.

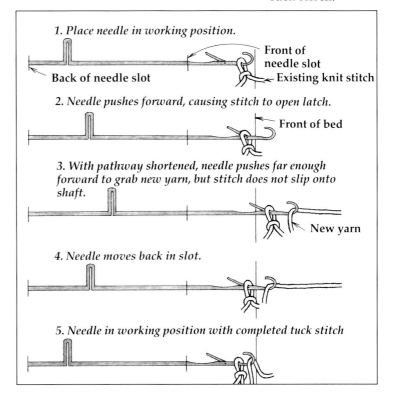

1. *Place needle in working position.*
   Front of needle slot
   Back of needle slot
   Existing knit stitch

2. *Needle pushes forward, causing stitch to open latch.*
   Front of bed

3. *With pathway shortened, needle pushes far enough forward to grab new yarn, but stitch does not slip onto shaft.*
   New yarn

4. *Needle moves back in slot.*

5. *Needle in working position with completed tuck stitch*

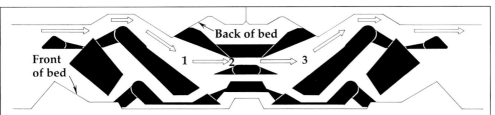

Back of bed
Front of bed
1   2   3

NEEDLE'S MOVEMENT IN CARRIAGE TO FORM TUCK STITCH.

When the carriage is set to slip, the cams shift to block the triangular pathway. Thus needles in working position are shunted straight through the carriage's lower channel without knitting, as shown in the drawings below. The needles may rise slightly in their slots, but they do not move forward and back to form stitches or collect tuck loops. Instead, the yarn simply slips across the needle and settles below its hook, forming a small float, or slip stitch, on the purl side of the fabric.

In practical terms, tuck and slip stitches need to be used in combination with knit stitches, which anchor them. That is to say, if more than two adjacent needles in a row try to tuck, there will be a tangle of unsecured loops lying across the needle hooks and the carriage will jam. And if all the needles in a row try to slip, nothing happens to any of them. The carriage simply makes a free pass. Thus, the more adjacent needles slipped, the longer the float between knitting needles.

On machines capable of automatically producing a given pattern of knit and tuck or slip stitches, you must set the cam lever to tuck or slip and use either a punchcard or an electronic design card to tell the needles what to do. According to the information the carriage receives from the selection system, it will simultaneously issue two sets of commands to the machine, one telling certain needles to form knit stitches and the second telling other needles to form tuck or slip stitches. The carriage can also be set to knit two colors at once or to slip or tuck when the carriage moves in one direction and to knit when it travels the other way, as shown in the drawing on the facing page. (Some Brother and Knitking machines preselect needles for automatic patterning. That is to say, as each row is knitted, the carriage selects the needles for the next row and places them in upper working position. This makes it easy to identify the exact placement of patterns and hand-manipulated techniques without having to count needles.)

When you manually select needles, it's possible to combine knit, tuck and slip stitches all in one row. For example, if you set the cams to slip and manually place certain needles in working position, others in upper working position and still others in holding position, the needles in working position will slip, those in

FORMATION OF A SLIP STITCH.

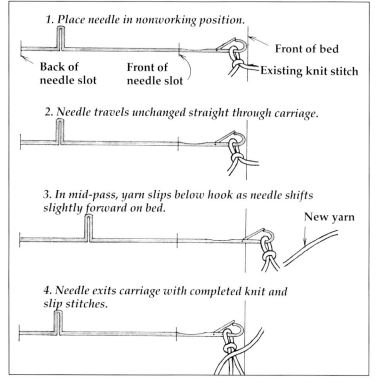

1. *Place needle in nonworking position.*

Back of needle slot   **Front of needle slot**   **Front of bed**   **Existing knit stitch**

2. *Needle travels unchanged straight through carriage.*

3. *In mid-pass, yarn slips below hook as needle shifts slightly forward on bed.*

New yarn

4. *Needle exits carriage with completed knit and slip stitches.*

NEEDLE'S MOVEMENT IN CARRIAGE TO FORM SLIP STITCH.

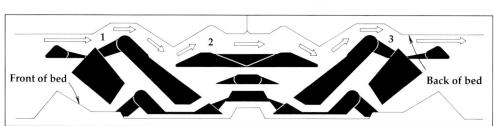

Front of bed   **Back of bed**

upper working position will knit, and those in holding position will tuck. Although using a punchcard or electronic design card would considerably speed up such a maneuver, it still requires manual intervention to "hand pull" the tucking needles since most carriages can only deliver two sets of instructions to the needles at once.

In order to enable needles in holding position to resume knitting, you can either manually or (depending on your pattern and machine) automatically return them to work. On all machines (except Passap), upper working position functions as a manual return position for needles in hold. You can manually control the number of needles returned to work by nudging some from holding to upper working position and leaving others in hold.

On very simple knitting machines, putting needles in upper working position is generally the only way to return them to working position without using transfer tools. However, most machines have levers or knobs that can be set to shunt all the needles down to upper working position so they can knit. These levers will return all needles in holding position since they cannot selectively return some and leave others in hold. Unfortunately, every brand has a different name for this control, but when you see a reference to Holding Cam Levers, Partial Knit Levers, N-H Buttons, Russell Levers, I/II Levers or Needle Return Buttons, you can be sure they are all names for the same thing. (Passap holds and returns needles with the BX setting with pushers.)

Manual intervention enables you at any point to override the command given to the needles by a punchcard or electronic design card. If you manually select needles when using an automatic selection system, you introduce a third stitch possibility since most selection systems provide for only two needle functions in a single row (for example, knit and tuck stitches or two differently colored knit stitches). As you will see in a number of the sample swatches in other chapters, overriding carriage commands by manual selection enables you to create new patterns. You'll also find that with manual selection, not all the needles in a row have to be considered for patterning and, conversely, you can manage patterns wider than the repeat capability of your selection system.

On a single-bed machine, all the needles face the same direction, and hence the stitches these needles produce also face the same direction. Thus, a single-bed machine is capable only of producing rows of knit and/or tuck or slip stitches. Without manual intervention, it cannot produce knit (or tuck or slip) stitches and purl stitches in the same row.

In order to automatically produce knit and purl stitches in the same row, you must have two beds of needles facing in opposite directions. That is, you must have a double-bed machine or be able to add a second bed to your single-bed machine. The two beds not only enable you to produce ribbing automatically, but also make it possible to work a variety of patterned, textured and structural variations on the fabrics that can be produced by a single-bed machine. A second bed can sometimes enhance the function of the main bed, making it work

NEEDLE'S MOVEMENT IN CARRIAGE TO FORM TUCK STITCHES SELECTIVELY.

At point X, selection takes place. All the needle butts enter carriage together, but, according to punchcard or electronic pattern, they are divided so that some knit and others tuck or slip, or some knit one color and others knit another color.

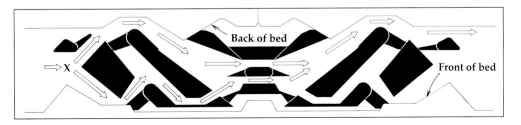

Back of bed

X

Front of bed

more easily and efficiently and extending its versatility with an expanded range of stitch sizes and combinations. But even if you don't have a second bed, you can still produce some double-bed effects by manually forming or reforming specific stitches (see pp. 69-81).

How machines change stitch sizes

Hand knitters accommodate various yarn weights by changing the size of their needles, and, generally speaking, the thicker the yarn, the larger the needle needed to knit it. On a knitting machine, the needles are sized and positioned on the bed for yarns within one of two specific ranges: standard and bulky or chunky. On standard-gauge machines, which are designed for fingering, sport and fine-weight yarns, the needles are set apart from one another either 4.5mm (as on Japanese machines) or 5mm (as on European machines). On bulky and chunky machines, the needles are twice as large as those on a standard-gauge machine and are set apart 8mm and 9mm respectively. These machines are designed for four-ply worsted weights and heavier fashion yarns. Recent additions to the market also include simple 6.5mm and 7mm mid-gauge machines, which are designed to handle the heaviest standard-gauge yarns and lightest chunky yarn (see the chart on p. 234).

Because the yarn must comfortably fit the hooks of the needles and the spacing between them, there is no single machine that can knit every type and weight of yarn. In addition, the weight of the machine itself will make a difference in the ease with which it knits certain yarns. For example, as capable as they are, none of the simple, all-plastic machines handles the extremely heavy yarns as easily as does a regular machine with metal cams. Nonetheless, standard-gauge and bulky knitting machines are each capable of working with a wide variety of yarns within their respective ranges.

The extent of the yarn range on any particular machine is determined by a stitch-size dial, which controls one pair of cams in the triangular pathway. Turning this dial shifts the cams to lengthen or shorten the pathway, causing the needles to take more or less yarn yarn into each stitch. (The Bond machine uses a series of four permanent "keyplates" to form triangular pathways of different lengths.) The stitch sizes on the dial of most machines range from zero to ten, with partial sizes in between. This stitch-size range can be finely tuned by adjusting the tension on the yarn before it enters the carriage and by the number of weights hung on the fabric as it is produced. Tension and weight together control how much a stitch relaxes (or expands) as it forms.

Knitting machines are generally calibrated to function best with a yarn size in the middle of their range, and they usually don't work as smoothly or easily with yarn sizes at either end of their spectrum. Thus, if you want to work with chunky yarn, use a chunky machine, and conversely, if you want to work with a sport-weight yarn, use a standard-gauge machine. It is true that most standard-gauge machines will knit four-ply worsted-weight yarn on every other needle, but this is not what these machines were designed to do, nor is it a feat for beginners. By the same token, chunky machines can technically knit sport-weight yarns, but they don't do very well with them — especially when it comes to ribbing. The new 6.5mm and 7mm machines may be the answer for working with yarns too large for standard-gauge and too thin for chunky machines, but at this point these gauges are made only in very basic models, for which ribbers are not currently available.

For the most part, you can use the same yarns for hand-manipulated techniques on the machine as you would choose for other machine-knitting projects, provided they are sturdy enough to withstand the handling, holding or twisting you intend to subject them to. When you are first learning to knit on the machine or to hand-manipulate stitches, light-colored, smooth-textured yarns will be the easiest to see and knit. In general, soft, stretchy yarns in two or three plies are best of all to work with on the machine. Although I feel that wool is the easiest, most forgiving fiber to work with, I know that not everyone else wants to or can work with it. For those who prefer nonwoolen yarns, there are lots of good synthetics and blends to choose from. Try to avoid inelastic yarns like cotton, linen and silk until you are sure of yourself and the technique. Whatever fiber you decide to work with, don't waste your efforts on cheap, bargain yarns. Completing a garment with some of these techniques will require a serious investment of time, and you should be sure that the quality of the yarn you choose is worthy of your efforts.

A glossary of tools

In addition to the basic tools supplied with all machines, the following are some that I have found useful and, in some cases, essential for certain techniques. As you become more involved with hand manipulations, you are likely to find that the right tool, no matter how simple, can make a task faster, less tedious and more efficient to perform.

Like knitting machines, tools are produced in standard and chunky gauges. Provided the gauges are compatible, you can use the tools from one machine on another, even if the machines are made by different companies. Any tool designed to remove and replace stitches on needles must be

the same gauge as the machine or half its gauge so that the tool's prongs line up with the machine's needles. All brands of Japanese standard-gauge (4.5mm) tools are interchangeable, and they can also be used on every other needle of the 9mm chunky-gauge machines. They will not, however, fit the 8mm bulky needles. Passap and White standard-gauge tools are interchangeable only with each other. In the text below, when gauge is unmentioned, the tools in question are available for both standard and chunky machines. When gauge is specified, the tool is available only in that gauge.

Tools for selecting, moving, holding and repairing stitches

Creating patterns on a knitting machine frequently involves selecting certain needles to knit while others slip, tuck or hold. Using selection tools makes this process considerably easier. Plastic needle pushers (number 1 in the photo on p. 13) enable you to select a number of needles at once, according to the arrangement of their "teeth." These tools are produced in a variety of configurations, enabling you to push or pull, for example, every second, third or sixth needle. There are a number of other arrangements available too, or you can make your own tool out of cardboard. To make a custom needle pusher, use the plastic every-other-needle pusher that came with your machine as a guide so that the teeth are properly spaced. Then cut away the teeth you don't need or add them where you do. Passap and White both have movable selectors, and Singer and Studio have a similar tool for chunky machines.

In many of the techniques presented in this book, stitches need to be moved from one set of needles to another, and for this purpose, moving tools are needed. Transfer tools (sometimes called eyelet or decker tools) are most commonly used for moving stitches. Pairs of one-prong, two-prong and three-prong transfer tools are generally supplied with all machines as standard equipment, but various other transfer tools are also available. Whenever you buy additional tools that might be used for techniques that require handling two groups of stitches simultaneously (like cables), try to buy these tools in pairs.

Some fixed transfer tools (2) have more than three prongs. Whether for Japanese or European standard-gauge or chunky-gauge machines, there are specific tools that can handle 15, 30 and 45 stitches and some that are spaced for every other needle.

Adjustable transfer tools (3) allow you to set each prong in a working or nonworking position, according to the spacing you need for a particular pattern. Passap makes an excellent adjustable 15-prong tool, and the Japanese machines all have 7-prong standard-gauge tools that can also be used as 4-prong tools on the chunky machines.

Garter bars (4) are used for turning the knitting over to produce garter stitch or ridges of reversed stitches and for evenly spacing increases and decreases across the fabric. Garter bars are used on single-bed machines to cross small cables and to hold the yarns for vertical weaving techniques. You can even use them as stitch holders if you add some kind of a cap to prevent the stitches from sliding off the prongs. I use the plastic spines sold in office-supply stores to secure report folders, snapping the spine over the prongs of the garter bar and holding it in place with a rubber band at each end.

Garter bars have long been available in standard gauge, and recently were introduced in chunky-gauge for Japanese machines, though unfortunately none of the latter was available for photographing at press time. (Because there is no garter bar for European machines, garter stitch is is produced by a transfer carriage, with interior increases and decreases executed by scrapping off and rehanging the fabric.) A standard-gauge garter bar can also be used on the chunky machines by using only every other prong. Similarly, the chunky garter bar can be used to remove every other stitch from a standard-gauge bed.

Standard-gauge garter bars generally come in three sections that can be joined to handle up to 200 stitches. There is also a mini-garter bar that holds 30 stitches, which is useful for working with narrow pieces. It can also be used as a stitch holder for vertical embroidery. Unlike other garter bars, its prongs fit between the sinker posts, enabling it to be used like a regular transfer tool.

There is also a garter bar manufactured for the 8mm bulky machine, which, in light of the general lack of 8mm accessories, is well worth having. None of the mid-gauge machines has a garter bar.

Some of the standard-gauge Japanese machines have what is called a shadow lace tool (5). This hinged, double-bed tool is designed to transfer groups of 20 stitches from one bed to the other for a technique the Japanese call shadow lace. (It can also be used to make adjacent transfers on a single-bed machine, but it is far more cumbersome than tools specifically designed for this purpose.) The stitches are removed from their needles with one side of the open tool. When it closes, the stitches are shifted to the other side of the tool and replaced on the opposite bed.

Special carriages are available for making lace, doing intarsia, transferring stitches from one bed to another and releasing stitches from the needles. (Since, from the top, these carriages look like a regular knitting carriage and the mechanics of their underside differ so greatly from one brand to the next, none is shown in the photograph.) Intarsia and release carriages are available for a variety of machines. Lace carriages that make lateral transfers are available only for Japanese single-bed machines, while transfer carriages are available for standard-gauge Japanese and

European machines. These carriages are generally not interchangeable between machines or brands.

In many hand-manipulated techniques, stitches need to be removed from the needles and temporarily placed on holding tools while other maneuvers take place. Capped stitch holders (6) are designed to securely remove and easily replace stitches on needles. These holders can also be used as transfer tools for moving groups of stitches. Depending on the manufacturer, these holders range from a 10-stitch to 70-stitch capacity and are available in 4.5mm, 5mm and 9mm gauges.

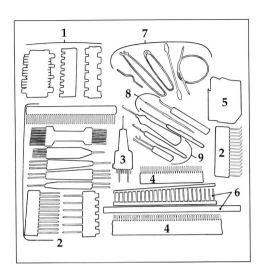

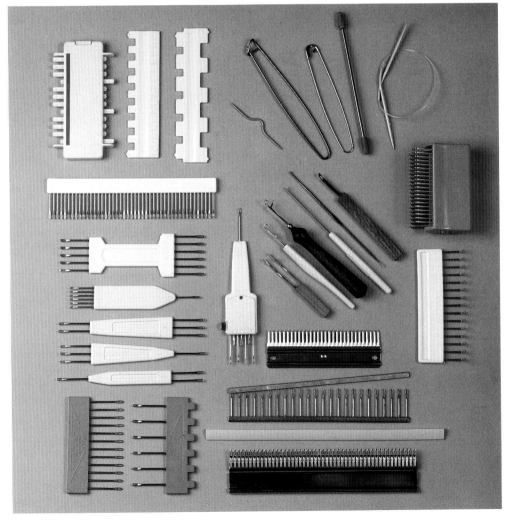

TOOLS FOR SELECTING, MOVING, HOLDING AND REPAIRING STITCHES.
(1) Needle pushers and selectors; (2) fixed transfer tools; (3) adjustable, 7-prong transfer tool; (4) garter bars; (5) shadow lace tool; (6) capped stitch holder and plastic spine for garter bar; (7) stitch holders; (8) pointed picks and threading hooks; and (9) latch tools.

In addition to safety pins and the clasped stitch holders used in hand knitting, knitting needles—especially flexible circular needles and cable needles (7)—make handy stitch holders for stitches being moved or held out of the way while the knitting continues. Held on circular or cable needles, the stitches can be individually slipped back onto the needles of the machine quite easily. Rubber tips are also available for capping the needles to prevent stitches from slipping off the ends.

In the event that stitches are dropped and need to be picked up and repaired, you will find the task more easily done with repair tools. Many machines come with pointed picks and ribber threading hooks (8) for this purpose. The Unicorn is a combination pick-and-transfer tool, with a pointed end that also has an eyelet for picking up tight stitches and transferring the retrieved stitches back to their needles.

All machines come with a crochet hook and a single tappet, or latch, tool (9), which is used to repair dropped stitches and to reform stitches for ribs or tuck. There are also double tappet tools with the latches paired side by side for speedy latch-ups or placed end to end for double-bed bind-offs and reversing stitches.

Weighting tools

Weights are important because, when hung on the fabric, they help stitches remain open and clear of the needles' latches. Like any tool, of course, they must be used properly. Too much weight on the fabric makes the stitches hard to handle and prone to run when dropped, while too little weight makes stitches split easily and transfer poorly. Weighting tools are shown in the photo on the facing page.

Claw weights (1) come in a variety of sizes and shapes and are easy to move as needed. Some weights have holes in their centers so that additional weights can be hung from them.

Ribber combs and weights (2) are usually supplied with the ribber or double-bed unit but can also be used for single-bed knitting. You can leave them in place after knitting ribbing and transferring the stitches to the main bed, or you can poke them through a fabric when needed for weight.

Combs with open hooks (3) are used for casting on when all the stitches need to be held under equal tension. These tools come in handy when working with lace knitting or with large, loose stitches that need weighting to keep them on the needles. These combs can be hung on the fabric after it has been cast on, and ribber weights or claws can be added as needed to the combs.

Wire edge hangers (4) can be used to weight small groups of stitches. Paper clips and deep-sea fishing weights are a handy alternative tool.

Yarn tails can be held securely by clothespins, stationary clips or fanciful "birds" (5).

Small quantities of yarns for weaving or intarsia can be wound on hand knitting argyle bobbins, netting shuttles, lace bobbins or plastic Easy Bobs (6). You can also suspend a ball of bulky yarn inside a zippered plastic bag and let the weight of the yarn help tension the stitches, or alternatively wind finger butterflies to use as small weights, as shown in the bottom left drawing on the facing page.

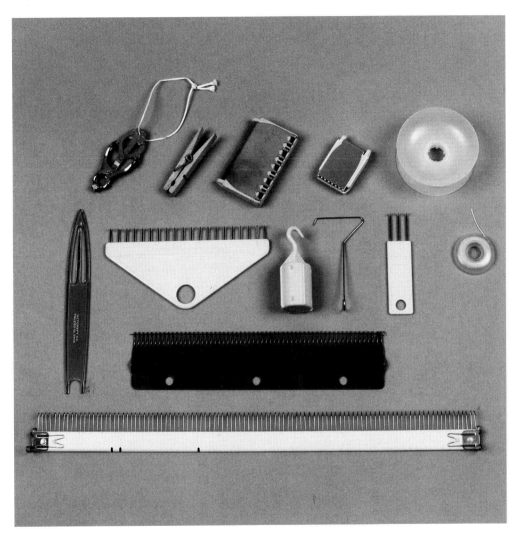

WEIGHTING TOOLS.
*(1) Claw weights;
(2) ribber comb and
weight; (3) comb
with open hooks;
(4) wire edge hanger;
(5) clothespin and
yarn bird clip; and
(6) netting shuttle,
at left, and Easy Bob
and yarn bobbins,
at right.*

*WINDING A
BUTTERFLY.*

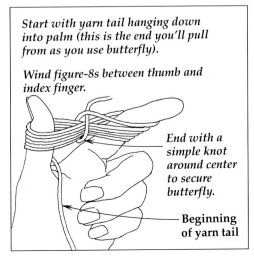

Start with yarn tail hanging down
into palm (this is the end you'll pull
from as you use butterfly).

Wind figure-8s between thumb and
index finger.

End with a
simple knot
around center
to secure
butterfly.

**Beginning
of yarn tail**

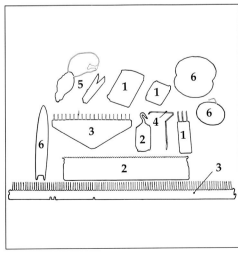

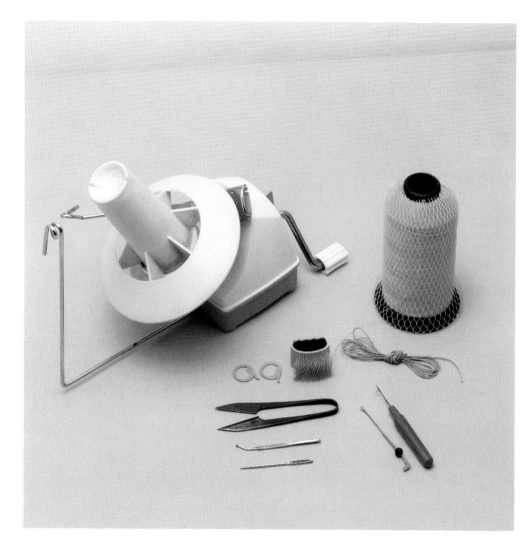

MISCELLANEOUS TOOLS AND FINISHING EQUIPMENT.
(1) Hand-knitting stitch markers; (2) ravel cord and cone of yarn with thread net; (3) beading needles; (4) ball winder; (5) thread snips and blunt yarn needles; and (6) bunka brush.

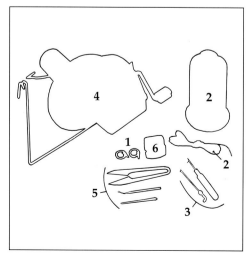

Miscellaneous tools and accessories

Stitch markers used in hand knitting (number 1 in the photo on the facing page) are easy to slip on and off stitches in order to identify the ones that need to be lifted, rehung or otherwise specially handled. They are also used to mark the location of increases or decreases in the fabric.

Sold in bright, easy-to-see colors in precut lengths, ravel cord (2) is generally used to knit one row between the scrap and main knitting, which can later be easily pulled out to separate these two sections. Nylon yarn on cones makes a good, inexpensive and disposable alternative. Expandable nylon thread nets (like onion bags), hairnets or sections of nylon stockings can be loosely wrapped around the cone to prevent the line from peeling off the cone too quickly.

Since the back of the fabric faces you as you work on the machine, a hand mirror is useful for checking the front of the fabric without removing it from the machine.

Beading needles (3) are used to place beads on stitches as they are formed. The needles most often used are actually tiny needles from hosiery knitting machines. Sewing-notions departments usually sell a latch-type snag-repair tool, which also works quite well for beading and is easier to hold onto because it is set into a handle.

Umbrella swifts hold looped skeins of yarn open for winding the yarn onto cones or into balls that pull from the center. Ball winders (4) and cone winders are available in both hand and motorized models. There are also some that will twist and ply several yarns together.

Calculators are inexpensive, invaluable, easy-to-use tools for any calculations involved in designing patterns on the machine. Counters, whether of the grocery-store clicker variety or official hand-knit row counters, are handy for keeping an accurate count of repeat units.

Pompom makers, knitting spools, daisy looms and hairpin-lace frames are useful for adding surface detail to the knitted fabric. They can be used to make flowers and frills to add to the knitting while on the machine or after it is finished. The Passap Mouse, a child's toy, is a spool knitter with latch needles that quickly knits cords.

Finishing equipment

Blunt yarn needles, thread snips (5), a tape measure, crochet hooks and straight pins are basic finishing equipment. Other useful tools include a washable fabric glue, which will prevent rayon and nylon yarn tails from working themselves loose, and a linking machine for putting garments together. A linker, used independently of the knitting machine, produces a chain stitch to join two edges, and it can also serve to add surface detail.

Mohairs and some wools respond well to brushing after knitting is finished. The little Japanese bunka brush (6) slips onto your fingertips for an especially gentle touch when brushing the fabric.

Finally, a good steam iron or steamer is essential for blocking and finishing knits. Most yarns need to be steamed only very lightly by holding the iron an inch or two above the surface of the fabric. Some yarns, like acrylics, may be damaged by excessive heat, and a pressing cloth should be used to protect those that are heat-sensitive.

Using this book

This is a book of possibilities rather than specific patterns. It is a reference book that will provide answers to your questions and, I hope, inspire you to invent your own patterns and techniques. The possibilities for combining, altering and expanding techniques and patterns are endless, as you will see when you begin varying the number of stitches, rows or repetitions in a pattern; the stitch size used; the direction of a particular motif; or the colors you choose.

The first two chapters should be read thoroughly first because they present information and concepts used throughout the book. In this first chapter, you will find an explanation of the notation system that is used with all the charts in the book (see pp. 20-29) and a listing of the abbreviations used with the charted directions for the patterns (see p. 31). In the second chapter, you will find a detailed explanation of the four techniques that are fundamental to the other techniques presented in the book.

The remaining chapters in the book can be read and explored in any order. Each contains a general description of the technique at hand and a "glossary" of patterns created with that technique. In order to help you evaluate the techniques

that best suit your needs for a particular project, the sample swatches in the book were deliberately kept as simple as possible so that designs would not compete with technical information. Every swatch is accompanied by a full set of written and, also in most cases, charted, directions for reproducing the pattern.

Finally, you will find at the beginning of the book's back matter a brief appendix on how to plan garments when using these patterns. You will also find a glossary of machine-knitting terms, a bibliography, a list of suppliers and an index.

Notation systems and charts

Charted symbols are the clearest, most concise form of directions for knitted stitches and patterns. Without this form of shorthand, it would take a second volume to present the row-by-row instructions for all the patterns in this book. Fortunately, a well-defined symbol always means one thing—no more and no less—and it contains the directions for all of the motions involved in producing the stitch it represents.

Hand knitters have a number of very clear notation, or symbol, systems that all but eliminate the need for verbal directions. Although some hand-knit symbols are often used in machine-knit directions, there is no notation system specifically designed for machine knitters, most of whom resist using hand-knitting symbols because they are difficult and time-consuming to adapt for the machine.

From a machine knitter's point of view, hand-knitting symbols are especially limited because they usually refer to the right side of the fabric. Since the right, or knit, side of the fabric almost always faces away from machine knitters as they work on the machine, they must mentally reverse all the charted symbols and any directional notations to arrive at what they will see on the back of the fabric. Logically, therefore, machine-knitting charts should be written to show the purl, or "wrong," side of the fabric, which is how all the charts in this book have been prepared and should be read. This means, of course, that any pattern or motif with a left or right direction to it will be seen in reverse on the face of the fabric, an important consideration when designing a pattern or placing a motif on a garment (see also p. 231).

Please spend some time studying the symbols on the following pages because they're used throughout the book in the charts that accompany many of the sample swatches. I have provided symbols for most, but not all, of the stitches in this book. These symbols generally look like the stitches they represent or mimic the motions required to produce them. For a few stitches that are combinations of several techniques or which cannot be practically or clearly described in symbols (double-bed manipulations, for example), I have relied on needle diagrams and verbal directions rather than symbols.

Some of these symbols may differ from those you've used before. Most of them, however, are fairly standard, though I've added a few of my own invention and modified others from hand-knit notation systems. For the most part, these symbols are grouped in the list below by effect. Specific directions for working with stitches and techniques are found in each chapter. This is required reading!

As you study the charts and diagrams on the following pages, keep in mind these points:

1. All charts represent the purl side, or back of the fabric.

2. Unless otherwise stated, all charts should be read from left to right and bottom to top.

3. Needles are numbered from left to right across the bottom.

4. Rows are numbered along the left side of the charts from bottom to top, just as fabric grows on the machine.

5. Needle numbers refer to the position of the needles on the chart and do not necessarily coincide with the position of the actual needles on the machine bed.

6. Always execute the motion or maneuver indicated by the symbol before knitting the row.

7. When transferring stitches, the first stitch placed in the hook of a needle is the stitch that shows on the face of the fabric.

8. On pp. 20-29, the basic symbol is shown out of context and also used in a sample chart.

Basic symbols

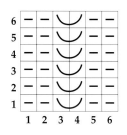

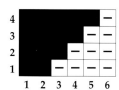

1. Empty needle in nonworking position.

In the charted example, a ladder forms across the space where needles 3 and 4 are in nonworking position. (The remaining stitches in the chart are purl stitches.) Some surface treatments can be more clearly charted if no background stitches are shown on the chart. In such cases only the stitches of special interest are shown, and the plain purl stitches are absent. Text accompanying the chart will always indicate when the background stitches are absent.

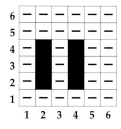

2. Needle in holding position.

In the first sample chart (at left), needles 2 and 4 will hold, forming tuck stitches in rows 2, 3 and 4 before they knit again. The second sample chart (at right) shows needles in holding position for show rowing. Rather than forming tucks, the needles shown in holding position hold stitches that are no longer knitting but will later either resume knitting or be bound off as a group.

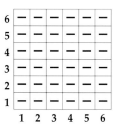

3. Purl stitch.

The sample chart shows the purl side of basic stockinette fabric (the side facing the knitter) that all knitting machines can produce automatically.

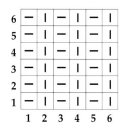

4. Knit stitch.

To produce knit stitches on the purl side of the fabric, purl stitches must be reformed manually, or a ribber must be used to produce knit and purl stitches automatically in the same row. In the sample chart, the stitches on needles 2, 4 and 6 are knit stitches and those on needles 1, 3 and 5 are purls, producing a 1x1 ribbing.

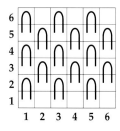

5. Tuck stitch.

The sample chart shows an alternating pattern produced with an every-other-needle, alternate-row tuck stitch. This pattern can be knitted by using a carriage with tucking cams and automatic selection, or by using the holding position to accumulate tucks.

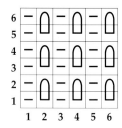

6. Reformed tuck stitch.

This symbol indicates that a tuck stitch has been reformed from a purl stitch with a latch tool. In the sample chart, the stitches on needles 2, 4 and 6 are reformed every two rows as tuck stitches. (See also pp. 77-80.)

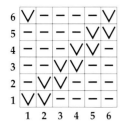

7. Slip stitch.

The sample chart shows a diagonal pattern of slip stitches, which will appear on the purl side of the fabric whether the slip stitches are formed by the carriage or formed manually.

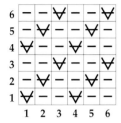

8. Reformed slip stitch on the knit side.

The sample chart shows a diagonal pattern of reformed slip stitches. When the carriage forms slip stitches, the floats always lie on the purl side of the fabric.

Placing the floats on the knit side can be done only by reforming the stitches. (See also pp. 69-70.)

Needle diagrams

Needle diagrams are a form of visual shorthand describing how the needles should be arranged on the machine. A vertical line represents a working needle, and a dot represents a nonworking needle. The long horizontal line in the diagram indicates the front of a single-bed machine, or the space between two beds on a double-bed machine. When the diagram refers to a double-bed setup, the vertical lines and dots above the horizontal line represent back-bed needles, and those below the line represent front-bed needles. On double-bed diagrams, stitch sizes or cam settings above the horizontal line represent the stitch size or cam setting for the back bed; those below the line refer to the front bed. Below are three sample needle diagrams.

1. This single-bed needle setup indicates that every third needle is in nonworking position. The needles themselves are unnumbered, as they are in other needle diagrams in the book, except where specific needles are referred to in written directions accompanying a given swatch.

In addition to numbers, some needle diagrams will also contain arrows and brackets to isolate specific groups of needles that will be treated differently from the rest (for example, those crossed for a cable). These specific needles are often referred to as x or y, or groups of needles may be labeled A, B, etc.

2. This double-bed diagram indicates that the beds are in full pitch and that the needles are arranged for 1x1 rib. Working needles are positioned directly opposite nonworking needles.

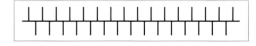

3. Because the needles on this double-bed setup are arranged for full-needle rib, the beds are in half-pitch.

Carriage directions

These arrows are used when the carriage direction is important.

 1. Carriage moves left to right.

2. Carriage moves right to left.

 3. Knit over and back, starting on the right.

4. Knit over and back, starting on the left.

Twisted symbols

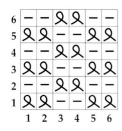

1. Twisted stitch.
A twisted stitch is one that is removed from its needle, twisted and returned to the same needle. In the first chart (at left), pairs of single twisted stitches alternate with regular purl stitches.

Multiple stitches can also be twisted together. The second chart (at near right) shows a pattern with pairs of twisted stitches; groups of three stitches are twisted in the third chart (at far right).

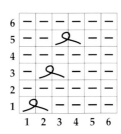 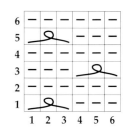

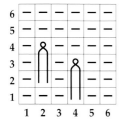

2. Twisted tuck stitch.
As its name suggests, a twisted tuck stitch is a stitch that forms one or more tucks and then is twisted before it resumes knitting. In the sample chart, needles 2 and 4 tuck for three rows. Then the original stitch on each needle and all three tuck stitches it has collected twist together before the needle knits in the next row.

Wrapped and woven symbols

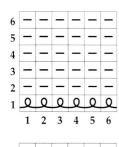

1. Basic E-wrap.
Yarn can be wound around the shafts of the needles, as shown by this symbol, either for purposes of casting on or for decorative effect. In the charted example, the first row indicates an E-wrap cast-on.

2. Knitted E-wrap.
When the E-wrap is manually knitted back as it is formed on each needle, it produces twisted knit stitches. In the charted example, the second row is wrapped and knitted back so that the entire row will appear twisted.

3. Knit weaving.

For this weaving technique, a supplementary yarn laces through knit stitches formed by the carriage.

⌒ Weaving yarn passes over a needle in holding position, bypassing needles in regular working position.

⌣ Weaving yarn passes under a needle in holding position, bypassing needles in regular working position.

In the sample chart, the yarn being knit-woven alternates above and below the first and last three needles. When knit woven in this fashion, the yarn will bind to the background fabric. In the center of the chart, the yarn lies under adjacent needles 4, 5 and 6, forming a float on the purl side of the fabric. Although purl stitches are indicated in this example, the background stitches are not always shown in the charts. When they are absent, accompanying text will indicate this.

1
1 2 3 4 5 6 7 8 9

4. Yarn wrapped around adjacent needles.

Yarn can be wrapped around the shafts of two adjacent needles in circular fashion for purely decorative effect. (You can, of course, wrap the yarn around more than two needles if you want.)

Yarn can also be wrapped around two or more needles, figure-eight style.

In the charted example, the stitches in Row 1 are hand knitted on each side of wrapped needles 4 and 5. In Row 3 this pair of wrapped needles is bordered by knit weaving. In Row 5, this pair of needles is wrapped figure-eight style, and the yarn forms floats between these and the next wrapped needles.

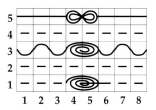

5
4
3
2
1
1 2 3 4 5 6 7 8

5. Vertical weaving with E-wrapping.

When the vertical weaving yarn is E-wrapped around needles, it produces a very textured purl surface.

The sample chart, whose background stitches are not shown, presents three vertical weaving patterns with E-wrapping. The first two diagrams (at left and center) show the yarn wrapping around one needle at a time and moving vertically or diagonally. The third example shows the yarn wrapping around two needles at a time. This technique could also be used as in #4 above, wrapping around the same two needles several times.

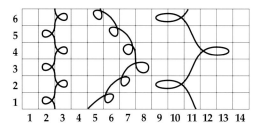

6
5
4
3
2
1
1 2 3 4 5 6 7 8 9 10 11 12 13 14

6. Vertical weaving with yarn laid across needles.

When the yarn is simply laid across the needles rather than E-wrapping them as in #5, the texture is less pronounced.

 Yarn laid across needle from left to right.

 Yarn laid across needle from right to left.

The sample chart, whose background stitches are not shown, shows three vertical weaving patterns using this method. The first two examples alternate the direction in which the yarn is laid across the needles. The third example shows the yarn consistently laid from left to right.

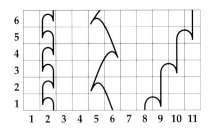

7. Stitches pulled through other stitches.

Stitches pulled through each other and returned to their own or each other's needles create low, rich textures. One or several stitches can be pulled through an adjacent stitch or stitches. The direction in which the stitches are pulled determines the slant of the overall effect.

 One stitch crosses through neighboring right-hand stitch.

 One stitch crosses through neighboring left-hand stitch.

 One stitch crosses through two neighboring right-hand stitches. The reverse symbol (at right) shows a stitch crossing though adjacent left-hand stitches.

 Two stitches cross through neighboring left stitch and are hung on two adjacent needles. The reverse symbol (at right) shows the stitch crossing through right-hand stitches.

  Two stitches (at far left, stitches 2 and 3) cross through a neighboring left-hand stitch (1), and Stitch 1 is rehung on Stitch 3's needle, while stitches 2 and 3 are rehung together on Stitch 1's needle. This maneuver creates an eyelet since Stitch 2's needle remains empty. The reverse symbol (at right) shows the stitch crossing through a right-hand stitch (3).

The charted example shows a pattern using each type of pulled-through stitch.

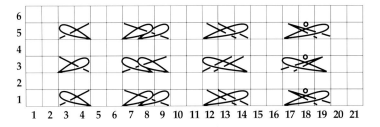

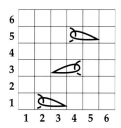

8. One stitch drawn through another but returned to its own needle. The symbol at left shows a stitch drawn through an adjacent stitch to the left, and the symbol at right shows the same maneuver worked to the right. This maneuver does not produce a real crossing. The chart shows the beginning of a diagonal pattern of stitches alternately drawn through the neighboring stitch to the right and left.

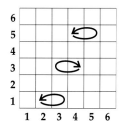

9. One stitch wrapped around another and rehung on its own needle. The symbol at left shows wrapping the stitch to the left, and the symbol at right shows wrapping to the right. When one stitch wraps around two or more stitches, the effect is one of gathering stitches together. The chart shows the beginning of a diagonal pattern of stitches alternately wrapped around the stitch to the left and right.

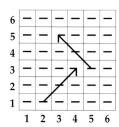

10. Diagonally woven stitches. Also called Chinese knots, these diagonally woven stitches pass in front of or behind, rather than through, each other. In the example, stitches 1 and 2 in Row 1 are woven with stitches 3 and 4, and the two pairs are returned to one another's needles. In the same row, stitches 7 and 8 are woven with stitches 9 and 10 and returned to each other's needles. In Row 4, the placement of the knots is staggered.

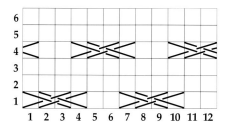

Lifted symbols

1. Arrow. An arrow indicates where to lift and hang a stitch or a sinker loop. When referring to a stitch to be lifted, the base of the arrow will be connected to the heel of the stitch (or stitches). When referring to a sinker loop to be lifted, the arrow will be connected to a sinker-loop symbol (see #2 on p. 26). The point of the arrow will always indicate the needle and row on which the stitch or sinker loop is to be hung.

In the sample chart, before knitting Row 3, Stitch 2 in Row 1 is to be lifted onto Needle 4 in Row 3; and before knitting Row 5, Stitch 5 in Row 3 is to be lifted onto Needle 3 in Row 5.

2. Sinker loop.
All stitches have sinker loops between them, but, for purposes of patterning, only those specifically marked with this symbol are of interest. This symbol is similar to the one used to indicate the ladder formed by a needle out of work (see #1 on p. 20), but it's smaller and formed between charted squares (that is, stitches) rather than in them.

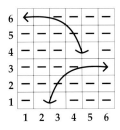

3. Arrow and sinker loop.
An arrow and sinker loop indicate exactly which sinker loops to lift and where to hang them.

In the charted example, the sinker loop between needles 2 and 3 in Row 1 is to be hung on Needle 6 before knitting Row 3. Then, the sinker loop between stitches 4 and 5 in Row 4 is to be hung on Needle 1 before knitting Row 6.

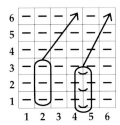

4. Arrow and circle.
The base of an arrow connected to a circle indicates that all the stitches or sinker loops included in the circle should be lifted and hung as a group.

In the charted example, three stitches (Stitch 2 in the first three rows) are all to be lifted and hung on Needle 4 before knitting Row 6. And three sinker loops, between needles 4 and 5 in the first three rows, are to be lifted and hung on Needle 6 before knitting Row 6.

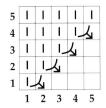

5. Lifted purl loop.
With this maneuver, the stitch in question remains on its needle.

Purl loop picked up from front-bed stitch and hung on back-bed needle.

Purl loop picked up from back-bed stitch and hung on front-bed needle.

In this double-bed example, purl loops from the main bed are hung on empty ribber-bed needles. (While all main-bed needles are working, the chart indicates ribber-bed stitches only.) After Row 1 is knitted, the purl loop between stitches 1 and 2 on the main, or back, bed is picked up and hung on ribber-bed Needle 2. After Row 2 is knitted, the purl loop between main-bed stitches 2 and 3 is picked up and hung on ribber-bed Needle 3, and so on. Were the main fabric knitted on the front, or ribber, bed and the purl loops lifted from the back bed to the front bed, the alternate lifted-purl-loop symbol would have been used.

Transfer symbols

1. Eyelet.
When a stitch is transferred to another needle, its original needle is left empty. If this empty needle is in working position and casts on and knits in the next row, an eyelet is formed. This symbol is always used in combination with another symbol, which indicates how the eyelet needle was emptied.

2. One-step transfers.

In the simple, one-step transfer, a stitch is decreased by transferring it onto an adjacent needle with another stitch. The decreased stitch lies on the fabric's purl side.

Simple transfers are always indicated by a combination of the eyelet and transfer symbols. The transfer symbols look like a diagonal letter T. If the transfer symbol sits to the right of the eyelet, it indicates a right transfer. When it sits to the left of the eyelet, it indicates a left transfer.

 One-step transfer to the right.

 One-step transfer to the left.

In Row 1 of the charted example, the stitch on Needle 1 is to be transferred to the right to Needle 2, causing Needle 2 to have two stitches and Needle 1 to be empty. If Needle 1 remains in working position, it will cast on with the next pass of the carriage, creating the eyelet shown in Row 1. In Row 1, the stitch on Needle 12 is also to be transferred, in this case, to the left to Needle 11, with an eyelet formed on the empty needle. Similar paired transfers, with resulting eyelets, are also indicated in rows 3 and 5.

3. Two-step transfers.

While this method is less common and more time-consuming than the the one-step transfer above, it is sometimes preferable because it creates a sharper line in a design. This crisper line results from the fact that while the decreased stitch still lies on the purl side of the fabric, the same stitch always lies adjacent to the eyelet.

To execute a two-step transfer, first transfer the second stitch to the first needle, and then return both stitches to the second needle. As with the basic method, the first needle is now empty and, if left in working position, will cast on with the next pass of the carriage, creating an eyelet.

 Two-step transfer to the right.

 Two-step transfer to the left.

The sample chart shows two-step transfers used in the same pattern as that for the one-step transfers above.

4. Slanting stitches.

Slanting-stitch symbols are usually found in combination with full-fashioned, multiple-stitch transfers (see p. 28). They are also used in double-bed charts to indicate traveling stitches (see chapters 7 and 8).

/ Stitch slanting to the right.

\ Stitch slanting to the left.

5. Full-fashioned transfer.

In a full-fashioned transfer, the empty needle is not adjacent to the needle with two stitches, as it is in a simple transfer. Rather, several stitches are transferred as a group with a multiple-transfer tool, thus separating the empty needle and the doubled stitch.

In the sample chart, the stitches on needles 1 through 5 are to be moved as a group one stitch to the right, leaving Needle 1 empty (to form an eyelet) and Needle 6 with two stitches. The full-fashioned transfer could, of course, involve more stitches and could also shift to the left. In any case, whenever slanting-stitch symbols are found between the eyelet and transfer-stitch symbols, they indicate a full-fashioned transfer.

6. Closed eyelet.

To prevent an eyelet from forming on an empty needle in working position, the purl bar of the stitch adjacent to the empty needle can be picked up and hung on this needle. This produces what I call a closed eyelet and still creates the slanted decorative effect of the transferred stitches.

The sample chart shows the same transfers as the full-fashioned transfer above, except that by filling the empty needle with an adjacent purl bar, no eyelet (or lace) will be formed.

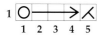

7. Crossed-eyelet transfer.

In a crossed-eyelet transfer, the decreased stitch is placed on a nonadjacent needle without moving any stitches in between. In this example, the stitch on Needle 1 is removed and hung on Needle 5. The empty needle is left in working position, so that an eyelet forms on the next pass of the carriage. The transferred stitch is stretched, creating a slightly puckered texture in the knitting.

8. Crossed closed-eyelet transfer.

This maneuver differs from #7 only in that the empty needle is filled with the purl bar from an adjacent stitch.

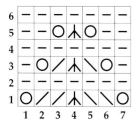

9. Three stitches held on one needle.

When two stitches are transferred to a common needle, a pair of eyelets is formed. Consequently, this symbol is always accompanied by a pair of eyelet or closed-eyelet symbols. The first stitch of the three on the needle will always show on the face of the fabric.

In Row 1 of the example, the stitches from needles 1 and 7 form eyelets, and Needle 4 holds three stitches. The slanted lines between the eyelet and tripled-stitch symbols indicate that these are full-fashioned transfers, as are the transfers in Row 3. In Row 5 there are no slanted lines, indicating that these are simple transfers.

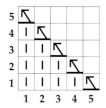

10. Stitches transferred from one bed to the other.

These symbols are used only in conjunction with double-bed work and appear on charts representing ribber-bed stitches.

 Stitches tranferred from the front to the back bed.

Stitches transferred from the back to the front bed.

In Row 1 of the example (a full-needle rib fabric worked with the beds in half-pitch), Stitch 5 is transferred to adjacent, main-bed Needle 4, and the empty needle is placed in nonworking position. In Row 2, Stitch 4 is transferred to main-bed Needle 3 and the empty needle placed in nonworking position, and so on. Were the stitches to be transferred from the main bed to the ribber, the alternate transfer symbol would be used.

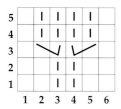

11. Making stitches by picking up purl bars.

These symbols are used in hand knitting to indicate making a stitch on the knit side. While there's a hand-knitting symbol for making a stitch on the purl side—the only side on which stitches can be made in machine knitting—this symbol incorporates a purl-stitch symbol with the check mark and is, I think, confusing to read. Therefore I am using these simpler symbols to indicate making a stitch on the purl side on a knitting machine.

Stitch made to the right by picking up the purl bar of the left stitch and hanging it on the right needle.

Stitch made to the left by picking up the purl bar of the right stitch and hanging it on the left needle.

In the example, which represents only the working ribber stitches in an embossed pattern, the additional ribber stitches required for the pattern are created in Row 3. In that row, the purl bar of Stitch 3 is picked up and lifted to empty Needle 2 to make a stitch, and the purl bar of Stitch 4 is picked up and lifted to empty Needle 5 to create a second new stitch.

Cable symbols

These basic symbols form the basis for the more involved cable crossings found in Chapter 8. While these symbols show cables formed by crossing two stitches over two other stitches, cables can, of course, be formed by crossing larger or smaller groups of stitches. The number of crossing lines in the cable symbol indicates the number of stitches involved.

Single cables

1. Left cable cross.

In this cable, two pairs of stitches are crossed: stitches 1 and 2 are hung on needles 3 and 4 first, and then stitches 3 and 4 are placed on needles 1 and 2. To execute this cable crossing, use a pair of double-eyelet transfer tools to remove and rehang the two pairs of stitches.

 I can use a shorthand symbol like the one at left for a four-stitch cable cross because simple arrows are

easier to read in charts than the full cable symbol. As with the full cable symbol, solid lines represent the last stitches returned to needles. These stitches show on the purl side of the fabric, which faces you as you work. The broken lines represent the first stitches returned to needles, and, because these stitches show on the knit face of the fabric, they name the crossing. The arrow pointing to the left may help you remember that this is a left cable cross.

2. Right cable cross.

This cable cross simply reverses the order of stitches crossed in the left cable cross, meaning that stitches 3 and 4 are moved first and hence show on the face of the fabric. Because the right-hand stitches are replaced first, this is called a right cable cross.

The shorthand symbol at left can also be used for a four-stitch right cable cross. In addition to cable symbols, instructions for crossings can be verbalized. In this case I'd tell you to "cross right, then left." That is, rehang the stitches in your right hand, then those in your left.

3. Cable cross with reformed stitches.

This is a left cross cable, but stitches 1 and 2 are reformed before being crossed with stitches 3 and 4. The face of the cable will show both purl and knit stitches crossing rather than just knit stitches. In most cable diagrams, only the crossing lines are

indicated. Unless exceptions like reformed stitches or eyelets are indicated in the diagram, you can assume that the stitches being crossed are the plain purl stitches regularly formed by the carriage.

Paired cables

The cable pairs below are opposing cables, that is, when one moves left, the other moves right, and vice versa. They are perhaps most easily thought of as having a center point between them.

4. Closed cable pair: inward cross.

This pair of cables crosses in (toward the center), then out (away from the center). On the knit face of the fabric, the pair appears joined, or closed. As an abbreviated verbal direction, I can simply say to "cross in."

I could also use the shorthand symbol at left for this cable. Note that, unlike those for single cables, the charted arrows for cable pairs should not be relied upon to remind you of the visual effect of the pair. In this example and that below, the arrows point in the opposite direction of the actual crossing effect on the knit face of the fabric.

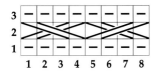

5. Open cable pair: outward cross.

This opposing pair crosses out (away from the center) and then in (toward the center). On the knit face of the fabric, the pair appears separated and open.

As an abbreviated verbal direction, I can simply say to "cross out." I could also use the shorthand symbol above for this cable.

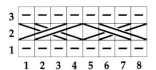

Abbreviations used in this book

A/R	Alternate row.		**O/W**	Out of work.
adj	Adjacent.		**P**	(Full) pitch.
alt	Alternate(ly), (ing).		**pat**	Pattern.
BB	Back bed.		**pos**	Position
beg	begin(ning).		**P/U**	Pick up.
B/O	Bind off.		**R(s)**	Row(s).
carr(s)	Carriage(s).		**RB**	Ribber bed.
CC	Contrast color.		**RC**	Row count(er).
C/O	Cast on.		**rem**	Remain(ing), (s).
COL	Carriage on left.		**rep(s)**	Repeat(ing), (s).
cont	Continue(d).		**ret**	Return(ed), (ing).
COR	Carriage on right.		**RP**	Resting position.
DB	Double bed.		**RT**	Right.
dec(s)	Decrease(ing), (s).		**S/O**	Scrap(ing) off.
E/N	Every needle.		**SB**	Single bed.
EON	Every other needle.		**SR**	Short row(ing).
EOR	Every other row.		**SS**	Stitch size.
EOS	Every other stitch.		**ST(S)**	Stitch(es).
E/R	Every row.		**tog**	Together.
FB	Front bed.		**tr(s)**	Transfer(s).
ff	Full-fashioned.		**UWP**	Upper working position.
fol	Following.		**WP**	Working position.
FNR	Full-needle rib.		**x**	Times.
GB	Garter bar.			
H	Half-pitch.		**#/Rs**	Every specific number of rows (for example, 8/Rs = every 8 rows).
HP	Holding position.			
inc(s)	Increase(ing), (s).			
K	Knit(ing), (ed).		***...***	Repeat stitches or directions between asterisks.
K/M	Knitting machine.			
KWK	Knit, wrap, knit back.		**[...]**	Brackets identify a group of stitches to be treated as a single unit.
L	Left.			
MB	Main bed.			
MC	Main color.		**MB**	Adjust cam settings and stitch size, as indicated, for the main bed (MB) and the ribber bed (RB).
NDL(S)	Needle(s).		**RB**	
NWP	Nonworking position.			
O/N	Opposite needle.			
opp	Opposite.			

CHAPTER 2

Basic Moves

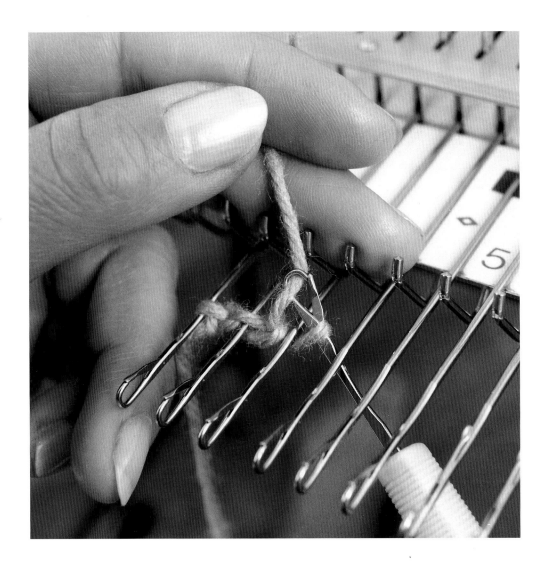

Four groups of techniques are at the basis of all hand-manipulated effects on the knitting machine. They appear over and over again in one way or another, and I call them "basic moves." These basic techniques are casting on and binding off, holding, lengthening and reforming stitches. While these moves have merit on their own, in the context of hand-manipulated effects they're used primarily in combination with other techniques to facilitate certain results or to overcome various limitations imposed by the machine. Because you'll find these techniques referred to throughout this book, it's important to begin thinking of them as fundamental skills to incorporate into your knitting repertoire.

Casting on and binding off are the most basic moves of all because without them, there would be no way to begin or end a piece of knitting. Yet cast-on and bind-off techniques can also be used to create lace eyelets and a variety of surface and edge decorations and shapes.

By lengthening stitches, you cause them to absorb more yarn and form larger stitches than the carriage could produce without intervention. Lengthening extends the otherwise finite stitch-size range established by the dial on the carriage and increases the machine's ability to handle heavy yarns and patterns dependent on larger stitch sizes. Lengthened stitches can be put to purely decorative use—for example, to create lace-like effects—or they can functionally serve to facilitate twisting or crossing stitch groups, or weaving stitches through other stitches.

By manually reforming stitches, you can produce stitches that differ from those automatically knitted by the carriage. That is to say, you can reform a purl stitch by hand as a knit, slip or tuck stitch. Thus, you can control the structure of individual stitches in a knitted fabric and even override the commands given to the needles by the carriage. Reforming stitches is the simplest way to produce such effects as a purl stitch at each side of a cable. And it is the only way to achieve other double-bed effects on a single-bed machine.

By placing needles into holding position so that the stitches they carry cannot knit, holding becomes a tool to produce a number of effects, among them, vertical slits, shaping, scalloped edgings and sculptural surfaces. Holding provides the ultimate control over every needle and stitch by enabling the knitter to select individually the needles that will knit and those that will not. Holding therefore makes it possible to produce adjacent areas in the knitting that contrast sharply in color, stitch size, patterning and shape.

Casting on and binding off stitches

Although there are dozens of ways to cast on and bind off stitches, I've included only those I use most often to produce a variety of edges with different visual and structural effects. Some of these methods are used exclusively to deal with a single stitch, while others can accommodate groups of stitches.

Casting on most often refers to the process of creating stitches to begin a knitted fabric. This process may involve putting a single needle into working position or establishing stitches on a hundred needles all at once. When extra stitches are cast onto an existing fabric on the machine, the process is usually referred to as *increasing,* even though there is no difference in the actual techniques used. Increasing stitches adds width to an existing fabric.

As with casting on, there are a number of ways to bind off, but the goal is always to secure stitches permanently so they cannot ravel when removed from the needles. Binding off usually implies ending a fabric by terminating all the stitches. Decreasing, another form of binding off, selectively terminates stitches to reduce their number and consequently the width of a fabric in progress. Decreasing is occasionally used for stitch patterning (see also Chapter 7).

Knowing a variety of cast-on and bind-off methods can confuse you if you don't understand why and when to use each one. This knowledge, however, can expand your creative choices because many of the same methods that serve a functional purpose can be used or adapted for decorative effects as well.

Whatever your goal in casting on or binding off, you need to decide before you begin which methods will be most effective, most attractive and most appropriate for your project. Consider the effect of each method and the needs of your project. Will the edge show as a final edge, or will it require further treatment? Do you need an open or a closed edge? A stretchy or firm one? Can the edge curl, or must it lie flat? Do the cast-on and bound-off edges need to match?

With a few exceptions, the following methods are for single-bed machines. Whenever a double-bed method is presented, the text will make note of it.

Cast-on methods

1. Open cast-on with ravel cord or cast-on comb.

Most new machine knitters find that when they try to cast stitches on a group of adjacent needles, the yarn simply lies across the hooks and creates a mess on the next pass of the carriage. The reason for this is that there is nothing to anchor the stitches so they can form properly. Hanging a comb on the loops that form on the first pass of the carriage or holding a ravel cord behind the sinker posts for the first five or six rows will give these open stitches enough definition to start the knitting.

Because this cast-on produces an open edge that can run—and you are bound to lose the first few rows in handling—always begin this method with 8 to 10 rows of

OPEN CAST-ON WITH RAVEL CORD.

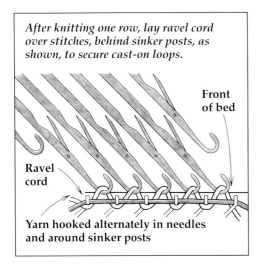

After knitting one row, lay ravel cord over stitches, behind sinker posts, as shown, to secure cast-on loops.

Front of bed

Ravel cord

Yarn hooked alternately in needles and around sinker posts

scrap knitting (see pp. 42-43). This raw edge always requires further finishing and is a good choice when you intend to crochet into the stitches, rehang an edge to continue knitting downward or ravel rows from the bottom up.

2. Every-other-needle cast-on.

This cast-on method is fast and produces an edge that is closed but not especially attractive and which tends to gather itself on the yarn running straight through the stitches. The edge is usually turned up in a hem, enclosed in a band or treated to a crocheted finish. This two-step cast-on is also used for the basic technique of increasing multiple stitches on the side opposite the carriage.

To cast on by this method, bring every other needle to working position and knit one row. Then bring the remaining, or alternate, needles to working position and continue knitting. The needles that cast on in the first row act as anchors for the stitches formed in the second row. If you plan to knit on every other needle in order to accommodate heavier yarns, you must cast on every fourth needle in the first row and then bring every second needle to working position to complete the cast-on.

3. Automatic weaving cast-on.

This cast-on is identical to the every-other-needle-cast-on above, but it is done in one step. It's possible only on machines with weaving brushes and a carriage that can be set to knit needles back from holding to working position.

To work this cast-on, push the required number of needles to working position and then move every other needle to hold. Thread the carriage, carry the yarn over the needles in holding position and tie the yarn end to the clamp on the side opposite the carriage. Make sure the yarn lies across the needle shafts, in front of the sinker posts. Knit one row, and the cast-on is complete. The needles that were in holding position have formed complete stitches. The needles that were in working position have taken on plain loops.

EVERY-OTHER-NEEDLE CAST-ON.

1. Begin with every other needle in working position and alternate needles in nonworking position. After you knit first row, yarn will lie across hooks of working needles.

Needle in working position   Needle in nonworking position   Front of bed

Yarn in needle hooks

2. Bring needles in nonworking position to working position and knit second row to complete cast-on.

AUTOMATIC EVERY-OTHER-NEEDLE CAST-ON.

Begin with every other needle in working position and alternate needles in holding position. Before knitting first row, lay yarn across shafts of needles in hold and tie yarn end to clamp on opposite end of bed. Knit one row to complete cast-on. This cast-on, after one row, looks like every-other-needle cast-on after two rows.

Yarn tied to clamp on side opposite carriage

Needle in working position

Needle in holding position

4. E-wrap cast-on.
This cast-on produces an attractive, fairly stretchy, closed edge that sometimes requires no additional treatment, although it is often finished with crochet to prevent curling or stretching. It is a good cast-on to use with latched-up ribbings (see p. 73 and p. 86) and can also be used for multiple increasing on the carriage side.

You can E-wrap in either direction, but it is most often described as being worked from left to right. Whatever the direction of the wrap, the method is the same, whether or not there are existing stitches on the needles. With the carriage on the right and the needles in holding position,

E-WRAP CAST-ON.

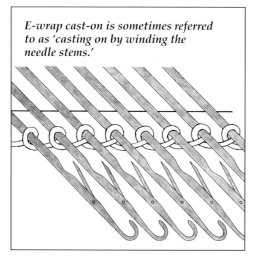

E-wrap cast-on is sometimes referred to as 'casting on by winding the needle stems.'

KNITTED-BACK E-WRAP CAST-ON.

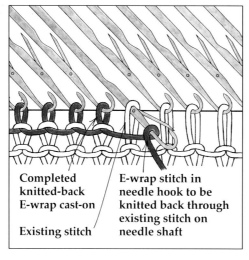

Completed knitted-back E-wrap cast-on

Existing stitch

E-wrap stitch in needle hook to be knitted back through existing stitch on needle shaft

tie the end of the yarn to the machine clamp on the left and wrap the yarn counterclockwise around the shaft of one needle at a time. After wrapping the last needle on the right, thread the yarn into the carriage and knit.

If your carriage cannot be set to knit needles back automatically from holding position, manually place them in upper working position after E-wrapping the shafts. Or, to eliminate any possibility of unknitted stitches, wrap in the needle hooks to begin with. This is easiest to do if the needles are pushed slightly forward of regular working position so that the hooks are clear of the sinker posts. In any case, the trick is to wrap the hooks or shafts tightly enough to create a firm, neat edge, but not so tightly that the needles cannot knit.

5. Knitted-back E-wrap cast-on.
The basic E-wrap can be done on empty or full needles, but this version of the E-wrap cast-on requires stitches on the needles to begin with. This generally means casting on and knitting eight to ten rows with scrap yarn and one optional row with ravel cord. The edge looks exactly as if it has been E-wrapped on empty needles, but the advantage of this method is that, when working with slippery, textured or otherwise tricky yarns, the knitting is weighted, which makes casting on much easier. As a hand-formed row in the main knitting, the stitches will have a cross-knitted, or twisted, appearance because of the way the yarn wraps under and over each needle before it is knitted back.

To cast on with this method, push all the needles forward to holding position so that the stitches slip behind the latches. E-wrap the hook of each needle, then use your thumb to push the needle butt back to working position, thus knitting the old stitch through a new E-wrapped stitch.

6. Knitted-back double E-wrap cast-on.
Similar to the knitted-back E-wrap method, this cast-on is faster than the other because two needles are wrapped at once. The edge produced looks quite like

that yielded by the single-wrap method and is comparably stretchy, but this edge has more free yarn spiraling from one stitch to the next. The edge is often treated to a crocheted finishing.

Like the basic E-wrap and the knitted-back E-wrap cast-ons, start this version with all of the needles in holding position, but wrap the yarn around the shafts of two needles at a time. As you wrap back over the needles, knit the first one down to working position. The second needle of the pair just wrapped becomes the first needle of the next pair.

7. Figure-8 E-wrap cast-on.
This E-wrap produces a more substantial, decorative edge than the other E-wraps, which is especially nice with latched-up ribbings. The edge does not need to be crocheted or otherwise finished.

To work this cast-on, first place the needles in holding position and carriage on the right, and tie the yarn to the left clamp in order to begin wrapping on the left side. The directions in parenthesis indicate an optional additional step that produces a knitted-back version of this cast-on. The second version produces a much more finished edge and makes it easier to control the figure-8 wrapping.

Begin by wrapping over the first needle, under the second; then back over the second and under the first. *Wrap over the first, under the second, over the third; then wrap back under the third and over the second. (Knit the first needle back to

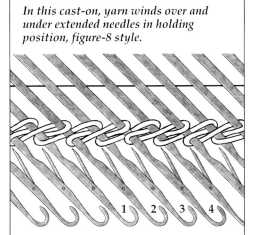

In this cast-on, yarn winds over and under extended needles in holding position, figure-8 style.

1 2 3 4

FIGURE-8 E-WRAP CAST-ON.

KNITTED-BACK FIGURE-8 CAST-ON.

KNITTED-BACK DOUBLE E-WRAP CAST-ON.

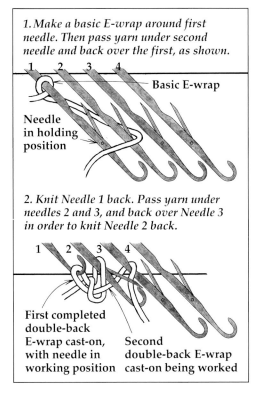

1. Make a basic E-wrap around first needle. Then pass yarn under second needle and back over the first, as shown.

1 2 3 4

Basic E-wrap

Needle in holding position

2. Knit Needle 1 back. Pass yarn under needles 2 and 3, and back over Needle 3 in order to knit Needle 2 back.

1 2 3 4

First completed double-back E-wrap cast-on, with needle in working position

Second double-back E-wrap cast-on being worked

Work a figure-8 cast-on (see the drawing above), and knit back to working position first needle in each group of three.

1 2 3 4 5

Initial wrap of figure-8 cast-on

Completed knitted-back cast-on stitch

Second wrap of figure-8 cast-on

Yarn being laid into needle hook to hand knit three wraps off needle and form stitch securing figure-8 edge

Final (third) wrap of figure-8 cast-on

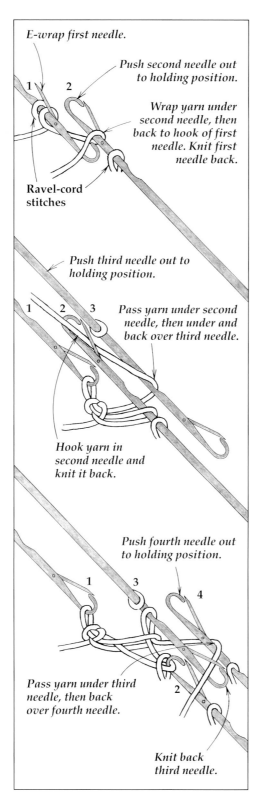

E-wrap first needle.

*Push second needle out
to holding position.*

*Wrap yarn under
second needle, then
back to hook of first
needle. Knit first
needle back.*

**Ravel-cord
stitches**

*Push third needle out to
holding position.*

*Pass yarn under second
needle, then under and
back over third needle.*

*Hook yarn in
second needle and
knit it back.*

*Push fourth needle out
to holding position.*

*Pass yarn under third
needle, then back
over fourth needle.*

*Knit back
third needle.*

working position.) Wrap under the second needle, over the third, under the fourth; back over the fourth and under the third. (Knit the second needle back to working position.)* Repeat from * to * over the remaining needles (always knitting back the first needle in each group of three).

Once the needles are all wrapped, thread the carriage and knit. If the edge has been very tightly wrapped, you may want to bring all the needles back out to holding position and let the carriage knit them back for the first row.

8. Doubled-back E-wrap cast-on.
This double-bed cast-on is less a true E-wrap than a sideways U-wrap because the yarn just passes under and then back over each needle. The edge produced is fairly firm and quite decorative. It is a good choice when you want added body at the cast-on edge.

To work this cast-on, knit eight to ten rows with scrap yarn and one row with ravel cord. Then start with the carriages on the right and the yarn between the beds and tied to the left clamp. Mentally number the needles consecutively from left to right and from bed to bed, as shown in the drawing at left. As you pass the yarn under each needle just before wrapping it, push the needle forward so that its ravel-cord stitch slides back behind the open latch, as in the regular E-wrap cast-on. Wrap around the hooks of the needles, then knit them back in this sequence:

1. E-wrap the first needle and push the second one to holding position. Then pass the yarn under and back over the second needle shaft and into the hook of the first needle.

2. Knit the first needle back to working position.

3. Push the third needle out to holding position. Then pass the yarn under the second and third needles and back over the third one and into the hook of the second needle.

4. Knit the second needle back to working positon.

5. Continue across the bed, passing the yarn under two needles, then back over the second needle to knit the first.

6. When all the needles have been wrapped, thread the yarn into the carriage and knit the first row of the ribbing with stitch size zero. Then move up a stitch size with each row to prevent the lower edge from flaring (see pp. 42-43 for more information on raising the stitch size).

9. Latch-tool cast-on.
Also known as a crocheted, tappet-tool or chain-stitch cast-on, this quick cast-on method produces a closed, slightly less elastic edge than the various E-wrap cast-ons. The edge usually requires a finishing row or two of crochet to prevent it from curling under. This cast-on is also suitable for multiple increasing on the carriage side.

To work this cast-on, move the carriage to the right, tie the yarn to the left clamp and bring the needles to holding position. (Note that although these directions call for working from left to right, you could also work from right to left.) Lay the yarn on top of the needle shafts, in front of the sinker posts. On the extreme left, do a

simple E-wrap on the shaft of the latch tool, then form a stitch on the tool by pulling the free yarn through the E-wrap. Push the tool from below up between the first and second needles and grab the free yarn above with the hook. Then pull the tool down through the loop to form a new stitch. Push the tool up between the second and third needles so that the stitch slides behind the latch and the hook can grab more yarn to form the next stitch. Continue chaining across the needles until you reach the last one on the right. Slip the stitch from the tool onto the needle. Thread the carriage, eliminate any slack and knit the first row.

If you are adept with the double latch tool, you can work with two colors at once by carrying them both across the shafts of the needles and alternating the color grabbed by the latch tool to form each stitch. The two-color method is generally used to apply surface detail by working a row across the main body of a fabric, forming a definite ridge on the purl side. The direction in which the ridge angles can be varied by working with the tool above the needles and the yarn below them—just the opposite of the directions given below. This produces a subtle difference, which is worth noting if you use this technique to highlight stripes or borders.

LATCH-TOOL CAST-ON.

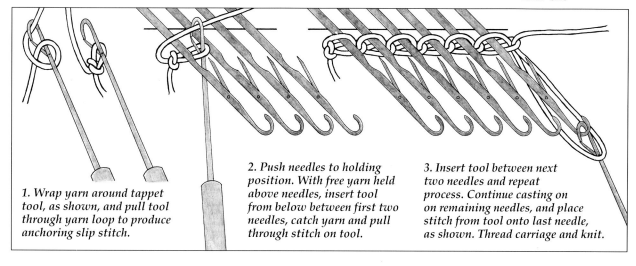

1. Wrap yarn around tappet tool, as shown, and pull tool through yarn loop to produce anchoring slip stitch.

2. Push needles to holding position. With free yarn held above needles, insert tool from below between first two needles, catch yarn and pull through stitch on tool.

3. Insert tool between next two needles and repeat process. Continue casting on on remaining needles, and place stitch from tool onto last needle, as shown. Thread carriage and knit.

10. Alternate crocheted cast-on.

This cast-on method produces an edge of several rows of crochet, rather than just one, which lies flat and needs no further finishing. If color is used, the edge can be quite decorative since its horizontal stitches border the vertical stitches of the main fabric (see the edge in Swatch 2 on p. 53).

Begin as you would for the basic latch-tool cast-on (p. 39), with the needles in holding position and the carriage on the right. *Chain, as for the latch-tool cast-on, from left to right, thread the carriage and knit one row to the left. Remove the yarn from the carriage. Set the carriage for a free pass and return it to the right side.* Repeat from * to * as many times as desired.

The additional rows of crochet will show on the purl side of the fabric unless you nudge the fabric forward on the needles and work the crochet behind it. If you want to introduce color, size or textural contrast, use a separate strand of yarn for the crochet rather than the free yarn from the carriage. Multiple rows of crochet can also be worked before binding off with the latch tool if you want to match both ends of a fabric.

11. Casting on by "hanging a rag."

This method is similar to starting with waste knitting except that it is a lot faster because you simply hang a preknitted scrap of fabric on the needles. You can push the needles through the fabric without having to hang each stitch precisely, then hang weights on the scrap and hand knit a row of ravel cord before continuing with the main knitting. When the ravel cord is later removed and the rag separated from the main knitting, the fabric will have an open edge, unless you choose to E-wrap or chain after knitting the ravel cord. The chief function of the rag in this case is to provide a vehicle for hanging weights and to ensure that the first row of the main knitting knits properly.

ALTERNATE CROCHETED CAST-ON.

Several Rs of basic crocheted C/O transform a functional edge into a decorative one. When successive Rs of chaining are worked behind each other, as they are in photo at right, effect shows on K face of fabric. When Rs are chained in front of each other, effect shows on P face.

To work: With all NDLS in HP and COR, crochet yarn over each NDL. Tr last ST from tool to edge NDL. Thread carr & K 1st R. *Remove yarn from carr & use free pass to ret carr to RT.

With all NDLS in HP, slide previous STS far enough forward on NDL shafts to work 2nd crocheted R behind 1st. First E-wrap latch tool with free yarn. Then crochet R, as shown, stopping short of last NDL.

Remove previous ST from last NDL & tr ST from tool onto NDL. Replace ST removed from NDL on same NDL. Thread carr and K 1 R.* Rep from * to * for desired length of edge.

This technique is also useful for multiple increasing in midfabric, when you want to be sure the first row of stitches knits without difficulty and you cannot use holding position and return levers to make the knitting easier (see also pp. 49-55). Because the rag can be well weighted, this is a good way to cast on small pieces of knitting like appliquées.

12. Casting on by hanging hand-knit ribbing.

True ribbing can be produced automatically only on a double-bed machine. It can be manually produced by latching up or reforming stitches, however, if you have a single-bed machine (see pp. 69-81). If you prefer hand knitting the ribbing to latching it up, you can easily transfer the last row of hand-knit stitches to the needles of the machine.

To cast on with this method, hand knit the ribbing on the recommended size needle, but use a needle a size or two larger to knit the last row. Then hold the needle with the ribbing parallel to the front of the machine bed. Poke a transfer tool through the first stitch on the hand needle and hook the tool onto the first needle of the machine. Lift the tool slightly so the stitch slips off the hand-knitting needle onto the machine needle. Repeat this process until all the stitches have been transferred to the machine.

If you need to increase in the first row, skip a needle on the machine every so often when transferring the stitches, being careful to avoid straining the stitches by forcing increases that skip too many needles at once. Remember that you can also increase at the edges of the first few rows. If you skip needles, go back and fill each empty needle with the purl loop from an adjacent needle to prevent forming a hole when you start knitting.

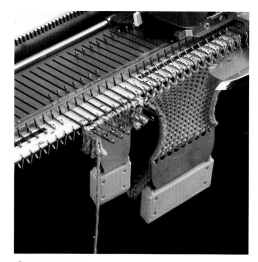

CASTING ON BY HANGING A RAG.

To work: Poke a scrap of fabric over NDLS in HP (shown on L in photo, with main K on RT). Weight scrap & set carr to K NDLS back from HP. Next pass of carr will K 1 R on main K & at same time form open C/O edge on NDLS holding scrap.

CASTING ON BY HANGING A HAND-KNIT RIBBING.

To work: After hand-knitting ribbing, position hand NDL more or less parallel to bed, insert tr tool through end ST & hook tool onto machine NDL. Lift tool slightly up & to L to slip ST from hand NDL to tool & NDL.

Scrap Knitting

Because it's so easy when working on a piece of knitting to change yarns and knit an extra ten rows, machine knitters rely on scrap knitting, or waste knitting, for a wide variety of tasks. Among its functions, scrap serves as an alternative to conventional cast-on and bind-off methods. I think of scrap knitting as the ultimate flexible stitch holder because it allows me safely to begin, end, move and manipulate knitting without worrying about the capacity of a particular tool. I use scrap wherever I can both to divide pieces of knitting for separate design treatments or different garment parts and to eliminate the physical bulk of bound-off stitches that are to be seamed, joined or reworked in some way.

Scrap knitting is particularly useful for casting on with yarns that are very textured or fragile, which tend to split, rip or get skipped in the cast-on process. While these yarns are tricky to cast on alone, they often knit just fine once there is some weighted knitting on the needles.

Always choose a scrap yarn that is the same size as the main yarn but in a contrasting color. The difference in color makes it easier to see and retrieve the live stitches in the main knitting. Avoid textured and fuzzy yarns for scrap knitting because, although they do not ravel as easily as smoother yarns, they often leave a permanent residue of fuzz when the scrap knitting is removed.

To cast on with scrap knitting, thread the carriage with scrap yarn. Use the cast-on method you prefer (see pp. 34-43) and knit eight to ten rows. If you then knit a row of ravel cord, nylon or some other smooth, strong yarn between the scrap and main knitting, the two will separate more easily and without fuzzy residue when the ravel cord or yarn is later removed. Leave several knot-free inches at each end of the row so that you can readily pull the cord or yarn out after treating the live stitches on the main fabric as required.

Scrap knitting is also helpful when stitches in the first few rows of main knitting need to be reformed or manipulated in some other way. Because it's difficult to execute such maneuvers without some weight on the knitting,

13. Basic double-bed, tubular cast-on with scrap and ravel cord.
This cast-on is a variation of the standard double-bed cast-on, and usually eliminates the broken stitches that can be caused by casting on too tightly or by the weight of the cast-on comb necessary with two beds. This cast-on also minimizes the inevitable stretching of the edge by the comb and weights. The tubular edge produced provides a neat place to hide a row of elastic if you are working with cotton yarn, which tends to sag.

This cast-on involves several steps:
1. With scrap yarn, knit one zigzag row (that is, with both beds knitting at the same time), hang the comb and weights, and knit enough rows for the comb to disappear between the beds. (Hanging the comb and weights in the scrap prevents the edge of the main knitting from stretching to accommodate the comb.)

2. Thread the carriage with ravel cord and knit two circular rows (that is, one row on one bed and then a row on the other bed) with a stitch size you think is appropriate for stockinette in your particular yarn.

3. Rethread the carriage with the main yarn and set the carriage to the smallest stitch size. Knit one zigzag row and then two circular rows.

I like to knit and weight some scrap to get the knitting started. And when I'm working double-bed ribbed cast-ons, I start with scrap knitting because it always produces a beautiful, firm edge that holds its shape and doesn't flare, regardless of the yarn that is used.

When the directions instruct you to "scrap off" rather than bind off, it means to knit about ten rows with scrap yarn, then remove all weights from the fabric, take the yarn out of the carriage and cut it, leaving a short tail. Hold the fabric down with your hand and run the empty carriage across the bed so the knitting drops from the machine. The last row of stitches in the main knitting is still live, but with enough rows of scrap knitting on top of it, it is secure and will not run. Since both the scrap and, in turn, the main knitting can run, however, don't skimp on the scrap rows. Always steam scrap knitting to fluff, or bloom, the yarn and retard raveling. As when casting on with scrap knitting, you can separate the scrap and main knitting with a single row of ravel cord or yarn to make it easier to separate the two pieces later.

If I know that a piece of knitting is going to be saved for a while or handled a great deal, I bind off the last row of the scrap knitting to prevent it from raveling. On my standard-gauge machines I use a linker attachment to speed things up by automatically binding off these stitches.

Keep in mind when using scrap that you're usually preserving open, or live, stitches in the main knitting, which require further treatment to keep them from running after the scrap is removed. To crochet the live stitches in the last row of the main knitting, simply fold the scrap back and work with these stitches as if the scrap weren't there.

Most knitters are anxious to remove the scrap as soon possible. Yet if it is left in place, scrap knitting generally doesn't interfere with further work on the piece and actually makes it much easier to retrieve and fix any mistakes. Scrap also allows you to change your mind when you're experimenting with something new.

4. Set the carriage to knit needles in holding position. Put all needles in hold and knit one row with stitch size 1.

5. Put all needles in hold and knit the second row with stitch size 2.

6. Continue knitting ribbing, putting the needles into holding position before each row and raising the stitch size by one number every row until you reach the desired stitch size for the rest of your rib. Although ribs are usually knitted on a stitch size that is half the size of the stitches chosen for the main fabric, do a sample first to determine which stitch size knits a rib with the best elasticity. Putting the needles into holding position helps

relieve the strain of tight stitches, making the carriage move more easily and enabling it to knit very small stitch sizes without breaking the stitches. And raising the stitch size one number per row helps eliminate flare.

If you're working with a tight, inelastic yarn and want to ensure perfect stitches, continue bringing needles to holding position before each row for the entire rib, even after you've reached the rib's correct stitch size. By doing this, you run less risk of splitting the yarn or tucking some of the stitches.

GATHERING-STITCH
BIND-OFF.

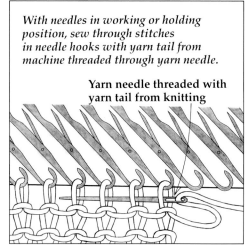

With needles in working or holding position, sew through stitches in needle hooks with yarn tail from machine threaded through yarn needle.

Yarn needle threaded with yarn tail from knitting

Bind-off methods

All bind-offs secure the edge stitches so that they will not run. Some bind-off methods produce a finished edge, while others yield an edge that may need additional crocheted embellishment or ribbing. The choice of bind-off method depends on the desired appearance of the finished edge, the elasticity the edge requires and your ability to maintain even tension when binding off, which is harder to do with some methods than with others.

Most bind-offs require the stitches to be somewhat elastic, which can be achieved by knitting the last row at a much larger stitch size than that used for the main knitting. Even when elasticity is not a concern, the bind-off tends to tighten and narrow the work if the last row is not enlarged. If the main knitting is done with one of the largest stitch sizes on your dial, you should refer to the section on drop stitch (pp. 65-67) in order to obtain a large enough stitch size for binding off.

1. Gathering-stitch bind-off.
The simplest way to remove stitches from the machine is to thread the yarn tail through a yarn needle and run it through

BASIC TRANSFER-TOOL
BIND-OFF.

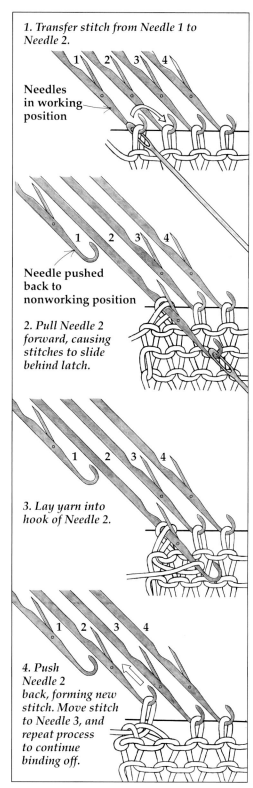

1. Transfer stitch from Needle 1 to Needle 2.

Needles in working position

Needle pushed back to nonworking position

2. Pull Needle 2 forward, causing stitches to slide behind latch.

3. Lay yarn into hook of Needle 2.

4. Push Needle 2 back, forming new stitch. Move stitch to Needle 3, and repeat process to continue binding off.

the stitches. The machine needles can be placed in either working position or holding position.

This bind-off is an obvious choice when you need to gather stitches for decorative or functional purposes. But you can also gather stitches just to hold them until you are ready to work with them later.

If you are working with bulky yarns, which are sometimes tricky to gather, run the yarn through every other stitch, then carry it back to the beginning and run it through the alternate stitches previously skipped. This bind-off makes the gathering easier and matches the every-other-needle and weaving cast-on edges.

2. Basic transfer-tool bind-off.

The transfer-tool bind-off is the first one that most knitters learn for decreasing multiple stitches and binding off. This edge is fairly inelastic, and evenly controlling the tension on it can be difficult.

To work this bind-off, use a single-eyelet transfer tool to move the first stitch onto the second needle and then pull the needle forward to holding position so the two stitches slide behind the latch (see the drawing at right on the facing page). Lay the free yarn into the hook of the needle, and then push the needle back to working position so the two stitches slide over the closed latch and a single new stitch is formed. The new stitch is moved to the third needle, and the process continues until all the stitches are bound off.

For most beginners, the basic transfer-tool bind-off tends to produce a narrow, tight edge because the tension on the stitches being bound off can be tricky to control. An alternative method, shown in the drawing at right, adds one simple step to the basic method that all manuals teach,

ALTERNATIVE TRANSFER-TOOL BIND-OFF.

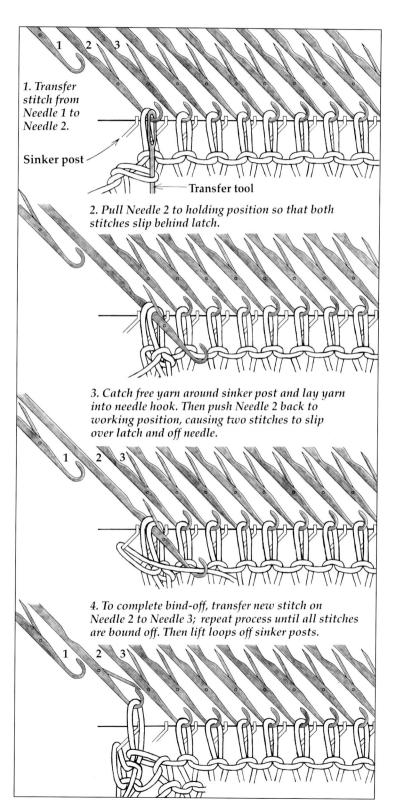

1. Transfer stitch from Needle 1 to Needle 2.

Sinker post

Transfer tool

2. Pull Needle 2 to holding position so that both stitches slip behind latch.

3. Catch free yarn around sinker post and lay yarn into needle hook. Then push Needle 2 back to working position, causing two stitches to slip over latch and off needle.

4. To complete bind-off, transfer new stitch on Needle 2 to Needle 3; repeat process until all stitches are bound off. Then lift loops off sinker posts.

and ensures that the bind-off will be evenly spaced and the stitches not be too tight. Before laying the yarn into the hook of each needle, pass it behind the adjacent sinker post. On machines that have flow combs rather than sinker posts, pass the yarn around the previous (empty) needle instead. If you are decreasing, remember to remove the loops from the sinker posts or empty needles before continuing to knit, since otherwise the knitting will bunch up against the bed.

3. Latch-tool bind-off.

The latch-tool bind-off, also called a tappet-tool or crocheted bind-off, is quick and easy to do. Each stitch is chained through the next, without adding any new yarn. This produces a row of horizontal stitches that lie perpendicular to the vertical stitches of the main fabric. The edge will match the latch-tool cast-on edge (see p. 39) and is, in fact, the same bind-off produced by an automatic linking accessory.

To bind off with this method, knit the last row with the largest stitch size possible and bring the needles all the way forward to holding position. Break the yarn, leaving a 6-in. long tail. Starting on the side opposite the tail, use the thumb of one hand to push needle butts back to nonworking position while the other hand manipulates the latch tool as follows: Insert the tool into the first stitch on the side opposite the tail so that, as the needle is pushed back to nonworking position, the stitch slips over the latch and onto the tool. Push the tool far enough forward for the stitch to slip behind the tool's latch. Insert the tool into the second stitch, push the second needle back to nonworking position and pull the second stitch through the first. Continue chaining one stitch through the next until you reach the end. Pull the yarn tail through the last stitch to secure the chain.

Because no free yarn is worked into the stitches with this bind-off, the edge tends to be very tight and may make the fabric too narrow. The stretch of this bind-off can be increased by working additional yarn into the chain of stitches and using the sinker posts—or if your machine does not have sinker posts, the empty needle to the left of each stitch—to space the bound-off stitches evenly and prevent tightening as additional yarn is used to chain the edge.

To work this variation on the basic bind-off, knit the last row with the largest stitch size, ending with the carriage on the left. Unthread the carriage, but do not break the yarn. Bring the needles out to holding position, keeping the fabric back against the bed. Your left hand should be holding the yarn to the left and behind the sinker post adjacent to the first needle, and the latch tool should be in your right hand.

Grasp the hook of the first needle with the hook of the latch tool, while guiding the needle butt back to working position with your left thumb. The stitch will slide off the needle onto the shaft of the tool. Lay the free yarn into the hook of the tool and pull the tool back to form a new stitch. Because the yarn has passed behind the sinker post, the bound-off stitch will be held against the front edge of the bed. Push the latch tool upward to place the new stitch behind the latch of the tool and then hook the tool onto the second needle, keeping the free yarn behind the adjacent sinker post. Use your thumb to nudge the second needle butt back into working position, so its stitch slides behind the latch of the tool. Lay the free yarn into the hook and pull the tool back so that the two stitches slide off over a new one. Continue in this fashion across to the last stitch. Break the yarn and pull the tail through the last stitch.

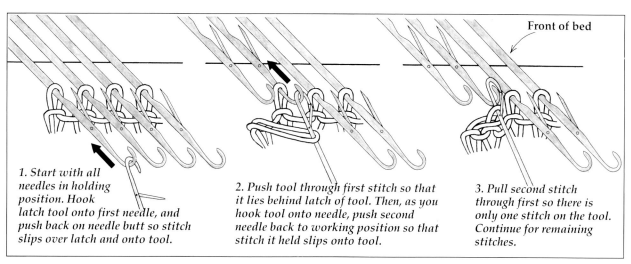

Front of bed

1. Start with all needles in holding position. Hook latch tool onto first needle, and push back on needle butt so stitch slips over latch and onto tool.

2. Push tool through first stitch so that it lies behind latch of tool. Then, as you hook tool onto needle, push second needle back to working position so that stitch it held slips onto tool.

3. Pull second stitch through first so there is only one stitch on the tool. Continue for remaining stitches.

LATCH-TOOL BIND-OFF.

LATCH-TOOL BIND-OFF.

To work: With all NDLS in HP, hook latch tool onto 1st NDL (above). Hold free yarn in L hand, keeping it to L of sinker post. Use L thumb to guide NDL back to WP so that ST slips over latch of NDL & onto tool.

Push tool through ST so that ST opens latch & lies behind it (above right). Catch free yarn in hook of tool & pull yarn through to form new ST.

Rep 3 steps, making sure always to keep free yarn to L of sinker post. From here on, always pull free yarn through 2 STS to form a new ST (right). Push tool through ST so ST lies behind latch. Hook tool onto next NDL at RT & rep all steps until all STS are B/O.

*BACK-STITCH
BIND-OFF.*

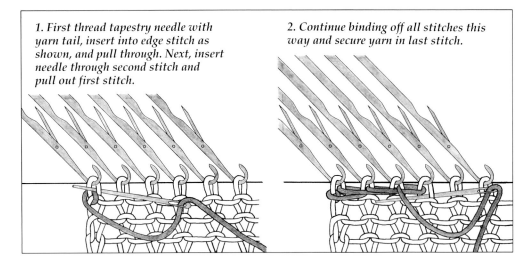

1. First thread tapestry needle with yarn tail, insert into edge stitch as shown, and pull through. Next, insert needle through second stitch and pull out first stitch.

2. Continue binding off all stitches this way and secure yarn in last stitch.

*LATCH-TOOL
RIBBED BIND-OFF.*

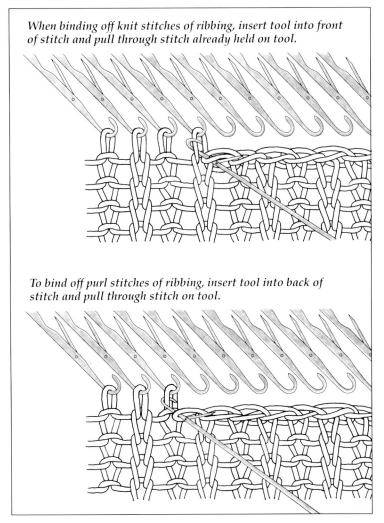

When binding off knit stitches of ribbing, insert tool into front of stitch and pull through stitch already held on tool.

To bind off purl stitches of ribbing, insert tool into back of stitch and pull through stitch on tool.

4. Back-stitch bind-off.

Back stitching produces a stretchier bind-off than either of the basic transfer-tool or crocheted methods. This bind-off is useful for seaming on the machine and for binding off edges where you want to be sure there is no narrowing of the fabric.

End with the carriage on either side, and cut the yarn to leave a tail at least twice as long as the width of the knitting. Some people prefer to place the needles in hold; others prefer working position. Use whichever needle position is most comfortable for you. If you are starting on the left, thread the yarn through a blunt yarn needle (or use your bodkin if it's handy) and sew down into the center of the first stitch and out at the left side. (If you're starting on the right, reverse these instructions.) Pulling the yarn around in front of the stitches, sew into the center of the second stitch and out the center of the first stitch. Next sew into the center of the third stitch and out the center of the second. Continue in this fashion across all the stitches on the needles and remove the fabric from the needles.

5. Latch-tool ribbed bind-off.
This latch-tool bind-off has as much stretch as the ribbing itself because it too is done in a knit-purl alternation. It is just as effective for binding off latched-up, single-bed ribbing as it is for true double-bed ribs.

Ribbed bind-offs are always a matter of great concern because most are not stretchy enough to fit over the head or a wrist. Many knitters try to avoid the problem by knitting the rib and then hanging the garment on the same needles and binding the two off together. While this approach eliminates the need to bind off in rib, it produces a seamed effect where the rib joins the garment. I prefer knitting my garment, transferring the appropriate stitches to the ribber and then knitting the ribbing directly onto the garment.

For double-bed ribbing, you can do a simple latch-tool bind-off, working from one bed to the other and turning the tool so its hook always faces the hook of the needle, but I find this method clumsy. Because the same stitches can be formed more easily by working on one bed, I always transfer all the stitches from the front bed to the back bed after knitting the last row of the ribbing. Important as it is to knit the last row before a bind-off with an enlarged stitch size, it is even more important when binding off in ribbing.

The actual bind-off process I use is very much like the simple latch-tool bind-off, except that when you remove a knit stitch, you insert the hook of the tool into the front of the stitch; and when you remove a purl stitch, you insert the tool into the back of the stitch. Alternatively, you could insert the hook of the tool in the front of the purls and the back of the knits. It does not matter which way you do it as long as you are consistent.

Holding stitches

Most knitters are familiar with putting stitches into holding position to do short rowing, or partial knitting. Holding position is often used as well to knit graduations for large-scale intarsia designs and to shape shoulder slants and most skirts knit sideways. Holding stitches is also useful for producing scalloped edges and patterned or sculpted surfaces, overriding carriage commands, introducing changes in stitch size or color in a single row, and helping the machine more easily knit tight stitches. Of all the basic moves, holding has the widest range of applications.

When you place a needle or group of needles into holding position, the needle butts avoid the working triangular pathway in the carriage cams and, instead, pass straight instead through the upper channel. Consequently needles in holding position stop knitting. The stitches on these needle remain live, however, and can resume knitting whenever the needles are moved back into working position or upper working position. While needles in holding position stop knitting, any other needles on the bed still in working position continue to knit, and these stitches continue to accumulate rows and thus length. Therefore, by moving groups of needles into holding position at various times, a fabric can be divided into various sections that are knitted independently of one another and treated differently in terms of structure and design.

Although every knitting machine is capable of holding stitches, models vary in their mechanics and flexibility (check your manual for information on your machine). Some machines, usually the very basic models, have an upper pathway that is permanently open and able to hold. Needles on these knitting machines can only be manually returned to working position. Most machines, however, have buttons or levers that open and close the upper pathway and which are pressed or manipulated when pattern instructions direct you to "set the carriage for holding" or "knit needles in holding position." (The Passap machine uses the BX setting on the lock and pushers to place needles into holding position.)

Placing needles into hold

Putting needles into holding position is always done manually. A single needle or a group of needles can be put into hold. And when a group of needles is to be held, the needles can be moved into holding position all at once or gradually.

HOLDING AN ISOLATED NEEDLE.

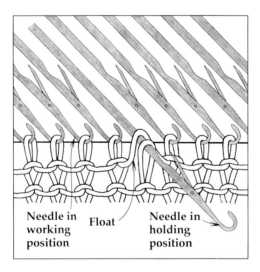

Needle in working position   Float   Needle in holding position

1. TWO KNITTED SECTIONS WORKED SEPARATELY BY USING HOLDING POSITION.

Using holding position to treat 2 sections of K differently produces vertical slits at points where NDLS are held. All these slits except 2nd from bottom were closed by hand after fabric was removed from the machine.

When a needle is placed into hold with working needles on each side of it, the carriage yarn simply floats over the shaft of the holding needle and knits a stitch on each of the adjacent needles. The number of floats a needle can collect before it must knit them off in a tuck stitch depends on the arrangement of working and holding needles, the yarn, weights and the machine itself. Eventually, the needle must be allowed to knit again because as the floats accumulate, they affect the tension on the adjacent stitches and can cause the neighboring needles to knit improperly.

When a needle is placed into hold at the side edge of the fabric, it does not collect floats, nor can it form a tuck stitch when returned to working position. Because there are no working needles at the outermost edge to anchor a float, the yarn remains free as the carriage passes by a needle in hold at an edge. Stitches held at the edge seem almost to have been bound off and forgotten, but in reality they are live. In fact, every time another needle joins or leaves a group of held stitches at the edge, it redefines the edge of the fabric.

The look and structure of the fabric is affected by the sequence in which needles are placed into hold and the length of time they are held. When a number of adjacent needles are to be held, you can either put them all into hold at once or start with a few needles in hold and gradually add the rest. The first approach creates a sharper division between the two sections of knitting, and the second method creates a slanting effect.

Consider an example: All the needles to the left of the center zero on the bed are placed in hold, and the needles to the right of zero knit 50 rows. Then the left group of needles returns to working position and knits 50 rows, while the right needles are held. Both groups of needles have knit 50 rows, but there will be a vertical slit between the two lengths of knitting. Each of the sections can be treated differently — that is, knitted with a different yarn, color, stitch size, division or cam setting — and the vertical slit separating them can remain open or be seamed later (Swatch 1).

If, instead of knitting 50 rows, each group of needles is alternately held and then knits for, say, two rows, the resulting sections can still be treated differently, and the slit can be avoided by wrapping. To do this, every time the carriage knits across the section and reaches the dividing point between the holding and working needles, catch the free yarn under the first holding needle before knitting back to the beginning edge.

If a group of needles is placed in hold gradually, rather than all at once, the resulting edge of the knitting will be slanted, not vertical. The gradual placement of needles into hold is used to shape shoulders and shirt panels knit sideways as well as to build intarsia design. Although this method does not produce a vertical slit between the working and holding needles, it does create a small but noticeable hole between the two sections. There are times when this hole will neither matter nor show, times when it may add to the design and times when it must be avoided by wrapping. Your design, yarn and cam setting can all help offset these holes, but it often boils down to a matter of taste. More often than not, the holes should be avoided.

Wrapping can be done by hand, as explained above, or automatically. Not surprisingly, automatic wrapping is the faster alternative, but it can be used only when needles are put into hold on alternate rows. To wrap automatically, begin with the carriage on the side of the

WRAPPING NEEDLES TO AVOID A SLIT.

1. Pull designated needles into holding position.

Needle in working position

Needle in holding position

2. With next pass of carriage, new stitches will form on working needles, and yarn will pass over needles in hold.

3. To close slit that will otherwise form in fabric, wrap yarn under first held needle before knitting back over working needles.

Yarn wrapping under first held needle

Loop that forms on first held needle will be knit together with existing stitch on that needle when held needles are put back into working position.

Loop closing vertical slit

bed opposite from where you will be holding. On the appropriate side of the bed, put into holding position one less needle than you ultimately need to hold. Knit one row, put one more needle into hold and knit back. If you need to hold five needles, for example, you initially hold only four, then knit one row and put the fifth into hold before the carriage is knitted back. The last, single needle that is held accounts for the wrap.

When you're gradually moving needles in and out of holding position, the tension on any adjacent working needles can be pesky to control. To avoid dropped or badly knitted stitches, keep your weights under working needles and move the weights often. Move them up the fabric as it grows to keep them close to the working needles.

Putting needles into holding position is always done manually, but returning them to working position can be done manually or automatically, depending on the machine's capabilities, the position of the other needles being used and the patterning involved in the effect you want. If you want a slanting effect, you must return the needles gradually, which has to be done manually. If the needles were gradually placed into hold to begin with, they should be returned to work in the same size groups.

If you want a vertical division between the two sections of fabric, you must return all the needles as a group, which can be done by simply setting the carriage to knit them back. However, if your patterning calls for some needles to be held and others to be returned to working position, you will

Seaming a Vertical Slit

Sometimes, instead of knitting, wrapping and joining two sections at once, it's faster, easier and just as effective to knit the sections separately and seam them later. If you seam the edges of a vertical slit, you'll need to sacrifice one stitch from each edge being seamed. The missing stitch is apt to show, and the fabric will be narrowed. If several seams are needed for a particular design, seaming will definitely affect the sizing of the garment. Therefore, it's always necessary to provide extra stitches specifically for seams as each section is knitted.

In Swatch 1 on p. 50, one group of adjacent needles was placed in hold while the others knitted, with the dividing line between the holding and working needles shifting for each section of the design. Extra seam stitches were added to each section as it was knit, and the sections were left unjoined for later seaming. To produce this, or a similar edge, follow the instructions below:

1. On the left of zero, transfer the stitch from Needle 1 to Needle 2. Put Needle 2 and all the needles to the left of it into holding po-sition. Needle 1 left is now empty, and Needle 2 left holds two stitches.

2. Make a seam stitch for the right half of the fabric by filling the empty Needle 1 left with the purl loop from Needle 1 right.

3. Set the carriage for holding and knit the right-hand section of the fabric, which now includes Needle 1 left.

4. Transfer the seam stitch from Needle 1 left to Needle 1 right, and then transfer both of them onto Needle 2 right.

5. Put Needle 2 right and all needles to the right of it into holding position.

6. On the left, return the stitch from Needle 2 left to Needle 1 left, and use its purl bar to fill Needle 1 right.

7. Include Needle 1 right as you knit the left half of the fabric.

8. Return the stitch from Needle 1 right to Needle 1 left, and then return two of the three stitches on Needle 2 right to Needle 1 right.

9. Needles 1, both right and left, now hold double stitches, the extra stitches for later seaming by hand.

need to place the returning needles manually in upper working position, where they will be able to resume knitting.

When dealing with the edges of a fabric, you can put a single needle in hold or return it to working position at either side, but you can usually manipulate groups of two or more needles only if they are on the side opposite the carriage. The angle of the slanted edge that results depends on the number of needles placed in hold and the rate at which they were moved into this position. For example, if you place a total of 20 needles in hold by moving groups of five, every other row, the slant

will be much shallower than if you placed the same 20 needles in hold two at a time, every other row.

When groups of stitches are held and gradually returned to working position at the edge of a fabric, a slanted edge is produced (Swatch 2). However, when the same method is applied within the body of a fabric, a diagonal texture results (Swatch 3). Although holding and returning groups of needles within a fabric seems contrary to basic guidelines for using holding position, sometimes creative innovation is just an exception to the rules — and the mother of many inventions.

2. CREATING A SLANTED EDGE WITH HOLDING POSITION.

To work: Slanted edge is 1st C/O as 3 Rs of crocheted C/O (see p. 39). Then begin K with all but 1 NDL in HP. *K 1 R & ret 1 NDL to work.* Rep from * to * until all NDLS are working.

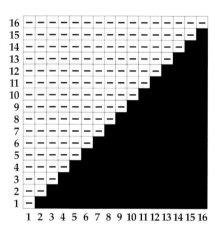

3. GRADUALLY RETURNING STITCHES TO WORKING POSITION WITHIN FABRIC.

Pat rep is produced by advancing 2 STS to RT for each new rep. If ST(S) to immediate RT of each held group does not K well, bring group to UWP before K each R. Bring groups of 4 STS to HP all at once; ret to UWP gradually.

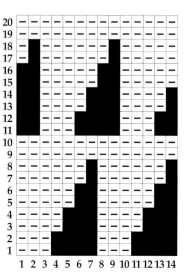

Pattern effects

Patterns created by holding tend to have either slanted edges (which can also grow into mitered sculptures when the slants are repeated in various ways) or three-dimensional, sculptured surfaces. With this latter group, the pattern may make the entire fabric look puckered or gathered, as in swatches 3 and 4. Alternatively, the dimensional texture may rise from a smooth, undisturbed background fabric, as in swatches 5, 6, 7 and 8.

These various pattern effects are determined by several variables — the number and location in the fabric of needles held and the number of rows they are held; whether the needles are placed into hold gradually, all at once as a group or in a patterned sequence; and how the needles are returned to working position. For example, if immediately after casting on, every sixth stitch is held for six rows and then allowed to knit, a scalloped edging is produced, with a textured tuck pattern across the middle of the fabric, as in Swatch 4. Generally, the longer a stitch is held, the more loops it collects and the bolder the texture.

4. CREATING A SCALLOPED EDGE AND TUCKED PATTERN WITH HOLDING POSITION.

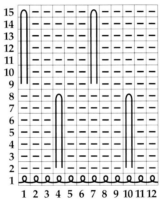

5. RUFFLED TRIM, EDGE AND FLOWER PRODUCED BY HOLDING.

To work: Basic ruffled trim at bottom right is made, starting with COR, by E-wrapping to C/O 3 STS, then holding 1 NDL and K 8 Rs, as shown on chart. Flower is K by rep basic scallop-trim sequence 9 times. End with gathering B/O (see p. 44-45), gather straight edge of trim & secure it tightly. Ruffled edge is worked in same way as trim, but all NDLS of main fabric except 2 edge NDLS are placed in HP, while extra Rs are K on 2 edge STS.

6. RAISED SCALLOP TRIM AND INSERT.

To work: For trim, COR, & E-wrap C/O 9 STS. *Immediately put NDLS 1, 2 & 3 into HP, & K 1 R. COL. Put NDLS 7, 8 & 9 into HP, & K 7 Rs over NDLS rem in WP, ending with COR. Ret NDLS 1, 2 & 3 to UWP, & K 1 R. Ret NDLS 7, 8 & 9, & K 3 Rs, ending with COR.* Rep from * to *. RT edge of large sample shows trim folded & hand-sewn to edge.

Vertical insert in large sample is worked in same way as trim, but all NDLS in fabric except 3 for insert STS are put into HP. Do not wrap adj STS for insert or trim.

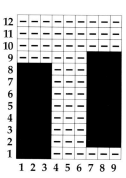

7. RAISED NOPPS.

Nopps can decorate a fabric as isolated motifs, 'popcorns' in vertical or horizontal Rs or as an allover pat. Nopps are formed on 2 or 3 STS, depending on how large you want them, and they're worked all at once before moving on to work neighboring nopp or other texture. They differ from popcorns since they do not require lifting STS.

× = wrap.

Start Cor

CARRIAGE MOTION FOR RAISED NOPPS.

To work: COR. Bring to HP all NDLS to L of 1st group of 2 or 3 NDLS on which nopp is to be formed. K 1 R. COL. *Bring to HP all NDLS to RT of NDLS designated for nopp. Then, if working with 2 STS, K 8 Rs total, ending with COR. If working with 3 STS, K 10 Rs, ending with COR. Bring NDLS for next nopp to L & all NDLS in between to UWP.* K 1 R. COL. Rep from * to *. (Last R of 1 nopp becomes 1st R of next nopp.)

8. ALLOVER RAISED NOPPS.

These nopps are K exactly like the raised scallop trim in Swatch 6, except they're wrapped at 1 edge every time carr is on that side. Other edge is wrapped only once (for 2-ST nopp) or twice (for 3-ST nopp). Nopps always lean to side with fewest wraps.

Nopps in bottom horizontal R of Swatch 7 were K for 8 Rs over 2 STS with plain STS worked in between. Nopps in upper horizontal R were K in same way, but without plain STS in between. Nopps in vertical columns were worked on same 2 NDLS with 3 plain Rs K in between (diagram above shows carr motion and wrapping). And allover fabric in Swatch 8 was worked using alternating groups of 3 STS & K for 10 Rs. Nopps in odd-numbered Rs were wrapped when COL, while those in even-numbered Rs were wrapped when COR.

9. *FERN LACE, WORKED BY HOLDING AND PROGRESSIVELY KNITTING SECTIONS OF THE FABRIC.*

Fern lace is generally used in sideways K sweaters or as an insertion. This example K 10 Rs over groups of 6 STS, but number of STS in groups can be larger or smaller, according to your taste and gauge.

To work: K 4 Rs with a tight SS (2 or 3 sizes less than for K stockinette with same yarn), ending with COR. Reset SS for stockinette. Put all NDLS except 1st 6 on carr side into HP; K 10 Rs on these 6 NDLS, ending COR. *Ret next 3 NDLS at L to UWP & K 1 R (COL). Bring 3 NDLS on RT edge to HP & K 9 Rs more, ending with COR.* Rep from * to * until all NDLS have K, always retaining a group of 6 NDLS. With tight SS, K 4 Rs over all NDLS, ending COL. Rep entire process from L to RT (reading COR as COL to reverse process), ending with 4 tight Rs to help retain shape of background fabric so it can support extra surface texture.

When a group of working needles in the center of the fabric is bordered by holding needles at each edge, the working needles can continue knitting without interference from the adjacent, held needles. Swatch 9 shows a Nihon Vogue technique in which the working-needle group continually shifts and increases to the left (or right), while the number of needles placed in holding position increases on the right (or left).

Overriding carriage commands

Holding position can also be used to override and augment a punchcard or electronic pattern by offering the needles an alternative to the cam selection. When you knit a punchcard pattern with the cams set to tuck and you push a group of needles back from holding to upper working position, the needles will all form knit stitches, regardless of the pattern on the card, because their butts are too far forward in the carriage to enter the working pathway governed by the cam lever. If you want to return stitches from holding to working position and still maintain the tuck patterning, you'll need to use an eyelet transfer tool to return each stitch manually to the hook of its needle in working position where it can enter the working pathway.

The fact that needles automatically or manually knitted back from either holding or upper working position will override cam settings can be used to advantage to produce knit, tuck and slip stitches all in the same row (Swatch 10). To produce all three stitches in one row, first set the cam lever to slip and set the carriage to hold. Then manually designate the needles you want to slip by leaving them in working position (these needles will slip, just as the cams instruct them to). Place the needles you want to knit in upper working position (where they'll knit, since they have no other choice), and move the needles you want to tuck into holding position (where the yarn will pass over the needle shafts, forming tucks when these needles eventually knit again, as they must). If you use a punchcard to select the slips and knits, you need only hand pull the tuck needles.

When knitting tuck or Fair Isle, whether with manual or automatic selection, you can create a vertical stripe of stockinette stitches if the same group of needles is pushed to hold before every row and the carriage is set to knit them back (Swatch 11). On tuck fabric, this override produces a stripe of stockinette stitch. On Fair Isle fabric, it creates a solid stripe in the pattern color. If different needles are selected each time, the stripe becomes a

pattern motif. This motif can be as large as you want, enabling you to produce designs larger than your machine's patterning repeat could do alone.

In addition to using holding position to override the carriage selection, you can also hold needles in working position. This is done by *not* selecting the needles you want to hold. The cams are set to slip, and the carriage is set to knit needles back from holding position. Any needles placed in hold will be knitted back, and those left in working position will effectively be held because they were slipped. This method is

10. *KNIT-SLIP-AND-TUCK PATTERN, USING HOLDING POSITION TO OVERRIDE CAMS AND WORK ALL THREE STITCHES IN ONE ROW.*

To work: Set cam to slip NDLS in WP & use a card punched as shown, or use larger rep that slips & K 4 STS. RT edge of each group slipping is placed in HP for 1st 4 Rs & ret to UWP as adj NDL is placed in HP for next bloc of slipped STS.

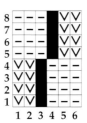

	1	2	3	4	5	6
8	−	−	−	■	V	V
7	−	−	−	■	V	V
6	−	−	−	■	V	V
5	−	−	−	■	V	V
4	V	V	■	−	−	−
3	V	V	■	−	−	−
2	V	V	■	−	−	−
1	V	V	■	−	−	−

MANUAL NEEDLE-SELECTION CHART.

PUNCHCARD.

11. *FAIR ISLE PATTERN WITH LARGE HAND-PULLED MOTIF.*

To work: In chart, X indicates a NDL brought to HP. Carr will always K these NDLS back with MC, overriding carr selection. Pat K every other ST & every other R, & is one usually found on Card 1 supplied with most KMs. Any small rep pat is appropriate.

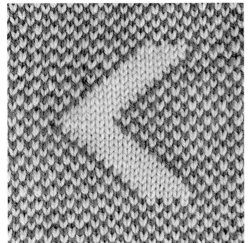

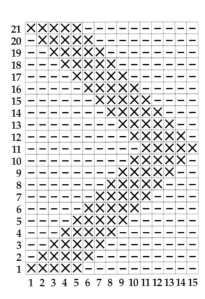

	1	2	3	4	5	6	7	8	9	10	11	12	13	14	15
21	X	X	X	X	−	−	−	−	−	−	−	−	−	−	−
20	−	X	X	X	X	−	−	−	−	−	−	−	−	−	−
19	−	−	X	X	X	X	−	−	−	−	−	−	−	−	−
18	−	−	−	X	X	X	X	−	−	−	−	−	−	−	−
17	−	−	−	−	X	X	X	X	−	−	−	−	−	−	−
16	−	−	−	−	−	X	X	X	X	−	−	−	−	−	−
15	−	−	−	−	−	−	X	X	X	X	−	−	−	−	−
14	−	−	−	−	−	−	−	X	X	X	X	−	−	−	−
13	−	−	−	−	−	−	−	−	X	X	X	X	−	−	−
12	−	−	−	−	−	−	−	−	−	X	X	X	X	−	−
11	−	−	−	−	−	−	−	−	−	−	X	X	X	X	−
10	−	−	−	−	−	−	−	−	−	X	X	X	X	−	−
9	−	−	−	−	−	−	−	−	X	X	X	X	−	−	−
8	−	−	−	−	−	−	−	X	X	X	X	−	−	−	−
7	−	−	−	−	−	−	X	X	X	X	−	−	−	−	−
6	−	−	−	−	−	X	X	X	X	−	−	−	−	−	−
5	−	−	−	−	X	X	X	X	−	−	−	−	−	−	−
4	−	−	−	X	X	X	X	−	−	−	−	−	−	−	−
3	−	−	X	X	X	X	−	−	−	−	−	−	−	−	−
2	−	X	X	X	X	−	−	−	−	−	−	−	−	−	−
1	X	X	X	X	−	−	−	−	−	−	−	−	−	−	−

often faster and more convenient than the conventional methods of holding when more needles need to be held than knitted, or when the selection changes every row or two.

One of my favorite uses for holding is something I call "bridging." This technique enables me to deal differently with all of the stitches in the same row by holding and then knitting each section in turn. I use this method when I knit popcorns by the continuous method, using the carriage yarn (see pp. 139-141). The needles for each popcorn actually knit several extra rows, but the needles between popcorns are allowed to knit only one row before being returned to hold. I call the distance between popcorns a bridge.

I also use holding position to interrupt the carriage to change stitch size from one group of needles to the next (see pp. 63-65). For pattern stitches like Chinese knots (see Swatch 42 on p. 111), I interrupt the carriage so that I can hand knit specific needles.

Easing strain on the machine

One of the best and most common uses for holding position has nothing at all to do with holding stitches. Instead, holding position can serve to help the machine knit more easily in potentially difficult situations. When the carriage is moved across needles in working position, it pushes them forward, places the yarn in their hooks and then pulls them back to form new stitches. Pulling needles back is easier for a carriage than pushing them forward. When you're knitting with particularly heavy yarns, small stitch sizes, several stitches on a needle or crossed and twisted stitches, the difficulty the machine has in pushing the needles forward is increased. Manually placing the needles in hold and setting the carriage to knit them back relieves the extra strain on the carriage, helping it knit more smoothly and minimizing the chance of dropped, broken or unknitted stitches.

After crossing cables, I always bring the needles out to holding position in order to relieve the strain of the crossed stitches. But if the cables are so tightly crossed that their needles touch and almost cross when pushed out to holding position, I ease them back to upper working position so they separate a bit and knit more easily. Placing needles in upper working position is a little slower and more deliberate than pushing them all the way forward on the bed to holding position, but it's easier for the carriage to knit tight stitches from this position. It's also the only option when you want to continue holding any other stitches for patterning or shaping, or if you're working on a very basic machine that is unable to knit back automatically.

Alternatives to holding position

There are times when it's neither convenient nor possible to use holding position, whatever the purpose. If you were manually working a tuck pattern, for example, you might not want to be bothered with returning specific needles from holding position to upper working position every time you wanted them to knit. Yet you would not be able to use automatic return levers if any needles were supposed to remain in hold. Similarly, you cannot use holding position when working with most lace carriages because they're unable to accommodate needles in that position and will jam, damaging both needles and carriage.

The most obvious alternative to holding position in such circumstances is to use a stitch holder and remove the live stitches from the needles altogether. Scrap knitting or stitch holders with eyelet prongs and covers are the most convenient holding tools because you can easily replace the stitches on the needles later. You can also use large safety pins, hand-knitting stitch holders and circular needles to hold stitches, or you can simply transfer one or more stitches to empty needles on the opposite bed, as was done in Swatch 12 (see also Swatch 100 on p. 169).

12. BUTTERFLY STITCH.

This popular hand-knit stitch requires 2 different methods of holding when K by machine.

To work: Center ST of each butterfly is placed in HP & collects tuck STS. ST on each side of center ST are tr to RB NDLS (or hand-knitting NDL if working on SB machine) to place floats on K side of fabric.

According to chart below at left, alternately form butterflies on group A and B NDLS from 1 row to next. Note that there is 1 NDL between A & B groups, which always K plain STS. Raise RB to 1st dropped position (about 1 in. from MB) & remove RB carr. *Tr STS 1 & 3 of each group A to RB to be held; these NDLS will not K. Put NDL 2 in each group A into HP & set MB carr to hold NDLS in HP. K 4 Rs & ret STS from RB to MB. Set carr to K NDLS in HP & K 2 Rs.* Rep from * to * with group B NDLS.

Larger version of pat at top of swatch was K with 2 STS, instead of 1, on each side of center ST tr to RB.

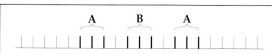

A AND B GROUPS OF NEEDLES FOR PATTERNING.

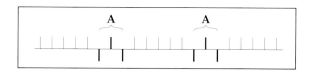

A NEEDLES TRANSFERRED TO RIBBER BED.

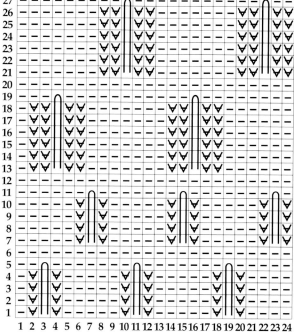

MANUAL NEEDLE-SELECTION CHART.

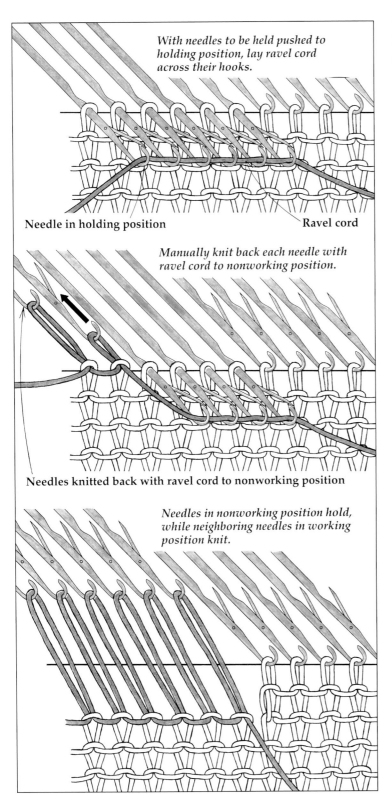

With needles to be held pushed to
holding position, lay ravel cord
across their hooks.

Needle in holding position   Ravel cord

Manually knit back each needle with
ravel cord to nonworking position.

Needles knitted back with ravel cord to nonworking position

Needles in nonworking position hold,
while neighboring needles in working
position knit.

You can also use nonworking position to
hold needles by manually knitting the
stitches with ravel cord, increasing their
size enough for the needles to remain all
the way back in nonworking position.
Even though there are stitches in the
hooks, the needles butts are too far back
on the bed to knit. If the needles tend to
slip forward as you knit, place some
masking tape across the bed in front of the
butts in nonworking position to prevent
them from moving. Make sure the bed is
clean enough for the tape to stick to so it
doesn't end up under your carriage. And
when you are through with the tape, be
sure to clean any sticky residue off the bed.
When you want those needles to knit again,
simply push the needles back into working
position and remove the ravel cord as
though you were ripping out a row of
regular stitches. Pull down on the knitting
as you push the needles forward because
the ravel-cord stitches are large and
springy and tend to slip out of the hooks.

*USING RAVEL CORD
AND NONWORKING
POSITION TO HOLD
NEEDLES.*

Lengthening stitches

The size and spacing of needles on a knitting machine are fixed and determine the range of yarns the machine can knit and the size of the stitches produced. At the same time, the needles' size and spacing limit some hand manipulations that require lateral stitch movement. Like the needles, the sinker posts separating the needles are also fixed. These posts regulate the length of the yarn connecting one stitch to the next and thus also affect the degree of lateral stitch movement possible.

These limitations, however, can be overcome with various methods of lengthening stitches. These methods include adjusting the stitch-size dial, leaving needles out of work, hand knitting stitches, working dropped stitches and lengthening the sinker loops between stitches.

Stitch size is adjusted by a mechanism, which is usually a dial on the face of the carriage. This dial moves the cams on the underside of the carriage, lengthening or shortening the triangular pathway and allowing the needles to take on more or less yarn as stitches are formed. The range of stitch sizes is determined by the movement of the cams. Whether a dial has four stitch sizes (as does the Bond) or a dozen to choose from, the largest stitch size is defined at the point at which the cams can be shifted no further to lengthen the triangular pathway.

Generally speaking, the stitch-size dial controls and maintains the consistent size of all the stitches in a row. Yet many hand-manipulated techniques require that certain stitches in a row be larger than others in order to twist, cross, bead or otherwise manipulate them without straining the yarn, the machine or one's

luck. Also, you may occasionally want to coax the machine into using slightly larger yarn than it was designed to knit. In both cases, you will need to enlarge stitches.

Individual techniques call for enlarging stitches by different methods. The method you choose depends on the capabilities of your machine, the nature of the yarn you're using, the movements the cams are already committed to and the effect that lengthening may have on the other needles and stitches.

The most common method for increasing stitch size is to work on every other needle so that the machine functions as though the needles are set twice as far apart as they really are. More yarn than usual thus spans the distance from one stitch to the next, and when the fabric is removed from the machine, the stitches become longer by absorbing the excess yarn between them.

But working on every other needle has some limitations. First, it can only extend the yarn-size range up to a point because the yarn must still be able to fit comfortably in the needle hooks. More important, the potential width of the fabric will be about half the width of a fabric knitted on every needle because the yarn between stitches is what ultimately contributes to their extended length. (Remember that the yarn extending across the alternate, nonworking needles accounts for less yarn than a fully formed stitch would.) Also, with some tightly twisted yarns, fabrics knitted on every other needle will have an unpleasant, vertically ridged look to them. But perhaps most important of all for hand-manipulated techniques is the fact that knitting on every other needle enables you to change the stitch size only for an entire row, not for individual stitches. The methods that follow present ways of controlling the size of individual stitches.

Leaving needles out of work

The principle of enlarging stitches by knitting on every other needle can be applied just as well to isolated needles as to an entire row. If a working needle or group of needles has an out-of-work needle on each side, the stitches formed adjacent to these out-of-work needles will be larger than they would have been had all the needles been knitting. The increased stitch size may not be especially noticeable when the fabric is removed from the machine and the excess yarn is absorbed by the stitches, but the stitch or group of stitches bordered by out-of-work needles will be much easier to move and manipulate. If two needles are left out of work on each side of the working needle or needles, however, the enlarged stitches will be more obvious.

To enlarge a stitch even more, bring the out-of-work needle to working position, allow it to knit with all the other needles and drop its stitch just before working the hand-manipulated maneuver you're undertaking. The knitted stitch will have taken up more yarn than would a simple float across an out-of-work needle. When dropped, this knitted stitch will provide extra slack for the other stitch being enlarged to absorb, making it even easier to move.

When you plan to let a needle drop the stitches it knits, make sure the needle is empty before you begin. That is, either skip over this needle when casting on, or transfer its stitch to an adjacent needle after casting on. Otherwise, if the needle is filled when you begin this maneuver, the existing stitch will drop, or run, all the way down the fabric.

If you need the extra slack only temporarily (to cross a cable, for example) and don't want to leave a ladder or increase the size of the stitches, you can drop the necessary stitches just a few rows before the slack is needed to produce extra ease. Then latch the stitches back up once the effect is worked and replace them on their needles. When dropping the stitches, catch them on a small stitch holder (like a hand-knitting cable needle or a toothpick) to prevent them from running too far.

Hand knitting stitches

If you manually guide a needle though the steps that form a stitch, you can control the amount of yarn taken up by the needle and hence the size of the stitch formed. To do this, first push the needle butt forward until the existing stitch on the needle opens the latch and slides behind it. Then lay yarn into the open hook. When you pull back on the needle butt to slip the old stitch off over the new one, you control the amount of yarn that goes into making the stitch. Unlike the carriage cams, you can pull a needle all the way back to nonworking position, which means that you can potentially create monstrously large stitches. Of course, you don't have to knit the needle all the way back. The size of the stitch is up to you and is regulated by how far back from working position you move the needle.

When you knit needles back to nonworking position, they are, in effect, in a rear holding position. If you want the needles to resume knitting, you must return them to working position. To do so, pull down on the knitting as you push the needles forward so the large stitches don't slip off the needles. Remember, too, to keep the fabric well weighted as you knit.

To hand knit an entire row of stitches, unthread the carriage and use the yarn to knit the row manually. Then, with all the needles back in nonworking position, move the carriage across the bed to rethread it and resume knitting. If the needles were knitted back to a point somewhere between working and nonworking position, set the empty carriage for slip or a free pass to get it over to the other side without dropping the stitches.

If you only need to hand knit specific stitches—in order to cross a cable, for example—you can use a separate strand of yarn. Knit normally with the carriage up to the designated row, and then, using the separate strand, hand knit the stitches that will be used to cross the cable. Sometimes it is difficult to judge exactly how much larger the stitches need to be to cross comfortably. If they're too large, they'll cross easily enough, but the enlarged stitches will show on the finished cable and ruin the look of it. With a separate strand, you can knit specific needles back to nonworking position for very large stitches that cross easily. These stitches can later be adjusted in size when the piece is off the machine by feeding the excess yarn out of the stitches, then knotting the ends or working them into the back of the fabric to secure them.

The drawback to this method is that each cable crossing uses a separate strand of yarn, which requires finishing later. Yet, with a little planning and swatching, you can figure out exactly how far back to knit the needles manually in order to get them to form stitches large enough to cross, but not so large that they require later adjustment. Then you can use one extra strand of yarn for all the cables, carrying it along the back of the work from stitch to stitch and row to row by loosely catching it over a needle every so often. When you finish knitting, you'll have only two ends to finish off instead of dozens. In either case, the extra hand-knit stitches do not usually show or affect the row gauge. I like this method when I have a lot of manipulations to keep track of and need to keep the enlarging process as simple as possible.

In addition to enlarging stitches, hand knitting stitches is an easy way to knit two-color designs on machines that do not have an automatic selection system. Place the needles that will be hand knitted into holding position before knitting each row. Then with a strand of contrasting yarn, manually knit each of the selected needles back to working position, keeping the

tension on the stitches as even as possible. You can use as many pattern colors as you want. This is also a great way to add extra colors to automatically selected patterns.

Chris Gibbons of Hallandall, Inc., in Rembrandt, Iowa, works an interesting variation on hand knitting two-color designs, which she calls "longstitch." This method similarly involves holding and manually knitting the contrast stitches, but in reverse order. To work this variation, use a strand of contrast yarn to knit the appropriate needles back to nonworking position, then knit two rows with the carriage. Return the needles to working position by easing the needle butts forward as you hold the fabric down. Select and manually knit the contrast stitches before knitting the next two rows. The manually knitted stitches will be twice as long as those produced by the carriage and will add interest because of their size. If the stitches are too long, try knitting three rows with the carriage.

Interrupting the carriage to change stitch size

Unless you're already knitting with the largest stitch size on the dial, the carriage can usually make all the stitch sizes needed to deal separately with groups of stitches in each row. For example, you

CARRYING SEPARATE STRAND ON BACK OF FABRIC FOR HAND KNITTING STITCHES TO EASE MULTIPLE CABLE CROSSINGS.

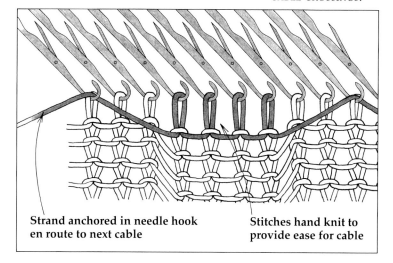

Strand anchored in needle hook en route to next cable

Stitches hand knit to provide ease for cable

might find that the main knitting looks just fine at stitch size 6, but that a group of stitches in the center would twist or cross more easily if worked on stitch size 8.

To use two different stitch sizes in the same row, move the carriage to the right and set it for holding. Put the group of needles whose stitch size will be changed and all needles to their left into holding position. Then set the stitch dial to the size needed for the stitches that act as a bridge to the section being enlarged (size 6 in the example above). Next knit one row from right to left over the needles in working position, and then push the working needles into hold as well. Move the carriage back to the right side of the fabric and turn the dial to the stitch size needed for the enlarged part of the fabric (size 8 in the example above). Nudge the needles in the center section down to upper working position. Knit one row from right to left, push these needles back into hold and return the carriage to the right side. Turn the stitch-size dial back to the size needed for the bridge stitches at left (6), and move this last group of needles into upper working position. Knit one row from right to left to complete the row, and then cross or twist the stitches as required. Since the stitch dial is already set for the main knitting, just continue knitting entire rows up to the next row requiring enlarging.

Had you worked the example above, the row counter would show five passes of the carriage, although only one row has actually been knitted. You can deal with this discrepancy either by turning off the counter before starting this process or by figuring the extra row counts into your plans. After each section knits, you must return the carriage to the right side of the bed in order to be sure of having backed up far enough for the yarn to start knitting on the first needle of the next group. To knit the next row across all the needles (from left to right), either use your automatic return levers or place all the needles into upper working position.

If, after knitting the first right-hand section on stitch size 6, you wanted to hand knit the needles in the center section all the way back to nonworking position to form giant stitches, you could do so with only three passes of the carriage. Leaving the carriage on the right, pull out enough free yarn to hand knit the center stitches. Then push these needles to holding position, and continue with the third section as before. Needless to say, you don't have to limit yourself to three sections. You can change the stitch-size dial or hand knit stitches as often as you want, knitting a plain bridge between the enlarged sections.

On machines with automatic return for needles in holding position, the slip setting is even faster and easier to use than the method just described. This is because, with the return levers set to knit needles in holding position, you only have to select the needles that will knit. The other needles remain in working position, but do not knit because the cams are set for slip. Additionally, there is less selection involved because you can leave needles in working position after they have knitted. To work the example above in this fashion, you would push the first group of needles at the right to hold, knit one row to the left and then return the carriage to the right side. Next you would select the center needles, repeat the process and finally move to work the third group of needles this way.

NEEDLES MANUALLY KNITTED BACK TO NONWORKING POSITION TO ENLARGE SELECTED STITCHES.

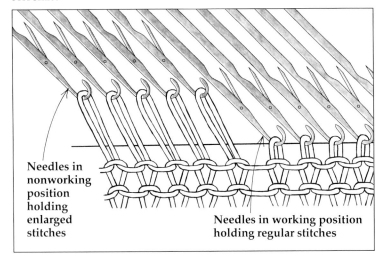

Needles in nonworking position holding enlarged stitches

Needles in working position holding regular stitches

Apart from the machine's capabilities and your personal preferences, you cannot use the slip method if you need to use holding position for garment shaping or forming tuck stitches. The reason for this is that the automatic return levers would cause all the needles in holding position to knit, including the ones you want to hold. Nor can you use the slip method if you have the cam lever set to tuck.

These interrupted methods are excellent when you need to avoid having separate strands on the back of the fabric where they would show, for example, in a cardigan or even an afghan. Because I dislike finishing off ends with the separate-strand method, I usually opt for interrupting the carriage unless I've already got too many other things to keep track of.

Drop stitch

Drop stitch is the name given to a double-bed technique for substantially increasing the size of any or all stitches on the main bed by having needles on the ribber bed cast on, knit and then drop. The extra yarn cast on and dropped from the ribber-bed needles is absorbed by the stitches on the main bed. This method introduces an entirely new range of stitch sizes beyond those supplied by the stitch-size dial. It is a useful technique for situations in which the other methods for increasing stitch size are impractical, produce uneven stitches or supply an inadequate variety of stitch sizes.

Whenever you work with drop stitch, you'll need to experiment with stitch size because the sizes vary, depending on the number of needles working on each bed. Whenever one bed has more needles working than the other, the stitch size on the bed with more needles working is usually larger. And, although the ribber carriage often has fewer needles working and is set for a smaller stitch size than the main carriage, when its stitch size is increased, so is the size of the dropped stitches produced.

To lengthen stitches by this method, first put the beds in half-pitch and weight the fabric well. Then, if you begin your knitting with ribbing, transfer any ribber stitches to the main bed so that the ribber bed is absolutely empty. Bring a few needles on the ribber bed into working position and knit one row. Look at the ribber needles, and you'll see that they have each automatically cast on a loop of yarn. Push these needles to holding position, then back to working position to drop the loops. Because a stitch can drop only to the point where it was cast on, these loops will drop only one row. As they do, the adjacent stitches on the main bed will absorb the yarn and become larger. Next, bring the remaining ribber needles to working position, knit several rows and disconnect the two carriages. Move the ribber carriage across the bed by itself so that all the ribber needles reach forward as if to knit, receive no new yarn in their hooks and drop their stitches. This yarn will be absorbed by the main-bed stitches in each of the rows just knitted.

Sometimes you'll want to knit and drop only selected stitches, for example, to ease a cable crossing. Other times you'll want to knit and drop an entire row. Dropping entire rows is necessary to create some very open fabrics and for effects requiring all stitches in one row to be enlarged.

You may be able to knit a number of rows before dropping the ribber stitches, or you may need to drop them after each row. For example, if you knit six rows and then drop the ribber stitches, these stitches will run for six rows, increasing the stitch size of the stitches in all six rows. If the carriage proves very hard to push, you may need to drop the ribber stitches more often, perhaps even after every row, in order to facilitate the knitting. The frequency with which you drop the stitches depends on the nature of the yarn and the stitch sizes you're using. Whatever rhythm you establish, be consistent.

After transferring all stitches to the main bed, you have several options for ribber-needle arrangements. You can set up the ribber needles for full-needle rib if you want to increase the size of every stitch on the main bed, row by row. In this arrangement, the yarn zigzags between the needles on the two beds and produces a loose, soft fabric, which is especially appealing with textured yarns and those that knit too tightly even with the largest regular stitch sizes. Other options for the ribber needles are an every-other-needle arrangement, changing pattern arrangements to knit open designs (as in Swatch 14) or an isolated individual needle for easing a cable crossing.

NEEDLE ARRANGEMENT FOR ADDING EASE TO CABLE CROSSINGS.

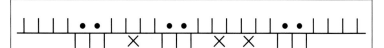

X indicates extra ribber-bed needles for drop stitch to ease cable crossing of four-stitch and six-stitch cables.

13. CONDO-STITCH AND DROP-STITCH FABRIC.

To work: Tightly K bottom Rs of swatch were worked in stockinette ST with SS 10. Center section was worked in drop ST, with both carrs set to SS 10 & K in both directions. Top section was worked in condo ST, with both carrs set to SS 10, & MB K in both directions, while RB K in 1 direction & slipped in other.

The full-needle rib setup can be used to duplicate the "condo" stitch, which hand knitters enjoy. When worked by hand, this stitch uses an unmatched pair of knitting needles to alternate rows of huge and tiny stitches. To work this stitch on the machine, set the ribber carriage to knit in one direction and slip in the other (it doesn't matter which is which). With this setup, you can alternate one row of stockinette with one row of drop stitch to achieve an extreme contrast of stitch sizes (Swatch 13).

Drop stitch can also be used to ease cable crossings in much the same way that I've already described for allowing out-of-work needles to knit and then drop. With the double-bed method, two carriages provide far greater control than a single carriage over stitch size. If the ribber bed is to be used only for drop stitches, it can be set to stitch size 1 or 2, while the stitch size on the main bed should be set more or less for stockinette. However, if the ribber bed is also to be used for rib or purl effects between cables, it will need to be set to a somewhat larger stitch size to accommodate these effects. Also, the drop stitches will have to be manually selected and released if some stitches are to be retained for ribbing.

To enlarge stitches for cables, *knit one less row than needed between cable crossings. Bring one empty ribber needle (or more) into working position opposite the center of each cable on the main bed. Knit one row, then release the loops just formed and return all empty needles to nonworking position. Cross the cables.* Repeat from * to *.

When crossing four-stitch (two over two) or six-stitch (three over three) cables, one ribber needle per cable will usually suffice. For crossing larger cables or when working with very inelastic yarn, you may need to use two or even three evenly spaced needles on the ribber bed for each cable. Knit a sample first and try to use as few needles as possible because you want to add only enough ease for the stitches to cross without strain. Too much ease will create overly enlarged stitches, which will stand out and ruin the look of the cable.

You can also use groups of needles on the ribber to create enlarged stitches for open-pattern effects or further manipulation. The pattern in Swatch 14, for example, was created by using different ribber needles every two rows, moving to the left or the right of the previous needles. If larger groups of needles were used, the effect would be lacier and more open.

By disconnecting the carriages and knitting with only the main carriage, you can also combine regular rows of stockinette with occasional rows of drop stitch for specific effects like twisting and crossing rows of giant stitches. If the very last row of a fabric is knitted with drop stitch, you'll also be able to bind off more loosely by hand or with a linker attachment.

Some ribbers have a small accessory carriage specifically designed to drop stitches, which eliminates the need to disconnect the ribber carriage. If you use this accessory carriage or disconnect the ribber carriage, all the ribber needles will drop their stitches. When you want to drop only selected stitches, you must do so manually.

Lengthening the loops between stitches

When stitch size is increased, it does not necessarily add length to the yarn that connects one stitch to the next. Yet there are some hand-manipulated techniques that rely on enlarging sinker loops between stitches rather than the stitches. Enlarged sinker loops add extra surface texture, independent of the background stitches, and they also allow greater lateral stitch movement for working other hand-manipulated techniques.

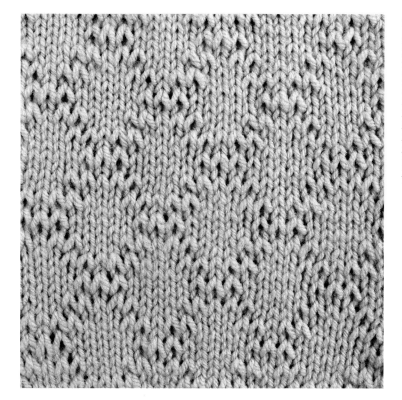

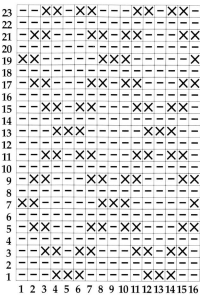

14. DROP-STITCH DIAMOND PATTERN.
On chart, X indicates selected NDLS on RB that K, drop & ret to NWP.

There are several methods for enlarging sinker loops, the most basic of which is simply leaving needles out of work. This technique, however, may also affect the appearance of the adjacent stitches or the design of the fabric by creating open gaps between stitches. Other methods for lengthening sinker loops all involve wrapping or hooking the yarn around some sort of a gauge to regulate sinker-loop size.

For occasional large loops, you can use the holding or slip methods for interrupting the carriage (see pp. 63-65), and pull out free yarn to form a loop between knitted sections. For many adjacent enlarged loops, you will need to hand knit stitches or manually knit-weave so that you will have easy access to free yarn between all the stitches.

In both cases, the yarn can be wrapped around your fingers, a dowel or a ruler each time you size the loops. You can also catch it onto the open hooks of a lace comb that has been suspended from a single-bed machine, or you can use the sinker posts or needle hooks of the ribber bed, as explained below. Because ribbers have several adjustable heights, this method provides for a variety of consistent loop lengths. You don't have to stabilize or hold onto a gauge, so your hands are free to deal with the yarn, quickly and easily. As long as the ribber is not raised all the way up, it should not interfere with the main carriage, and it can be dropped out of the way when you don't need it.

The beaded swatch (Swatch 15) used the interrupted-slip setting to work enlarged loops with the free yarn. Loops formed in this way provide a good base for attaching feathers and threading beads (see p. 124) because the loop provides a double strand of the yarn to work with.

To hand knit or to knit-weave the stitches from one enlarged loop to the next, first unthread the yarn from the carriage. Use the yarn to weave or hand knit two rows, catching sinker posts or wrapping around gauges as desired. Work from the carriage to the opposite side of the bed and then work your way back to the carriage, where you can rethread and continue knitting. You can create heavier loops by catching the same sinker post in both directions, or you can stagger the loops by catching alternate posts in each direction.

E-WRAPPED LOOPS FORMED BY WRAPPING EVERY OTHER NEEDLE TO ALTERNATE SINKER POSTS ON RIBBER.

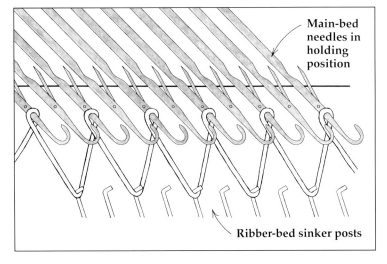

Main-bed needles in holding position

Ribber-bed sinker posts

Reforming, or latching up, stitches

One of the first things that all machine knitters learn to do is repair dropped stitches with a latch tool by imitating the knitting action of the needles. You can easily repair stitches to look exactly like all the others on the bed, or you can deliberately drop and reform them to contrast with the surrounding stitches. The terms used for this process, *reforming* and *latching up,* are synonymous. *Reforming* refers to the general process of recreating a stitch by hand after the carriage has knitted a row. *Latching up* describes the basic maneuver in this manual process.

Reforming stitches enables you to produce ribbed welts and also isolated purl stitches to highlight cables and other textures. It can enhance cam-selected pattern stitches and produce effects beyond the regular capabilities of a single-bed machine. Reforming stitches does not, however, duplicate double-bed knitting or replace the need for a ribber.

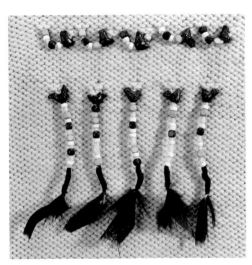

MAKING ENLARGED SINKER POST LOOPS.

To form a group of enlarged sinker loops: After removing yarn from carr, weave over & under 1st 7 NDLS on carr side. In photo, 1st loop has been formed by wrapping free yarn around RB sinker post. Continue knit-weaving or hand-knitting MB NDLS to next enlarged loop location.

15. BEADED FABRIC.

Beads & feathers in lower portion were added to fabric after it was removed from KM. Beads at top were added immediately after enlarged loops were formed, with end of loops then hung on 3rd NDL to L to secure them with next pass of carr.

To work: COR. K 1st group of NDLS, *ret carr to RT edge & before K next group, catch free yarn around a RB sinker post. K 2nd group of NDLS*, & rep from * to *. Continue until each group of NDLS has K & then remove loops from sinker posts or K 1 R. You don't need to add beads until later unless you want to hang end of a beaded loop onto 1 of NDLS to secure it.

To form an entire row of enlarged loops: After wrapping E/4 MB NDL & alt RB sinker post from RT to L, wrap 2nd time from L to RT & ret free yarn to carr to continue K.

The need to reform stitches arises from the fact that all the needles on a single-bed machine face the same direction, and therefore the stitches they form face only one way. These stitches are all seen as knit stitches on the face of the resulting fabric and purl stitches on the back.

In order for any of the stitches in a row of a single-bed fabric to face the other direction—that is, for stitches on the face of the fabric to be purls—the stitches must be reformed by hand. If the machine is automatically to "form" these stitches, it must have a second bed with needles positioned and working in the opposite direction from the needles on the main bed. For this reason, ribbing can be automatically produced only on a double-bed machine.

If you are working on a single-bed machine with a pattern calling for purl stitches on the fabric's face (or for knit stitches on the back), you must remove the stitches in question from their needles, manually produce the effects and return the stitches to their needles.

The latch tool is the primary tool for reforming stitches, although crochet hooks are sometimes used and eyelet tools can be helpful at the end of the latching-up process. The latch tool looks and functions like a knitting-machine needle, except that it can be turned in any direction and hence form both knit and purl stitches.

Double latch tools latch two stitches at once, which means that you can work twice as fast. But, when working with some yarns, these tools tend to pull the stitches together, reducing the length of the sinker loop in between. This pulling together of stitches usually takes care of itself when the fabric is washed and blocked, but it's a good idea to wash and block a sample swatch before beginning a project to see if pulling will be a problem.

To counter the crowding of stitches with the double latch tool, you may also want to try leaving a needle out of work between the two stitches being latched up. The nonworking needle creates a ladder of floats, which provides extra slack for the double latch-up, making it easier to handle. The resulting two stitches worked in this manner, however, will be larger than they would be otherwise.

A single stitch or groups of stitches can be latched up. (Because of the way in which the first and last stitches in a row are formed as the yarn turns back on itself, however, the stitches at the outside edges of the knitting are difficult to reform and are usually left alone.) Some pattern effects call for latching up a single stitch or multiple stitches in a given row immediately after that row is knitted. Other effects require that a stitch or stitches be dropped and allowed to run down the fabric for latching up all at once. Still other patterns or effects depend on creating columns of floats, or ladders, in the fabric; these ladders are later latched up.

The columns of floats, or enlarged sinker loops, that create ladders are formed when a stitch is dropped or when a stitch is transferred and the empty needle is left in nonworking position between working needles. A ladder formed by a dropped stitch grows in length downward from the point at which the stitch is dropped until it stops raveling, which, unless you manually intervene, could even be back to the cast-on edge. A ladder formed when there is an empty, nonworking needle grows as the knitting progresses from the point at which the needle was emptied or put out of work.

When a needle knits and then drops its stitch, the ladder it produces is looser than the ladder produced by a nonworking needle. As a result, the stitch reformed from the looser ladder will be larger and softer than the stitch reformed from the other ladder.

You can begin a ladder at any point in the work by transferring a stitch to an adjacent needle and placing the empty needle out of work. Alternatively, when casting on, you may be able just to leave the needle out of work at the point at which you want the ladder to form unless it interferes with other patterning effects. Floats, or enlarged sinker loops, form across the space left by the nonworking needle as the other needles continue to knit. When you bring the needle back to working position, it will cast on and end the ladder. However, unless you fill the empty needle with the purl loop from an adjacent stitch, there is apt to be a noticeable hole at the top of the ladder (see pp. 175-177).

Although you can latch up ladders in a fabric after it is removed from the machine, it is harder to manipulate the tools and control the tension on the stitches being reformed. While even tension is usually not a problem if you are latching up ladders when the fabric is still on the machine and the stitches are well weighted, it's still not a good idea to wait too long to latch up. I usually latch up a ladder every tenth row, or I coordinate latching up with a particular motion like crossing a cable (though, of course, some patterns call for latching up at particular points in the knitting).

When latching up, for example, every tenth row, replace the reformed stitch on the needle and continue knitting another ten rows. The next time the stitch drops, allow it to run only ten rows, that is, to the point where you last latched up. Again latch up the stitch, replace it on the needle and continue knitting.

Although ladders are usually latched up, they don't have to be. The ease that ladders add to a fabric can be used to create lacy stitch designs, provide looser stitches for seaming and facilitate stitch movement. Ladders form crease lines for folds, markers for pleating and lifting stitches, and spaces through which to embroider or lace ribbons. In Swatch 16, the width of the ladders was increased and decreased to form leaf shapes. The lower leaf and vertical ladder to its left were later filled in with needle weaving. Because ladders tend to be absorbed as slack by adjacent stitches, you might hemstitch the side edges if you want the ladder to remain fully open.

Finally, remember that if you need to rip back rows that include reformed stitches, you must reform these stitches in reverse before ripping out these rows. You can reform individual stitches in reverse, row by row, or you can try the following

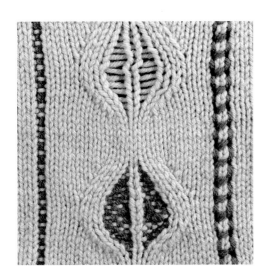

16. OPEN AND FILLED LADDERS.

The leaves are simply shaped ladders, with lower one filled with needle weaving. Vertical ladder at L was laced through, & ladder at RT was hemstitched.

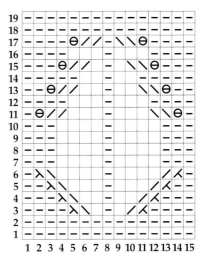

shortcut. Insert an eyelet tool into the column of stitches whose topmost stitch needs to be reformed, as many rows down as you need to rip out. Drop the stitch from the needle and let it run down to the eyelet tool, which will stop it. Then replace the stitch from the eyelet tool onto the needle. The floats produced by dropping will be easily removed as you rip out rows.

Reforming a single stitch

To reform a stitch for a particular pattern effect, insert a single transfer tool into the stitch directly below the one to be reformed and drop the stitch from the needle, as shown in the drawing below. The stitch can be repaired as a purl stitch, or it can be reformed as a tuck, slip or knit stitch on either side of the fabric.

To reform the stitch as a purl, lift the stitch and the float back onto the needle. Place the stitch behind the latch and the float in front of it, and hand knit the float through the stitch.

To reform a purl stitch as a tuck stitch, lift the stitch and the float back onto the needle, simply placing them in the needle's hook or on its shaft if you have the carriage set to knit needles back from holding position (Swatch 17). They will knit together in the next row, making a tuck stitch. The zigzag and the rib in the bottom of the swatch were done with reformed tuck stitches, but only the zigzag was done by this method.

To reform a purl stitch as a slip stitch on the purl side of the fabric, lift the stitch and the float onto the needle, and then remove the float. To reform a purl stitch as a slip on the knit side of the fabric, pull the tool toward you enough to drop the float, then hang the stitch alone onto the hook of the needle.

REPAIRING OR REFORMING A PURL STITCH.

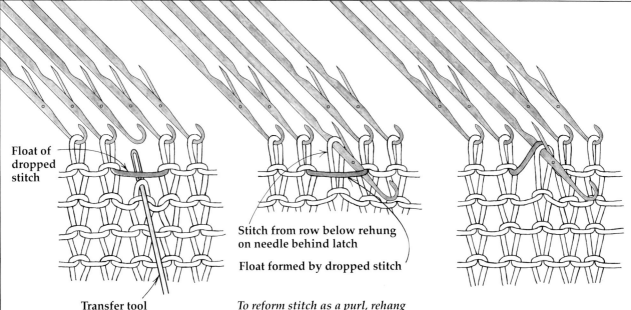

Float of dropped stitch

Transfer tool

Insert transfer tool into stitch directly below one being reformed and pick up float of dropped stitch.

Stitch from row below rehung on needle behind latch

Float formed by dropped stitch

To reform stitch as a purl, rehang stitch and float on needle, with stitch behind and float in front of latch. Hand knit float to reform purl stitch.

To reform stitch as a tuck, rehang stitch and float on needle behind latch. They will form tuck stitch with next pass of carriage.

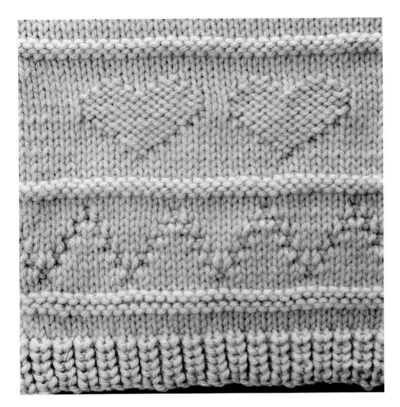

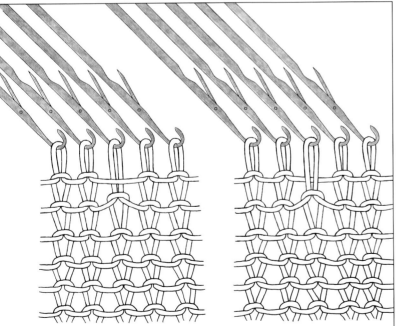

To reform purl as slip stitch on purl side, rehang stitch on needle and then drop float.

To reform purl as slip stitch on knit side, drop float before rehanging stitch on needle.

17. PATTERNING OF REFORMED STITCHES.
Rib & zigzag pats at bottom of swatch are produced with reformed tuck STS. (Zigzag STS are reformed on A/R, & rib is formed by latching up columns of STS.) Hearts & horizontal bands are worked with reformed STS.

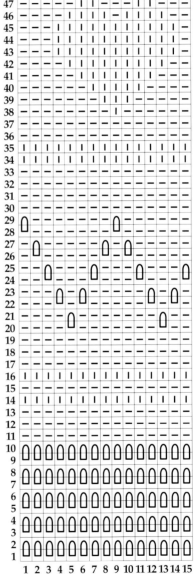

Reforming and Beading

It's quite easy to add beads to embellish a fabric when you reform stitches. You can use a tappet tool, a beading needle or a crochet hook as long as the tool will fit through the hole in your beads.

To begin the process, put a bead onto the tool, behind the open latch (or simply onto the hook if you're working with a crochet hook). Insert the tool into a stitch in the first row directly under the machine needle, then drop the stitch off the needle, pull it through the bead and rehang the stitch on the needle. If the bead seems crowded, you can give it a little more space by inserting the tool into a stitch in the second row down. Pull the stitch through the bead and then reform the float above it as a slip or tuck stitch before rehanging the stitch on the needle. With this method, a slip stitch will produce a float that shows in front of the bead on the knit side of the fabric; a tuck stitch will lie above the bead.

You can vary this procedure by working from the knit or purl side because the bead tends to create an open space, which makes it visible from either side. If you are reforming slip stitches, you want the float to pass behind the bead, which would determine from which side of the fabric you work. You can also move stitches from adjacent needles to create larger bead openings, or you can accumulate several tuck stitches on the needle to create a textured effect around the bead. In Swatch 18, stitches were latched up above the beads to create a pattern of knit stitches.

REFORMED BEADED KNIT, SLIP AND TUCK STITCH.

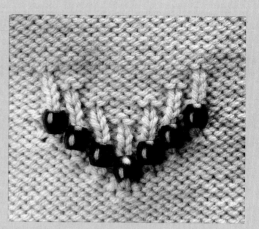

18. BEADED FABRIC WITH REFORMED KNIT-STITCH EMBELLISHMENT.

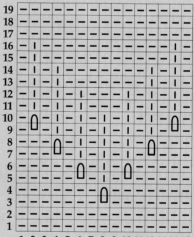

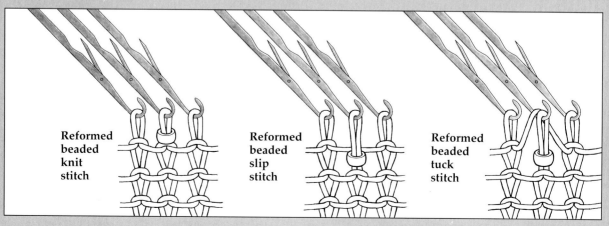

Reformed beaded knit stitch

Reformed beaded slip stitch

Reformed beaded tuck stitch

To reform a purl stitch as a knit stitch, drop the stitch and the float onto a latch tool, rather than a transfer tool, placing the stitch behind the latch and float in the hook. Pull the loop through the stitch and hang the new stitch back on the needle. In Swatch 17 on p. 73, the hearts were reformed as knit stitches on the back of the fabric. Thus, on the fabric's face, they appear as purls on a knit background.

Reforming a ladder of stitches

While a single stitch is reformed with a transfer tool, a column of stitches must be reformed by using a latch tool to mimic the knitting action of the needle. If you use the latch tool from the right side of the fabric to reform or repair a ladder, the stitches will be reformed exactly as the carriage would knit them. If you reform a ladder from the wrong side of the fabric, all the stitches, including slips and tucks, will become knit stitches and thus appear as purls on the face of the fabric. The slip stitches will still have their characteristic float on the knit side of the fabric, but they will have purl stitches behind them. Both slip and tuck stitches reformed from the wrong side of the fabric will appear as if they had been knitted on a ribber bed.

Reforming a ladder of purls or knits.
To reform purl stitches as purls, work from the knit side of the fabric (see the bottom drawing at right); to reform purl stitches as knits, work from the purl side of the fabric. In both cases, if you are dropping a stitch to form a ladder, insert the latch tool into the stitch you want to be the lowest one in a column. Make sure the stitch lies behind the tool's open latch, and release the stitch from the needle directly above. You may have to pull down on the fabric to get the ladder started. Once the ladder runs down, it will be stopped by the shaft of the tool. Next, catch the first float of the ladder with the tool's hook and pull it through the stitch on the latch tool. Continue to pull one stitch through the next and then replace the last stitch in the needle.

If you are working on the wrong side of the fabric to reform purls as knits, grab the hook of the needle with the hook of the latch tool. Making sure the stitch is behind the latch of the tool, tip the tool so that the stitch closes the latch and slides over it, into the hook of the needle. If you are working on the right side of the fabric to

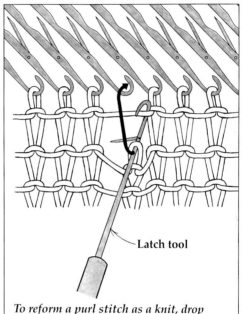

Latch tool

To reform a purl stitch as a knit, drop stitch and float onto a latch tool, placing stitch behind latch and float in hook. Pull float through stitch and rehang on needle.

REFORMING A SINGLE PURL STITCH AS A KNIT STITCH.

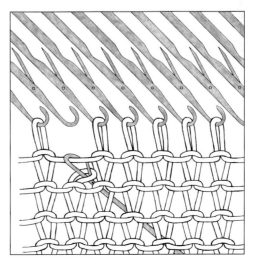

REFORMING A LADDER OF PURL STITCHES AS PURLS.

REPLACING LAST STITCH OF REFORMED PURL LADDER ON NEEDLE.

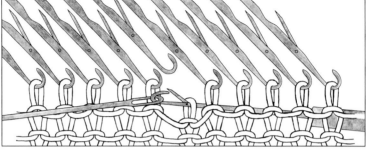

In order to replace the last stitch on needle, you must be working on purl side of fabric. To transfer stitch from latch tool to eyelet transfer tool, first position stitch on shaft of latch tool behind open latch. Hook transfer and latch tools together, as shown, and pull back slightly on latch tool to make stitch slide onto transfer tool. Replace stitch on needle.

19. REFORMED KNIT-STITCH DIAMONDS.

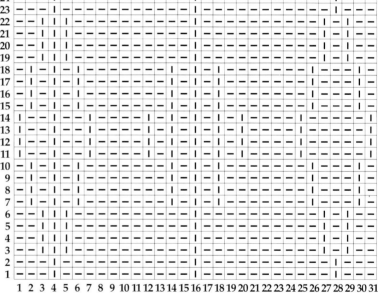

	1	2	3	4	5	6	7	8	9	10	11	12	13	14	15	16	17	18	19	20	21	22	23	24	25	26	27	28	29	30	31
24	−	−	I	−	−	−	−	−	−	−	−	−	−	−	−	I	−	−	−	−	−	−	−	−	−	−	−	−	I	−	−
23	−	−	I	−	−	−	−	−	−	−	−	−	−	−	−	I	−	−	−	−	−	−	−	−	−	−	−	−	I	−	−
22	−	I	I	I	−	−	−	−	−	−	−	−	−	−	I	I	I	−	−	−	−	−	−	−	−	−	−	I	I	I	−
21	−	I	I	I	−	−	−	−	−	−	−	−	−	−	I	I	I	−	−	−	−	−	−	−	−	−	−	I	I	I	−
20	−	I	I	I	−	−	−	−	−	−	−	−	−	−	I	I	I	−	−	−	−	−	−	−	−	−	−	I	I	I	−
19	−	I	I	I	−	−	−	−	−	−	−	−	−	−	I	I	I	−	−	−	−	−	−	−	−	−	−	I	I	I	−
18	−	I	−	I	−	−	−	−	−	−	−	−	−	−	I	−	I	−	−	−	−	−	−	−	−	−	−	I	−	I	−
17	−	I	−	I	−	−	−	−	−	−	−	−	−	−	I	−	I	−	−	−	−	−	−	−	−	−	−	I	−	I	−
16	−	I	−	I	−	−	−	−	−	−	−	−	−	−	I	−	I	−	−	−	−	−	−	−	−	−	−	I	−	I	−
15	−	I	−	I	−	−	−	−	−	−	−	−	−	−	I	−	I	−	−	−	−	−	−	−	−	−	−	I	−	I	−
14	I	−	−	I	−	−	−	−	−	−	−	−	−	I	−	−	I	−	−	−	−	−	−	−	−	−	I	−	−	I	−
13	I	−	−	I	−	−	−	−	−	−	−	−	−	I	−	−	I	−	−	−	−	−	−	−	−	−	I	−	−	I	−
12	I	−	−	I	−	−	−	−	−	−	−	−	−	I	−	−	I	−	−	−	−	−	−	−	−	−	I	−	−	I	−
11	I	−	−	I	−	−	−	−	−	−	−	−	−	I	−	−	I	−	−	−	−	−	−	−	−	−	I	−	−	I	−
10	−	I	−	I	−	−	−	−	−	−	−	−	−	−	I	−	I	−	−	−	−	−	−	−	−	−	−	I	−	I	−
9	−	I	−	I	−	−	−	−	−	−	−	−	−	−	I	−	I	−	−	−	−	−	−	−	−	−	−	I	−	I	−
8	−	I	−	I	−	−	−	−	−	−	−	−	−	−	I	−	I	−	−	−	−	−	−	−	−	−	−	I	−	I	−
7	−	I	−	I	−	−	−	−	−	−	−	−	−	−	I	−	I	−	−	−	−	−	−	−	−	−	−	I	−	I	−
6	−	−	I	I	I	−	−	−	−	−	−	−	−	−	−	I	I	I	−	−	−	−	−	−	−	−	−	−	I	I	I
5	−	−	I	I	I	−	−	−	−	−	−	−	−	−	−	I	I	I	−	−	−	−	−	−	−	−	−	−	I	I	I
4	−	−	I	I	I	−	−	−	−	−	−	−	−	−	−	I	I	I	−	−	−	−	−	−	−	−	−	−	I	I	I
3	−	−	I	I	I	−	−	−	−	−	−	−	−	−	−	I	I	I	−	−	−	−	−	−	−	−	−	−	I	I	I
2	−	−	I	−	−	−	−	−	−	−	−	−	−	−	−	I	−	−	−	−	−	−	−	−	−	−	−	−	I	−	−
1	−	−	I	−	−	−	−	−	−	−	−	−	−	−	−	I	−	−	−	−	−	−	−	−	−	−	−	−	I	−	−

	1	2	3	4	5	6
12	−	−	−	I	−	−
11	█	−	−	I	−	−
10	█	−	−	I	−	−
9	█	−	−	I	−	−
8	█	−	−	I	−	−
7	█	−	−	I	−	−
6	I	−	−	−	−	−
5	I	−	−	█	−	−
4	I	−	−	█	−	−
3	I	−	−	█	−	−
2	I	−	−	█	−	−
1	I	−	−	█	−	−

20. REFORMED TUCK-STITCH RIB.

reform purl stitches, you need to transfer the stitch from the latch tool to an eyelet tool to replace it on the needle. Swatch 19 creates a diamond pattern of knits and purls, while Swatch 20 combines latching up and holding to create a widely spaced rib with tucked texture. Both of these swatches were worked from the wrong side of the fabric to form knit stitches on a purl background.

Reforming a ladder of tuck stitches.
Ladders can also be reformed as tuck stitches, working from either the front or the back of the fabric. If you latch up from the back, the stitches that form the tucks will be knit stitches. Working from the

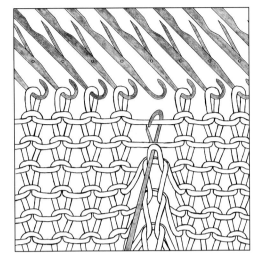

REFORMING A LADDER OF TUCKS AS KNITS, WORKING ON BACK OF FABRIC.

Working Garter Stitch on the Machine

Garter stitch is one of the easiest hand-knit stitches to work because all rows are simply knitted, with the fabric turned over at the end of each row to work from right to left. The result is a fully reversible fabric, both faces of which are composed of alternating rows of knit and purl stitches. As easy as this stitch is to do by hand, it is tricky to work on the machine. Although all rows are knitted by the carriage, the fabric does not automatically turn over at the end of each row. When the fabric is turned by hand, however, the reversal causes the characteristic garter-stitch ridge to form where knit stitches are followed by purls (and vice versa).

Purl stitches can be reformed as knit stitches individually, in groups or by entire rows. Individual stitches and groups of stitches are usually reformed using a tappet tool. I sometimes reform small blocks of garter stitch by working with two separate latch tools. one on each side of the fabric.

REFORMING GARTER STITCH WITH A PAIR OF LATCH TOOLS.
To reform the knit-purl alternation of garter stitch, one method is to pass the stitch back and forth from one tool to the other in order to work from alternating sides of the fabric.

To reform stitches with these two tools, begin reforming the first stitch with the lower tool on the purl side of the fabric. Let the stitch slip back to open and lie behind the latch of this tool. Pass the second latch tool under the next float from the knit side, and hook the two tools together to transfer the stitch from the first tool to the empty second tool. Remove the first tool. Reform the next stitch in the column from the back of the fabric. Slip the tool under the next float and

21. REFORMED TUCK STITCHES IN STRIPES.
(Pattern courtesy of the Silver Knitting Institute of Japan.)

right side will produce purled tuck stitches identical to those formed by the carriage.

Unlike reforming a single tuck stitch, where a stitch and a float are placed together on a needle, you must use a latch tool to reform a ladder of tucks. Begin by inserting the tool into the bottom stitch in the column. Then insert the tool under two floats and catch the second one with the hook of the tool, as shown in the drawing on p. 77. Pull this stitch under the first float and through the stitch on the tool.

For more pronounced texture, you can insert the tool under several floats before catching and pulling one through the

transfer it to the empty tool on the purl side. Continue reforming in this fashion until the entire ladder is latched up. The differing direction of the tools creates alternating knit and purl stitches up the column.

An entire row of stitches is usually not reformed since this is a lengthy, tedious undertaking. Instead the whole piece of knitting is more often turned over on the machine with a garter bar or scrap knitting so that the right side faces the knitter. If, after turning the fabric once, you continued knitting, you would simply have reversed the face of the fabric.

All garter bars come with instructions for their use, but they take practice and patience to master. They are usually divided into sections, which can be joined to work with wide widths or an entire row. Start practicing with a single section of garter bar and work your way up to using the tool fully assembled to accommodate the entire width of the bed.

To avoid dropped and split stitches, the prongs of the garter bar must align perfectly with the needles on the machine. Hence check your machine for bent needles and replace them before you begin.

To reverse one row with a garter bar, turn the work, knit one row, turn the work again

USING THE GARTER BAR TO TURN OVER THE FABRIC.

To work: Hold GB with lengthwise ridge on top (near right) & hook GB onto NDLS. Start at either end, pulling fabric forward so STS slide over latches & onto prongs of tool. If you try to work both ends toward middle, you're apt to split STS or catch them on NDL hooks. Then unthread carr, set it to hold NDLS in HP & move to opposite end of bed.

Turn GB over so that horizontal ridge faces NDLS (far right). Align NDLS with grooves on back of GB prongs.

(Note that these photos show a standard-gauge bar using every other prong on a chunky machine.)

stitch on the tool. The rib at the bottom of Swatch 16 on p. 71 was made by reforming every other stitch in tuck.

Swatch 21 is a very clever use of stripes and reformed tuck stitches. A needle was left out of work wherever a ladder was needed to reform stitches. Then the entire fabric was knit, alternating two rows of color A with two rows of color B. After these rows were knit, one stitch on each side of the nonworking needle was dropped, the stitches raveled to the first row and both stitches caught together in the latch tool. The latch tool was passed under both bars of color A to catch both bars of color B in the hook. The entire

ladder was latched up, working with double bars of each color, in one large tuck stitch and hung on the center (formerly nonworking) needle. One color always tucked, the other formed the stitches.

The recessed "ditches" formed by columns of latched-up tuck stitches are ideal for adding crocheted effects on the surface, especially when you don't want the crocheted detail to be raised above the rest of the surface. Surface crochet is ideal for adding vertical lines to simple designs and turning stripes into multicolor plaids. The reformed tuck stitches are also less likely to pucker than latched-up knit stitches reformed every row.

so the purl side faces you, and continue knitting. Two turns produce one ridge with a knitted row in between. To produce continuous garter stitch, turn the work after knitting each row. In figuring patterns with garter-stitch ridges, you will always need an even number of rows and turns to return the purl side of the fabric so that it faces you.

If you do not have a garter bar or if only part of a row needs to be reformed, you can produce garter stitch by manually reforming stitches. To reverse one row, knit two rows and then reform the last one. To produce continuous garter stitch, you would have to re-

form every second row. Whether you reform stitches or use the garter bar, the effect is the same, but working with the garter bar is much faster.

To produce double ridges, a faster variation on the basic garter stitch, you can again either use the garter bar or manually reform stitches. To work with a garter bar, turn the fabric with the bar at the point where you want the double-ridge effect, knit two rows, and turn the fabric again. To work double ridges by hand, reform the individual stitches in the double-ridge area, knit four rows and reform the last two rows of stitches in the same area.

Slowly rotate GB to make it perpendicular to NDLS (far left). Be sure every ST is caught by a NDL. If you missed a ST, use a crochet hook or transfer tool to lift ST onto NDL. If you missed many STS, rotate GB forward & try again. When all STS are caught, pull GB straight down to remove it (near left). Do not tip it forward as you pull or the NDL hooks will catch in eyes of prongs. Pivot GB toward bed, keeping NDL hooks in grooves. When GB is nearly parallel to NDLS, gently pull it toward you until STS catch in NDL hooks.

REFORMING A LADDER OF SLIP STITCHES TO SHOW ON KNIT FACE, WORKING FROM PURL SIDE.

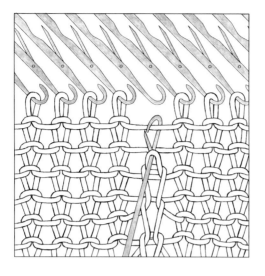

22. REFORMED FAIR ISLE.
Rib is reformed tuck STS. Checkerboard is a pat of reformed P STS.

Reforming a ladder of slip stitches.

To reform a ladder of slip stitches, latch every other float by passing the tool over one float and latching the next. For a stronger effect, you can latch every third or fourth float, for example. If you work from the wrong side, the slips will appear on the knit face of the fabric, but the stitches that show behind them will be purls. If you work from the right side of the fabric, the slip stitches will appear on the back, or purl, side just as they would if they had been formed by the carriage.

Slip stitches are never automatically formed on the knit face of a single-bed fabric, but it is possible to place them there with knit stitches showing behind them by adding some extra steps to the latching-up process. Work from the knit side and after each knit stitch is formed, *take it off the latch tool with a transfer tool from the purl side. Lift the transfer tool above one float and then return the stitch to the latch tool. Reform the next float as a knit stitch.* Repeat from * to *. In the drawing above left, every other stitch was slipped. For a more pronounced texture, you could skip two or three floats before returning the stitch to the latch tool. The difference between this method and the other, working from the purl side, is that not only are the slips on the right side of the fabric, but they also lie on top of knit stitches.

As seen in Swatch 22, you can reform stitches in two-color work. The rib at the bottom of the sample was originally knitted as a vertical Fair Isle one-by-one stripe. The second-color stitches were reformed every other row as tuck stitches, from the wrong side of the fabric. The first-color floats were treated as tuck loops.

The Fair Isle checkerboard design was also reformed from the wrong side so that the pattern stitches appear as purls on a knit background. The effect is unique, but producing it is a slow, clumsy process because the tappet tool must be used in the space between the floats and the stitches being worked on. You can work only three or four rows down at a time before you have to reach in with a transfer tool, remove the last stitch from the tappet tool and replace it on its needle. Alternatively, you can reform after every row or latch in tuck, though this produces a ribbed effect.

Because knitting machines are incapable of producing knit-purl patterns in two colors, I think this procedure is worth the trouble for small patterns and isolated effects. Whenever you use this method, start latching up with the first row of stitches in the contrast color rather than the last row of stitches of the previous color, unless, of course, you want to highlight the dividing line with an obvious, two-color ridge.

To reform a wide ladder with a double latch tool, catch the first float at the bottom of the ladder with one hook of the tool and the second float with the other hook of the tool, as shown in the top drawing at right. If you try to start with one large float, you'll latch up a single, oversized stitch, which has very limited usage, instead of creating two separate stitches. Once you've started the ladder with these two steps, you can simply latch up both stitches at once, catching each float in both hooks simultaneously. Two separate, though parallel, stitches will be formed.

Finally, while not actually a method for reforming stitches, duplicate stitch (also called Swiss darning) is visually related to reformed stitches. As its name suggests, this technique duplicates with embroidery already existing stitches and is useful for repairing mistakes and for adding small, colorful details to finished knits. To work this effect, use a tapestry needle threaded with contrasting yarn or embroidery floss and sew over the stitches of the fabric as shown in the bottom drawing at right. Duplicate stitch can add touches of third and fourth colors to Fair Isles, embroider a bouquet on a plain garment or turn a simple stripe into a mock plaid.

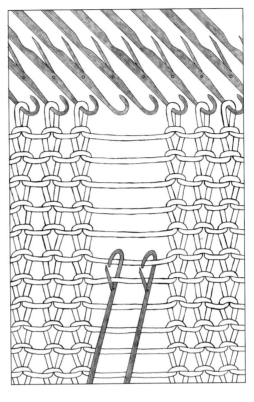

USING A DOUBLE LATCH TOOL TO LATCH UP A SIDE LADDER.

DUPLICATE STITCH.

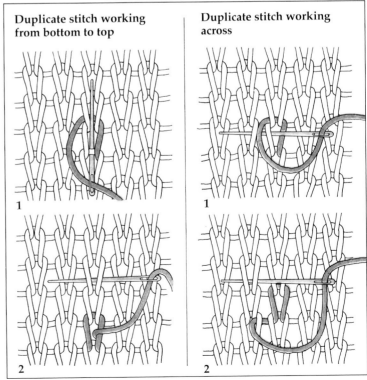

Duplicate stitch working from bottom to top

Duplicate stitch working across

A
Glossary of
Hand-Manipulated
Stitches

CHAPTER 3

Twisted Stitches

Twisted stitches are just what their name suggests: stitches that have been removed from their needles, twisted or rotated, and then returned to a needle or needles above. The stitches produced by twisting create low, rich textures in the fabric. While these stitches have long been popular with hand knitters, machine knitters have not known how to duplicate twisted effects because the technique is never discussed in machine-knitting manuals or sourcebooks.

Until the bulky-gauge machine's recent growth in popularity sparked an interest in hand-manipulated techniques, twisting stitches was thought too slow a process on the multi-needled, standard-gauge machine to be of interest to machine knitters. It's true that some twisted-stitch patterns are far too time-consuming to be practical for knitting an entire garment, even on a chunky machine. Yet most of these patterns are faster to work than cabling and produce excellent results when combined with other techniques, isolated as panel designs or piggy-backed on cables for added impact.

Knit, slip and tuck stitches can all be twisted, whether as individual stitches, pairs of stitches (the most common) or groups of up to three or four stitches. It is possible to twist stitches 180° or 360° to the left, right or in any combination. While most twisting is done on single-bed machines (because there is more room to work without the interference of a second bed), double-bed stitches can also be twisted. Although a little clumsier to maneuver, double-bed twisting is essentially worked like twisting on a single bed, but it produces a deeper, more pronounced texture.

The simplest way to twist a stitch or stitches is to use a bodkin or an eyelet transfer tool. Remove the stitch from its needle, twist it by rotating the tool and then return it to the same needle or to a new needle if the pattern calls for this.

The number of stitches you can twist together depends on the size of the stitches, the stretchiness of the yarn and the tools used for twisting. In order to twist groups of three or four stitches or to create softer, open fabrics with large, loosely twisted stitches, you will probably need to lengthen the stitches, relying on one of the methods explained on pp. 61-68. The more stitches you twist together, the bolder the effect, but the more you twist any stitches (that is, the more times you rotate the tool), the tighter and more compact the stitches become. And, if stitches are over-twisted, you may not be able to return them to their needles, or the carriage may have difficulty knitting them back.

SYMBOLS FOR
TWISTED STITCHES
(SEE ALSO P. 22).

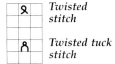

☒	Twisted stitch
☒	Twisted tuck stitch

Single-bed twisted stitches

The simplest twisted stitch is a knitted-back E-wrap, a cast-on method explained on p. 36. This is, in fact, the only way to twist a stitch as it is being formed on a knitting machine. Otherwise, you must knit stitches with the carriage and then rework them to twist them. The knitted-back E-wrap can be used to create cross-knit ribs (see the bottom part of Swatch 23) by alternately wrapping all the needles from left to right, knitting right to left and then returning the empty carriage to the right side with a free pass. Then, after ten rows, for example, the cross-knit rib is produced by reforming every second or every third stitch.

While any stitch can be twisted, twisting a single stitch does not usually show. Twisting two adjacent stitches, however, creates a clear, visible texture. Even more visible than twisted plain knit or purl stitches are twisted tuck stitches, whether clustered or isolated on a plain knit background. These stitches stand out beautifully because the tuck loops add extra texture and body to the twist (see the top part of Swatch 23).

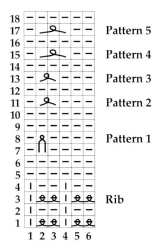

23. TWISTED RIB, AND TWISTED KNIT AND TUCK PATTERNS.

To work: For twisted rib, *E-wrap alt Rs, wrapping from L to RT, ret yarn to carr & knit from RT to L. Remove yarn from carr & free-pass carr to RT.* Rep from * to * for desired length. Reform every 3/ST as K ST.

For twisted-tuck pat in Rs 7 & 8 (above rib), individual tuck STS were twisted 180° with a bodkin. In 2nd pat, pairs of K STS were twisted 180°, & in 3rd pat they were twisted 360°. In 4th pat, groups of 3 K STS were twisted 180°, & in 5th pat, they were twisted 360°.

To twist one tuck stitch, (or any single stitch, for that matter), use a bodkin to remove the stitch and all its tuck loops from the needle. Twirl the bodkin like a miniature baton to twist the stitch to the right or to the left, 180° or 360°, and then return the stitch to its needle. The bodkin is perfect for single-stitch twists because the stitch can be returned from either end of the tool. Whether hand-pulled or automatically selected, repeating tuck-stitch patterns can be enhanced by twisting any or all of the tuck stitches (Swatch 24).

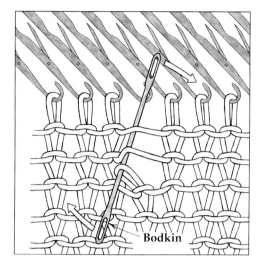

TWISTING A SINGLE TUCK STITCH WITH A BODKIN.

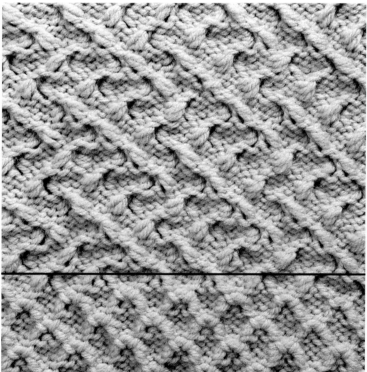

24. TWISTED TUCK-STITCH PATTERNS.

While pat at bottom of swatch is not twisted at all, but simply tucked by carr according to punchcard, upper half of swatch alt 2 different twist sequences. First twisting sequence (Twist A) begins with 1st 2 tuck STS twisted to L, then next 2 tuck STS twisted to RT, & alt in this fashion across R. Second twisting sequence at top of swatch (Twist B) simply reverses direction of twisting the alt pairs of STS.

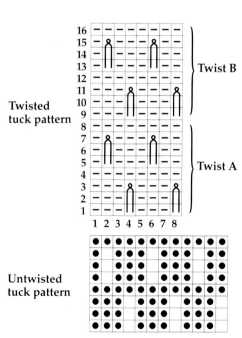

PUNCHCARD.

Pairs of knit stitches that are twisted 360° (full twists) form raised knots of texture. These same pairs twisted 180° (half-twists) produce the more common twisted patterns, which closely resemble cables and are, in fact, related. The latter are also the closest in appearance to hand-knit twisted stitches (Swatch 25).

The tools used to twist a pair of stitches depend on the degree of the twists. Full twists are worked with an eyelet transfer tool, twirling it like the bodkin. Half-twists require two matched eyelet-transfer tools: one to remove the stitches from their

needles, and the other inserted from above before twisting to ensure that, after twisting, a tool faces the right direction for replacing the stitches on the needles (top and middle photos, facing page).

There is also a single-tool method for working half-twists with pairs of stitches, but it is tricky to master and unsatisfactory if the stitches are at all tight. After twisting the stitches, hold the tool slightly above the needles on which you want to place the stitches. Keep the tool just high enough above the needles to create some tension on the stitches. With your free

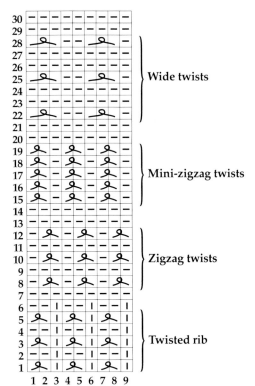

25. TWISTED RIB, ZIGZAG TWISTS AND WIDE TWIST.

To work: For twisted 1x2 rib, reform every 3rd ST as K ST, &, on A/Rs, twist next 2 STS tog, working all twists in same direction.

For zigzag twist, twist 2 STS tog on A/Rs, alt direction of twist from 1 R to next.

For mini-zigzag twist, twist 2 STS tog E/R, alt direction of twist from 1 R to next.

For wide twist, twist 3 STS tog every 3/R, working all twists in same direction.

hand, push the needles butts far enough forward so that the needle hooks poke through the back of the stitches. Then pull the tool away (bottom photo, facing page).

Three-stitch twists are less common than paired twists. Yet they too can be worked with the two-tool method.

Most hand-knit twist patterns space out the twisting to every other row to give the stitches time to recover and adjust before being twisted again. Since the same tightening of the fabric results on the machine, it's useful to keep the twisting to every other row. This is the cadence of twisting worked in all the sample twisted-pattern swatches in this chapter. You can, of course, space out the twisting even more if you like.

TWISTING TWO STITCHES WITH AN EYELET TRANSFER TOOL

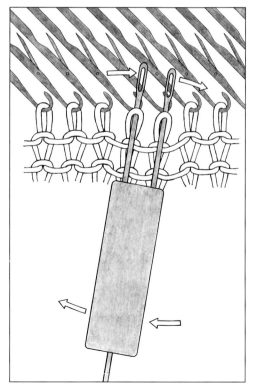

TWISTING A PAIR OF STITCHES 180° WITH TWO TOOLS.

To make a half-twist, a pair of matched, 2-pronged eyelet tr tools is needed. After removing STS from NDLS on 1st tr tool (at bottom in photo at left), insert 2nd tr tool into STS from above. Then remove lower tool.

Twist tool 180°, in this case toward RT, until eyes of tool can be hooked on empty NDLS (photo at left). Ret STS to NDLS.

SINGLE-TOOL METHOD FOR TWISTING A PAIR OF STITCHES 180°.

After twisting STS, single-tool method leaves tool facing wrong direction for redepositing STS on NDLS. But by holding STS taut, with prongs parallel to NDLS, you can poke NDLS through back of STS & remove tool.

The left or right direction of the twist depends on the pattern used. In a vertical design, it is unimportant whether the twists are made to the left or right, but they must be worked consistently throughout. However, when a design involves diagonals, the direction of the twists must be coordinated with the slant of these diagonals (Swatch 26). In other words, if part of the design slants to the right, the stitches forming it should twist to the right; and if a line slants left, the stitches forming it should similarly twist to the left. When the direction of the twisting is contrary to the slant, the ridge of texture formed lies underneath, like a shadow effect, rather than defining the top surface of the fabric as it should.

When knitting a diamond design, you will find that the direction of the twists changes at all vertical and horizontal midpoints. The direction of the central twist is unimportant, but it should be consistent from one pattern repeat to the next.

Double-bed twisted stitches

The most challenging twisted-stitch patterns are those knitted on two beds. The stitches on the main bed form a purl background for the knit ribber stitches, which are twisted according to the given pattern. Such double-bed knnitting produces a clearly defined contrast of knits and purls. Introducing plain purl stitches between the twisted knits produces a fabric that is closest in appearance to hand-knit twisted-stitch patterns.

Because of the second bed, the actual twisting process can be clumsy at first. Also, keeping track of your place in the pattern when working on two beds requires extra concentration because you cannot rely on following what you've already done. I always work from a well-numbered chart so I can tell at a glance exactly which ribber stitches need to be initiated, eliminated or moved to adjacent needles. (The main-bed needles are not shown on these charts). Although these patterns are not appropriate for beginners, a great deal of double-bed experience is not necessary.

For double-bed patterns, you'll be knitting on every needle on the main bed; hence the stitch size on the main bed should be set about as it would be for stockinette. Since there will be fewer needles in use on the ribber bed, its stitch size should be somewhat smaller than that on the main bed. Try two numbers less for starters, and adjust from there if this seems too tight or too loose. The beds must be in half-pitch and the fabric properly weighted for double-bed knitting. You may want to start with a rib and transfer the stitches that will not be used in a given pattern to the main bed. Alternatively, you can start with single-bed stockinette and create the necessary stitches on the ribber.

Initially, stitches are created on empty ribber needles by picking up the purl loop of a main-bed stitch. Once there are stitches established on the ribber, you should create new ones as needed by picking up the purl loops from adjacent ribber-bed stitches.

To eliminate, or decrease, ribber stitches when they are no longer needed for patterning, transfer them to double up with adjacent stitches. Do not transfer ribber stitches up to the main bed since this move will show in the fabric and destroy the line of the design. At the end of the knitting, however, you will have nowhere else to put the ribber stitches except to double them up with main-bed stitches in the very last row, where they will hardly show. If the number of stitches is the same from one row to the next but they shift to the left or right, simply use a transfer tool to move the stitches to the needles indicated on the pattern chart.

Let's assume, for example, that you'll begin with a rib, ending with the carriage on the left. You then need to transfer all of the ribber stitches onto the main bed so that all of the main-bed needles hold stitches and the ribber bed is empty. Look at the first row of the chart for Swatch 27. All stitches on this chart represent ribber-bed stitches. Wherever a stitch is indicated by the vertical line representing a knit stitch, you

must create a stitch on the ribber bed by picking up the purl loop of the opposite main-bed stitch and hanging it on the appropriate ribber-bed needle. Knit one row to the right (completing the first row of the chart), twist the new ribber stitches and knit back to the left (completing Row 2).

The ribber stitches are unchanged in Row 3, so you'll simply knit to the right, and then twist the stitches again, as indicated in Row 4. Knit back to the left and look carefully at Row 5 of the chart. This row calls for increasing the number of ribber stitches by picking up the purl bars of the

26 AND 27. SINGLE-BED AND DOUBLE-BED TWISTED DIAMOND GRIDS.

Swatch 26 (top photo) is a SB fabric, with twisted K STS on field of K STS. Swatch 27 (bottom photo) is a DB fabric with a purl background knitted on MB & twisted K STS formed on RB.

To work SB fabric: All twists are worked on pairs of STS on A/Rs. Observe rules explained in text about direction of twists.

To work DB fabric: Note that chart represents only RB NDLS. Vertical-line symbol indicates K STS formed on RB. Simple slanted lines indicate STS repositioned on RB. Incs & decs are shown by standard symbols.

Before K R 1, make STS on RB NDLS 5, 6 11 & 12, as shown on chart. All incs, moves & decs are done before K odd-numbered Rs. All twisting is worked before K even-numbered Rs.

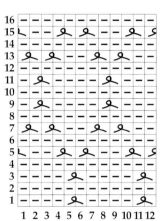

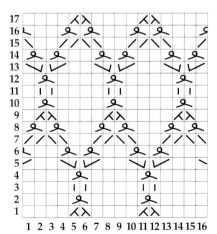

existing ribber stitches and hanging them on the adjacent needles. Remember not to create these additional stitches by picking up the purl bars of the opposite (main-bed) stitches because it shows and ruins the effect. Knit Row 5, twist in the appropriate direction and then knit Row 6.

Row 7 does not call for creating or increasing stitches, but it does require you to move the existing pairs of stitches one needle to the right or left. Row 9 calls for decreasing each group from four to two stitches. Make these decreases by transferring the first and fourth stitch in each ribber group onto the second and third needles. Do not transfer them to the main bed (although you are obliged to do so after the very last row). The remaining rows in the chart are read in the same way and call for increasing, decreasing or moving stitches on the ribber bed, every two rows.

All double-bed twists are two-stitch, 180° twists, accomplished by using the two-tool method and knitting two rows after twisting. Full 360° double-bed twists are so tight visually that they interfere with the pattern itself and physically make the twisting nearly impossible to manage. It would therefore be very unusual to find them called for in a pattern.

The greatest difference between single-bed and double-bed twisting is that, in double-bed work, you do not coordinate the direction of the twist with the direction of a diagonal line, but rather twist the tool in the opposite direction. That is, if a line of the design is to slant to your right, you must rotate the tool to your left to compensate for the fact that the ribber bed faces you upside down. If you don't compensate, the stitches will have a ragged appearance that fights the overall design. Also, whenever the design contains

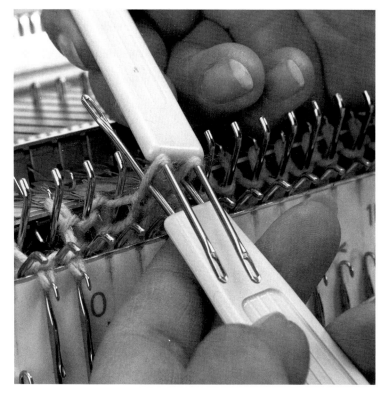

DOUBLE-BED TWISTING.
After removing RB STS on a tr tool (at top in photo at left), insert 2nd tool from below & remove upper tool. After twisting tool 180° (photo above), tool correctly faces RB NDLS so STS can be returned.

intersecting diagonal lines, make sure there is an even number of empty needles between the twisting pairs of stitches at the outset, or you'll be unable to cross them when they approach each other.

Swatches 26 and 27 on p. 91 show the different effects achieved by working the same twisted pattern on a single bed and on double beds. Separate charts are provided, with the double-bed chart annotated to indicate when to increase, decrease or move stitches on the ribber bed. Once you understand the double-bed method, you can work any single-bed chart on two beds.

Although it doesn't matter which side the carriage is on, I've also indicated whether to knit from left to right, or from right to left in order to help simplify the process by setting a standard to follow. I always like to twist the stitches when the carriage is on

the right. When the carriage is on the left, I make whatever changes are necessary in the needle arrangement — that is, beginning, ending or shifting stitches. You cannot do both maneuvers at the same time.

The French knots and basketweave in swatches 28 and 29 are atypical twisted stitches. The French knots are created by twisting oversized sinker loops between stitches. The basketweave pattern, which resembles a cable-stitch effect, is, in fact, twisted by shifting stitches left or right.

To work the French knots, the ribber was raised to its highest, nonworking position (one notch below the height where the carriages would connect for double-bed knitting). I wrapped over every fourth needle on the main bed and under or behind the alternate fourth sinker post on the ribber. I wrapped two identical rows so that the free yarn returned to the carriage

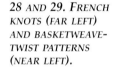

28 AND 29. FRENCH KNOTS (FAR LEFT) AND BASKETWEAVE-TWIST PATTERNS (NEAR LEFT).

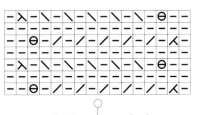

Center zero on bed

and could be rethreaded to knit one row. Next I removed the loop from the first sinker post and, lifting it up and out of the way, used an eyelet transfer tool to remove and hold the stitch from the opposite needle. I twisted the loop onto the tip of the transfer tool (almost like an E-wrap) and placed the twisted loop and stitch together on the same needle. I completed all knots and knitted a number of rows to the next French-knot location, where alternate fourth needles and sinker posts were wrapped in the same fashion to stagger the knots. Because the stitch was removed from the needle before twisting the loop onto the tool, the texture appears on the knit side of the fabric.

MAKING FRENCH KNOTS.

Begin process by K some Rs on MB, ending with COR. Push every 4th MB NDL to HP. Raise RB to highest NWP. Remove yarn from carr & work RT to L, wrapping yarn from, for example, every 4th MB NDL to alt 4th RB sinker post. At L edge, reverse & wrap same NDLS & posts back to RT. Rethread carr. K 1 R.

To form knots, use single-pronged tr tool to lift loops off 1 sinker post & then remove ST from MB NDL directly opposite (center NDL in each group of 3 MB NDLS), as shown in the top photo.

Lift enlarged sinker-post loops over tip of tool so they lie on K face of fabric. Then E-wrap tip of tool, in front of ST. Ret E-wrap & ST to empty NDL to complete knot (bottom photo).

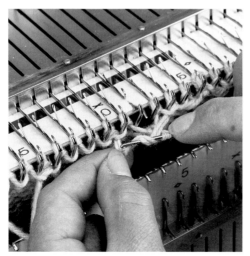

If you find that the needles holding the knots do not knit well on the first pass of the carriage, leave those needles in holding position for the first row and then knit them back by hand. In the sample, I alternated placement of the knots, but you could put them wherever you want. If you want an isolated motif of knots, use a separate piece of yarn to form the loops, rather than carrying the free yarn across the back of the fabric, introducing unneccessary floats that can catch.

A multiple-eyelet transfer tool makes it very easy to knit the twisted basketweave pattern shown in the top photo on the facing page. Because these stitches are not actually twisted, it is tempting to call this technique a cable method. However, since it is worked with a single tool rather than with two, as true cabling requires, the method is more closely related to twisting than cabling. Because the stitches are not individually twisted, the symbols for twisted stitches are not used on the chart. Rather, the chart shows a lateral move with a double stitch on one end of the row and a closed eyelet on the other.

To produce the basketweave effect, choose a tool that will select every other needle. The twists will alternate left and right from row to row, (with two rows knitted between each row of twists), and you will need to keep track of which needles to use for each twist. When twisting toward the right, select every other needle, making sure to include the first needle to the right of zero on the bed. Start at the right end of the bed and move the first group of selected, alternate stitches two needles to the right. Continue in this fashion with all remaining groups, working from right to left. Each stitch will cross behind one stationary stitch to its right before being placed on the next empty needle. When you have finished, the first needle on the right edge will hold a doubled stitch, and the last needle on the left will be empty. To prevent an eyelet from forming, fill the empty needle with an adjacent purl bar and then knit two rows. The next twist is made to the left by selecting and twisting the alternate needles, including the first needle to the left of zero. Knit two rows and repeat the entire sequence.

In Chapter 8 (Swatch 139 on p. 212), you'll find a layered, open-grid design that looks very much like this basketweave, but it requires actual cable crossings with two tools. These crossings can be worked with a single tool, but the resulting fabric is unusable because it biases when all the twisting is done in the same direction. Because the direction of the twists alternates for basketweave, however, biasing is not a problem with this pattern.

Finally, in addition to twisting stitches and sinker loops, you can also twist loose bundles of yarn to create cords and roped fringes. Although this is a finishing technique rather than a knitting technique, the cords and fringes are visually (if not physically) related to twisted-stitch fabrics. Twisted cords make fast, easy belts and ties, and twisted fringes have more body than plain fringes.

To make twisted cords and fringes, tie all of the strands you'll be twisting into a knot and secure the knot to a doorknob or some other stationary point. Divide the strands into two groups and knot the free end of each group. Hold each group taut, and separately twist each one to the right until the yarn is so tightly twisted that it loops back on itself when you relax the tension. (You can also insert a pencil above the botttom knot in each group, and twirl the pencil to twist the yarn.) After slightly relaxing the tension on each group, hold them together and roll them between your palms to twist them to the left. When you let go, the yarn usually stays twisted together. If the two groups tend to untwist, tie a simple, overhand knot at the bottom of the bundle to secure the yarn.

MAKING BASKETWEAVE TWIST. You can twist either RT or L. In top photo, twist is worked to L. Remove EOS, taking care to include that on 1st NDL to L of center zero.
  Shift tool 2 NDLS to L & ret STS to empty NDLS (bottom photo). Notice that last NDL on L of group holds 2 STS, while last NDL on RT is empty. Fill empty NDL with P bar of adj ST to RT.

CHAPTER 4

Wrapped and Woven Stitches

You can wrap yarn around needles and stitches, lace it through needles and stitches, or weave stitches through other stitches. The purl-side textures created with these techniques range from allover patterns of floats and interlacing fibers to puffs of yarn and loopy fringes that obscure the underlying fabric.

In machine knitting, weaving and wrapping yarns are secondary yarns that do not actually form stitches but rather travel behind, in front of, or around the stitches formed by the main yarn to decorate the fabric. Because these yarns simply weave over and under the needle shafts or wrap around stitches, they need not need fit in the hooks of the needles. Hence yarns that are extreme in size and texture, which would normally be unsuitable for a given machine, can be used for weaving and wrapping. Ribbons, bits of fleece, strips of fabric, leather and even fur can all be used (Swatch 30).

Weaving yarns can be worked horizontally in a technique called knit-weaving, or they can be be used vertically to produce embroidered effects. Wrapping yarns can be E-wrapped at the edges of a fabric or around individual needles within the body of the fabric. Wrapping yarns can also be wound around needles and/or stitches to create decorative effects and fringes. Despite

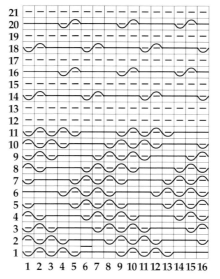

30. Yarns suitable for weaving and wrapping.

Because weaving & wrapping yarns need not fit into NDL hooks, yarns normally unsuitable for machine knitting can be used. Bottom of sample is woven with rayon ribbon; top is woven with strips of fake fur.

WRAPPING AND
WEAVING SYMBOLS
(SEE ALSO PP. 22-25).

♀	E-wrap
♀	Knitted-back E-wrap
⌒ ⌄	Yarn woven over and under needles
◎ ∞	Wrapped adjacent needles
⋈	E-wrap vertical weaving
⋊ ⋉	Vertical weaving, working to L or RT
⋈ ⋈	Stitch pulled through stitch to L or RT
⋈⋈ ⋈⋈	Stitch pulled through 2 stitches to L or RT
⋈ ⋈	Two stitches pulled through 1 stitch to L or RT
⋈ ⋈	Two stitches pulled through 1 stitch, with eyelet, to L or RT
⊿ ⊾	Stitch pulled through stitch, from L or RT, and returned to same needle
↻ ↺	Stitch wrapped around other stitch, to L or RT, and rehung on same needle
⋈	Diagonally woven stitches

their obvious differences, weaving and wrapping techniques are presented together in one chapter because they are related and are often worked in concert.

Both horizontal and vertical weaving techniques and several methods of wrapping produce texture on the purl side of the fabric, with a slight shadow, or "grin through," often seen on the knit side. You can also create woven and wrapped effects on the knit side of the fabric by removing the stitches from their needles before working the effect, then replacing them on their needles and continuing to knit.

To empty the needles temporarily in order to work woven and wrapped effects on the knit side, the stitches must be removed with transfer tools or held on stitch holders. If a number of stitches are involved, a garter bar or scrap knitting can be used. Both the garter bar and scrap knitting also make it possible to remove an entire row of stitches, which offers the option of turning the fabric over before replacing it on the needles. Applying woven and wrapped textures to the knit side of a fabric always involves the extra steps of removing stitches from their needles and then replacing them. Because this two-step procedure becomes tedious if worked excessively, knit-side accents are best used only occasionally.

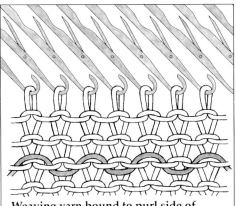

Weaving yarn bound to purl side of fabric wherever it passes over or under a needle

Weaving methods

In both horizontal knit-weave and vertical embroidery weaving, the secondary weaving yarn laces through the background fabric to create texture. The weaving yarn is generally heavier or more textured than the main yarn, but it need not be, nor need it be any particular type of yarn. Whatever the yarn used, however, the bulk of the extra woven strand (especially the horizontally knit-woven strand) requires that the stitch-size dial be raised from that used for nonwoven areas — generally by one number for most weaving patterns and by more for patterns with lots of close interlacements and few floats. If most of the fabric is to be knit-woven, work with the increased stitch throughout. If there are to be only occasional knit-woven areas, increase the stitch size at those points alone. For vertical embroidery, there's no need to increase the stitch size unless you're working with an extremely bulky strand or many parallel strands that nearly cover the surface of the fabric.

If you want to use the same yarn for both the background and woven (or for that matter, wrapped) effects, you need only remove the yarn from the carriage when the pattern calls for weaving (or wrapping), manually work the effects, then return the carriage in a free pass to the opposite side to rethread and continue knitting. If you repeat the woven (or wrapped) effect in a second row, that effect will be more pronounced, appearing as if the yarn were doubled. Additionally, working two rows of woven (or wrapped) effects means that you end up on the carriage side and hence do not need to worry about finishing off cut ends or making free passes to rethread the carriage.

WEAVING YARN
BOUND TO FABRIC IN
1X1 INTERLACEMENT.

Horizontal weaving, or knit-weaving

Knit-weaving is a fairly standard technique for machines with automatic selection and a carriage equipped with knobs to carry the weaving yarns ahead of the carriage and brushes to place it on the shafts of the selected needles. If you have a more basic machine, you can still do knit-weaving entirely or partly by hand.

This technique involves a background yarn threaded into the carriage and a weaving yarn caught by a knob or guide at either end of the sinker plate (your manual will explain any instructions or settings unique to your machine). When the carriage moves across the bed, the main yarn forms stitches and the weaving yarn laces between them, sometimes between all the stitches, at other times between groups of stitches, forming floats. If the knit-weaving is to be repeated in another row (or rows), the weaving yarn must be unhooked and moved to the other side of the carriage so that it travels ahead of the carriage to weave each successive row. Some machines have a weaving accessory that automatically switches the yarn after each row, but this is done manually on most machines.

In knit-weaving, the weaving yarn passes either over or under a needle, depending on the pattern of holes on a punchcard,

the markings on an electronic card or your manual placement of the yarn. Whenever the weaving yarn shifts from lying over a needle to under the next (or vice versa), it is caught by the stitch at that point and bound to the purl side of the fabric.

A combination of closely interlaced background floats (where the yarn passes over and under one or two needles) and wider floats (created when the yarn passes over or under several adjacent needles) provides the contrast that defines most horizontal weaving patterns. In addition to any major patterns created by the floats, a secondary pattern is also formed in the background stitches and can be varied by allowing the weaving yarn to pass over and under the same needles in every row (as it does at the top of Swatch 31 or to alternate the interlacement from one row to the next (as it does at the bottom of Swatch 31).

Although elaborate pattern sequences should be knitted on machines with automatic selection, simple patterns can easily be knitted on machines that have weaving brushes and knobs but no punchcards. By following a stitch-by-stitch, row-by-row chart, you can hand-pull the needles for the background and float effects. Before each row is knitted, simply pull to holding position all the needles that the weaving yarn should pass over.

31. ALTERNATIVE BACKGROUND EFFECTS.
Different background effects can be produced by weaving over & under either same NDLS (top) or alt NDLS (bottom).

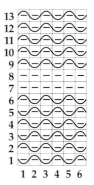

Repeating
1x1 interlacement

Alternating
1x1 interlacement

Make sure the carriage is set to knit needles in holding position and let the knobs carry the weaving yarn ahead of the carriage. This yarn will pass over all needles in holding position and under those left in regular working position.

A basic over-one/under-one background pattern is easiest to work with a minimum of concentration if you always begin each row by selecting the first needle on the carriage side (and every alternate needle from there on). With an even number of needles, the background effect will alternate as at the bottom of Swatch 31 on p. 99. With an odd number of needles, the effect will be vertically striped, like that at the top of this same swatch.

You can use a needle pusher to select every other needle or every two needles for background interlacement and then individually select additional needles that you want grouped to form floats. Make sure the background interlaces consistently from selvage to selvage. That is to say, if you begin a row by selecting the first and third stitches, make sure you select every other odd-numbered needle across the entire row. Even when a row is interrupted by pattern floats, be sure to select the correct background needles on the other side of the floats. If you should select the wrong needles, you will disturb the background interlacements.

KNIT-WEAVING AN ISOLATED INLAY MOTIF.

This motif has no floats. Instead the pattern is created by alt background interlacement, & shifting position of the 2 weaving yarns. Though design's edges are straight, they could have changed from R to R by weaving over or under more or fewer NDLS.

The brushes on the carriage sinker plate ensure that the yarn is properly placed as it runs ahead of the carriage. However, even if your machine does not have weaving brushes, you can weave by pushing all the needles out to holding position, closing their latches and manually lacing the yarn over and under their shafts. Then, if your machine cannot automatically knit needles back from holding position, you'll have to place them manually in upper working position before the carriage knits each row. Because there are so many different machines in use, it's difficult to guarantee that this method will work with every one of them. Therefore, if you run into problems, check your manual or confer with your local knitting-machine dealer.

Knit-woven effects.
Knitting-machine manuals tend to present knit-weaving as an allover, selvage-to-selvage technique that produces a fabric with limited horizontal stretch. This increased stability often causes the fabric to be stiff and firm enough for upholstery and placemats. To avoid this stiffness when the design yarn weaves from selvage to selvage, you can knit the background fabric on every other needle or use a weaving yarn lighter in weight than the main yarn. Because the design formed by a lightweight weaving yarn will be less pronounced, this offers a wonderful opportunity to add a subtle touch of metallic or specialty yarn to a plain fabric, while improving its drape and suitability for various uses.

If designs are planned for isolated accents rather than for selvage-to-selvage coverage, you can weave with as many different yarns as you want in each row and also apply the technique to multicolored inlay designs. Very often, designs that would be suitable for intarsia, or tapestry, are also appropriate for inlay weaving, that is, isolated knit-weaving. While intarsia must produce its own structure as it creates a design, a woven inlay is supported by a background fabric. Hence isolated knit-weaving is faster to knit and much easier to control than intarsia.

Depending on how you select the needles, you can minimize the floats or make them the focus of the weaving design. Swatch 32 eliminated the floats entirely in favor of the background interlacement to create a brocade design. To produce such a brocaded design, the carriage is threaded with the main yarn, and the needles selected for the design are hand pulled according to a chart. The weaving yarns are not carried ahead of the carriage by the weaving knobs but instead are controlled entirely by hand. The main yarn knits after the weaving yarns have been laid across or manually laced through the selected needles. (It's a good idea to wind each of the weaving yarns onto a bobbin or yarn holder of some kind to keep them from tangling.) You can chart your design on gauged graph paper or, if your machine has a charting attachment, draw it right onto a pattern sheet. If you're using a charting attachment, just follow the needle scale indicating the needle numbers on the bed for placing each color.

Because the purl side is usually the right side of a knit-woven fabric and the side on which all the floats show, you cannot allow a needle to catch two overlapping weaving yarns. Nor can you float these yarns across from one area to the next since these floats will show. With brocade knit-weaving, you may have a sense of never being in the right place at the right time to make changes in color placement or design shape. Sometimes cutting and restarting a yarn from the opposite direction is the only way to ensure that one shape increases while the adjacent one decreases, without overlapping the yarns or skipping needles.

Tapestry weavers have learned to avoid some of these problems by using their yarns in contrary motion, rather than in parallel motion (see the drawing at right), as is done for intarsia. That is to say,

32. BROCADE DESIGN WITHOUT FLOATS.
To eliminate floats, each section of this design was woven with a separate strand of yarn, whether working with a contrast yarn or main yarn.

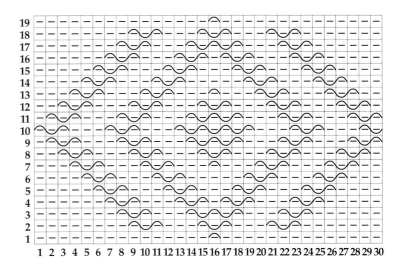

PARALLEL AND CONTRARY MOTION.

Four weaving yarns working in parallel motion

Four weaving yarns working in contrary motion

tapestry weavers start each new strand of yarn from the opposite direction of the adjacent yarn, and maintain that order even when additional new yarns are added. This technique also works well for knit-weave because the weaving yarn does not form stitches and requires very little slack for take-up.

Another technique I find useful for minimizing confusion with an isolated brocade motif on a one-over/one-under background is to select designs with an odd number of needles in each section of the pattern. These designs are easy to widen or make narrow as needed without changing or affecting the background pattern. In addition to providing continuity of background stitches, the odd number also eliminates irregular floats, which muddle the edges of designs as they change shape.

The four border designs in Swatch 33 were woven using a three-prong transfer tool, varying the number of needles the tool passed over or under. Each prong was threaded with a separate strand of yarn (in the photo the first and third strands are black, and the second one is white, but they could have been the same color). The bottom photo on the facing page shows how the tool was maneuvered between extended needles to weave all three strands simultaneously. With all of the needles in holding position, each prong (and the yarn it carries) passes up and down, over and under the needles as the tool is manipulated across the bed. If you're new to working with this three-prong tool, focus on moving the first prong, and the others will follow suit.

The first border in Swatch 33 was woven by moving the tool down between three needles, under one and then up between the next three, over one, and so on. The other borders are variations on this theme, and the last one introduces the idea of twisting the yarns together as they float beneath the needles. This technique combines well with the vertical weaving methods that follow.

Other knit-woven features.
Knit-weaving is the easiest way to provide marker rows for hanging pleats, lifting stitches and locating specific rows on which to position other effects or pattern details later in the fabric. Because the weaving yarn laces through stitches rather than forming them, marker rows can easily be pulled out later without affecting the structure of the fabric. Ravel-cord markers are the easiest to remove, but you can use any yarn that is strong and smooth enough to pull through the stitches without breaking or leaving a fuzzy residue.

To create a visual marker, a simple over-under order is all that's needed. In some cases, weaving over and under several needles at a time is faster and easier to remove than weaving over and under individual needles and also provides a clear enough marker to follow.

If you want more weaving yarn to show between the stitches on the front of the fabric and offer additional possibilities for manipulating the weaving and background yarns in combination, you can create ladders with the weaving and main yarns. Do this at the start of the knitting by transferring stitches to adjacent needles and pushing the empty needles into nonworking position.

Because manual weaving is a good way to carry yarn across the surface of a fabric from one spot of texture to another without having to cut and restart the yarn each time, it is often combined with or used to support other techniques. When choosing or designing a pattern for knit-weave, remember that the greater the number of adjacent needles the weaving yarn passes over before traveling under a needle (or vice versa), the longer the floats will be. These floats offer all kinds of possibilities for latching up, twisting, beading, cutting for fringes and lifting onto needles (see Chapter 5 for further discussion of lifted stitches).

33. BORDER DESIGNS.

To work: Thread each eye of 3-prong tr tool with separate strands of yarn. In these examples, 1st & 3rd strands are black, 2nd is white.

1. *Pass 3-prong tool down between 3 NDLS, under 1 to RT & then up between next 3 NDLS. Pass tool over 1 NDL to RT*, & rep from * to *.

2. Pass 3-prong tool down between 3 NDLS, then *under next 3. Bring it up between next 3 NDLS, pass it over 1 and back down*. Rep from * to *.

3. Work same as for 2 above, except that tool passes under groups of 5 NDLS, instead of 3.

4. Work same as 2 above, but twist entire tool 2 or 3 times as it passes under groups of 5 NDLS.

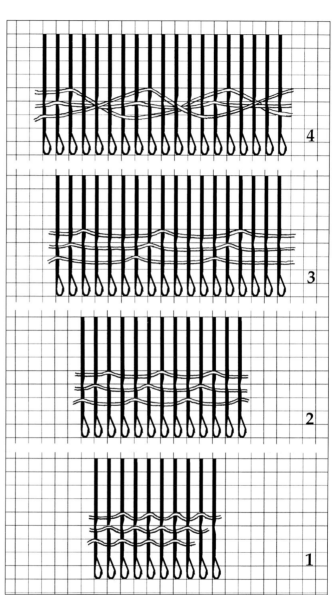

WEAVING THREE STRANDS AT ONCE.

Three-prong tool has just passed under 1 NDL to RT of last NDL wrapped & is moving up between next 3 NDLS.

Vertical, or embroidery, weaving

Vertical weaving, also called embroidery knitting, laces a secondary yarn through the purl surface of a fabric from row to row rather than from stitch to stitch, as in horizontal weaving. This technique is generally used for decorative spots of embroidery and occasionally for covering an entire fabric surface. Because the yarn is always manually placed in either the hooks of the needles or over their shafts, weaving brushes are not needed for this technique. Hence, unlike horizontal weaving where the machine's features determine the extent of its knit-weaving abilities, all machines are capable of vertical weaving.

If you want to use coned yarn for vertical weaving, the cone should be placed on the floor in front of the machine at your feet or beside your chair. If you prefer to work with cut pieces of yarn, these pieces should be two to three times the length of

the vertical knitting, and the more diagonal movement in a design, the more yarn you're likely to use.

To weave vertically once you've begun knitting, lay a strand of the weaving yarn across the hook of a needle. If you're working with a cut length of yarn, be sure to leave a tail long enough to finish off later or catch the strand in the middle and use it doubled. (Working with a doubled strand will give a more pronounced effect to the weaving and also eliminate one end to be finished off later.) Knit two rows, then draw the weaving yarn upward and lay it into the same needle in which it was placed before. The yarn can be laid on the needle in one of two ways. It can simply be placed across the hook of the needle, which is called a plain wrap and produces a vertical, ridged effect. Or it can be passed under the needle before laying it over the hook, like an E-wrap, which creates a twill-like, diagonal texture. The choice of method is a matter of personal taste, but whichever you choose, be consistent.

For vertical designs, the weaving yarn is laid over the same needle each time. For diagonal designs, the yarn is laid over a needle to the left or right of the one previously holding it. For both vertical and diagonal designs, two rows are generally knit between each series of wraps. Wrapping every row is usually too often and stiffens the fabric. While knitting a number of rows between wraps creates a softer, more open effect, it also produces longer vertical floats, which are apt to catch. Pay special attention to how you wrap when diagonals change direction to prevent reversing or mixing up plain wraps and E-wraps.

For vertical or diagonal designs with several parallel lines (Swatch 34), you can thread the strands of yarn through the eyes of a transfer tool to keep them properly spaced and easy to handle. By moving the tool between extended needles, one motion places yarn into several needles at the same time, just as it did when weaving horizontally. For designs wider than the

34. VERTICALLY WOVEN DESIGNS WITH PARALLEL PATTERNING.

Texture on L was formed with plain wraps, while design in center uses E-wraps. Wide example on RT also uses E-wraps but shifts L or RT each R, adding zigzag effect to texture.

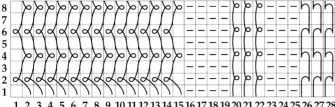

capacity of your eyelet tools, thread the yarns through the eyes of a stitch holder, garter bar or homemade cardboard guide. If the yarn tends to feed through the stitch holder or garter bar too quickly, hold a piece of cardboard or a ruler against it with an elastic band or a pair of spring-type clothespins, trapping the yarn in between.

Push all of the required needles foreward enough to catch the weaving yarn in their hooks. A punchcard machine that preselects needles for each row, an intarsia carriage or a "P" carriage (available for some Japanese machines) will speed up the needle-selection process. However, each of these options

will probably also push the needles so far forward that you must lay the yarn across the needle shafts, rather than in their hooks. Working with the selected needles in holding position is the fastest way to work as long as your machine has the ability to knit them back automatically. Otherwise, you'll have to push them back to upper working position before each row.

For designs in which the relative spacing of yarns changes at some point (Swatch 35), feed the yarns through the slots (rather than the eyes) of the garter bar or stitch holder. Doing so enables you to rearrange the yarns as often as necessary by simply

35. DESIGN WITH CHANGING SPACING BETWEEN YARNS.

Relative spacing of 5 vertical-weaving yarns in this example changes EOR.

REARRANGING YARNS IN A VERTICAL-WEAVING DESIGN.

In a design whose yarns change relative position, a garter bar can keep the yarns properly spaced. Thread yarns through bar's slots (rather than its eyes) so they can be easily moved. A plastic spine for binding reports caps off the bar & keeps yarn in place.

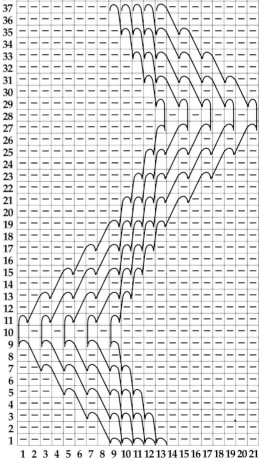

36. HANDLING YARN TAILS ON ISOLATED KNIT-WOVEN EFFECTS.

Ending yarn tails on both diamonds were drawn through to back of fabric & finished off. Beginning tails on L diamond were also finished off but were used as fringe on RT diamond.

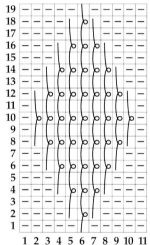

moving them to a different slot. To keep yarns from slipping out of their respective slots, you'll need to cover the top of the tool you're using. Unlike a stitch holder, the garter bar has no cover, so you'll need to improvise. The plastic spines sold by most stationery stores for report folders work well, and cost under a dollar. If yours doesn't clamp the garter bar tightly enough, secure each end with an elastic band.

While horizontal weaving increases or decreases in width according to the number of needles used in each row, vertical patterns grow row by row. Since each strand of a solid pattern can follow only one vertical path, changing the width of such a design means initiating or ending a separate strand of yarn each time a shape widens or narrows. For occasional,

37. DOUBLING AND TRIPLING VERTICAL WEAVING YARN FOR INCREASED EFFECT.

Weaving yarn is used singly at bottom of swatch, doubled in center & tripled at top. C/O for wrapped STS is figure-8, E-wrap C/O.

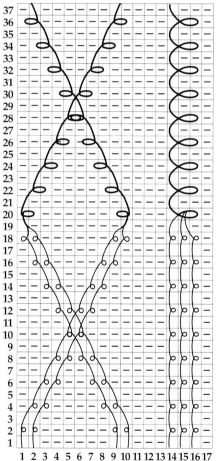

simple motifs you can certainly finish off extra yarn ends or even leave them for fringed effects (Swatch 36). Complex designs that change width, however, are more easily handled with horizontal weaving. Beginning and ending the many additional strands required with vertical weaving makes the finishing process impractical and adds excessive bulk to the edges of the design.

When vertical weaving is used on fabric edges, it adds body and inhibits curling. You can individually E-wrap the first few stitches every two rows, or form a single E-wrap around two or three needles at once for a bolder effect. Threading separate strands through an eyelet-transfer tool allows you to E-wrap all the needles in one motion, which is faster and less clumsy than handling each yarn separately. To avoid snagging the yarn in an incorrect needle, always let the rigid prongs of the tool, rather than the yarn threaded through them, pass between the needles. Unless you choose a contrasting yarn to wrap edge stitches (as I have for the example), the wrapping will not show very much, but it will nonetheless provide body and a bit more bulk to the edge.

For the bottom right half of Swatch 37, separate strands were used to E-wrap the three edge stitches individually, every other row. In the top right half of the swatch, all the strands were tripled together to wrap the three edge needles as a group. Similar variations were used to weave the motif in the sample's center.

By removing specific stitches from their needles, laying the weaving yarn behind the stitches and then replacing the stitches on their needles, vertical weaving can be used to produce an embroidery effect on the knit side, as shown in the drawing above right. Although the same end result could be sewed on later with a needle and strand of yarn, it's easier and more precisely done right on the machine because you don't have to count stitches or rows, and the fabric is under tension (Swatch 38).

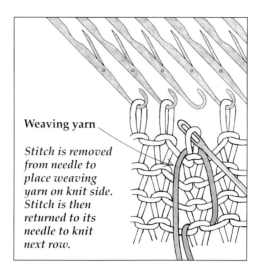

Weaving yarn

Stitch is removed from needle to place weaving yarn on knit side. Stitch is then returned to its needle to knit next row.

USING VERTICAL WEAVING TO CREATE AN EMBROIDERY EFFECT ON KNIT SIDE.

38. VERTICAL-WEAVING EFFECT PLACED ON KNIT SIDE OF FABRIC.

In this sample, weaving yarn is placed on K side of fabric by removing ST from NDL before it is vertically woven.

To work: Begin by laying center of long strand over NDLS marked X on chart, working each half for 1 side of diamond. Where 2 yarns intersect at point of diamond, weave 1 to front & let other travel on back.

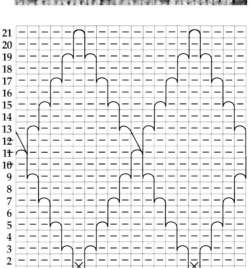

In addition to using a variety of yarn sizes and textures with vertical weaving, you can add interest to your designs by changing the direction in which the yarn is laid into the needle hooks and the number of needles used. You can also leave needles out of work to create ladders, which will, as it does with horizontal weaving, allow more of the weaving yarn to show on the knit side. Also, by wrapping the yarn several times around a group of needles and beading, crisscrossing or twisting the strands between wraps, you can create effects like those in Swatch 39. And, if you're using an eyelet tool to weave several strands together vertically, you can also use the tool to weave horizontally and combine the two techniques.

Not all weaving is decorative. I use vertical weaving to bind long Fair Isle floats to the purl surface of the fabric so they do not catch and pull. I also use this technique when I'm carrying a yarn up the back of a fabric and cannot catch the yarn itself on a needle because it's a different color and might show on the front. The vertical weaving strand can be used to "cage" the other yarn against the back of the fabric. When you use vertical weaving for these purposes, work with a strand of the main yarn to prevent the extra wraps from showing, catching it over a needle every other row. When the main yarn is very heavy, avoid adding extra bulk by splitting the plies of the yarn or using sewing thread or a matching, lighter-weight yarn for the caging or vertical wraps.

Weaving stitches with other stitches

Instead of weaving a separate strand of yarn through knitted stitches, it's actually possible to weave the stitches themselves. Stitches can be woven in front or in back of one another, forming slip-stitch patterns, which show on both sides of the fabric.

It's usually necessary to enlarge some or all of the stitches being woven with one another in order to make the effect stand out clearly and prevent the stitches from twisting or bunching together. Lengthening stitches also makes it easier to work more elaborate patterns and to allow the stitches to weave for a longer

39. VERTICAL WEAVING VARIOUSLY COMBINED WITH WRAPPING.
To work: 1. Separate strands are used to E-wrap edges of motifs & plain wrap center crossing point, where both yarns catch center NDL.
2. Separate strands crisscross before E-wrapping every 2/Rs, with RT strand wrapping on L & L strand on RT.
3. Separate strands crisscross & alt E-wrap every 4/Rs.
4. Separate strands twist around each other before E-wrapping edge NDLS every 6/Rs.

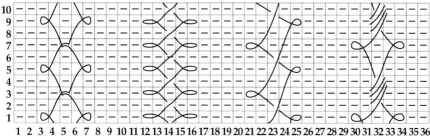

distance. For isolated or intermittent effects, the stitches can be enlarged by knitting needles back to nonworking position. For allover, repeat designs, it's faster and easier to enlarge stitches by the drop-stitch method (see pp. 65-67).

Although it's usually necessary to lengthen stitches to weave them together, some designs can be worked, and even enhanced, with unlengthened stitches. In Swatch 40, the stitches were not lengthened for weaving because each stitch wove only six rows before knitting again. The puckering created by the unlengthened stitches added interest to the design.

USING VERTICAL WEAVING TO `CAGE' OTHER YARNS.

40. PUCKERED WOVEN DESIGN WITH UNLENGTHENED STITCHES.

To work: *Bring NDLS 1, 2 & 3; 7, 8 & 9; & every alt group of 3 NDLS to HP. K 2 Rs. Use tr tool to weave STS* (as explained in main text). Rep from * to * 2x, alt weaving, as shown on chart.

K 2 Rs over all NDLS (RC 8). **Bring NDLS 4, 5 & 6; 10, 11 & 12; and every alt group of 3 NDLS to HP. K 2 Rs. Use transfer tool to weave STS**. Rep from ** to ** 2x, alt weaving as shown on chart. K 2 Rs over all NDLS (RC 16). Continue for desired length, alt directions * to * with ** to **.

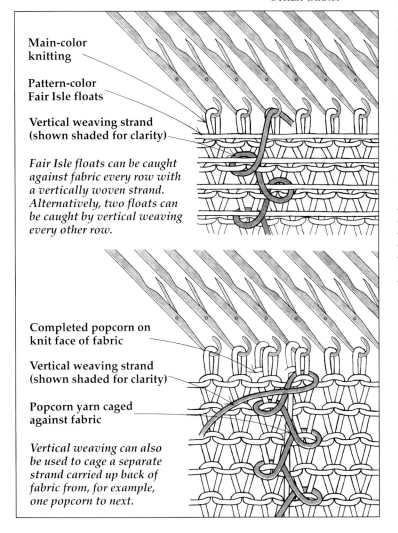

Main-color knitting

Pattern-color Fair Isle floats

Vertical weaving strand (shown shaded for clarity)

Fair Isle floats can be caught against fabric every row with a vertically woven strand. Alternatively, two floats can be caught by vertical weaving every other row.

Completed popcorn on knit face of fabric

Vertical weaving strand (shown shaded for clarity)

Popcorn yarn caged against fabric

Vertical weaving can also be used to cage a separate strand carried up back of fabric from, for example, one popcorn to next.

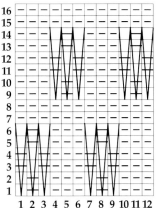

41. *WOVEN DESIGN WITH OCCASIONAL LENGTHENED STITCHES TO COUNTERBALANCE PUCKERING.*

Even though each vertically woven ST travels only 6 Rs in a block, the block's size contributes to distortion. Note that it takes twice as many Rs as STS to achieve a balanced appearance in this pat.

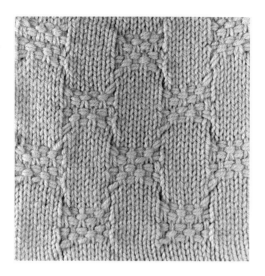

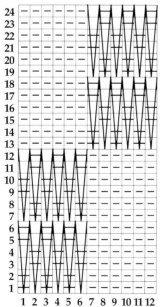

Slight puckering with this weaving technique is common, even when the stitches have been lengthened, because knitted and woven stitches take up different amounts of yarn. When the puckering enhances a design, so much the better, since not having to lengthen stitches eliminates a step and speeds up the weaving process. For small repeats, like those in Swatch 40 on p. 109, you won't have any problems with not lengthening stitches. Larger designs (like Swatch 41) however, should include a row of stitches lengthened enough to weave for several rows before they have to resume knitting or be lengthened again.

Begin large designs like Swatch 41 by knitting one row to enlarge any stitches to be used for weaving, and then put all enlarged stitches into holding position. Knit two rows. The yarn will float over all of the needles in hold. *Use a transfer tool to remove the first stitch and both its floats from the needle. Immediately replace the stitch on the same needle, first dropping the floats off the transfer tool so they fall to the knit side. Repeat this for every alternate stitch in the group. Then just lift the floats off all the remaining alternate needles so they lie on the purl side.* Make certain that all of the selected needles are still in hold, and knit two more rows. Repeat from * to *, reversing the choice of needles whose floats lie on the knit and purl sides. After several repeats, the needles will have to knit again or the fabric will start to bunch up on the needles.

The four stitches that form the Chinese knots in Swatch 42 are woven at angles to each other in a simple, two-step process. You can use either a single or double latch tool, depending on your skills and preferences. It's essential that these stitches be enlarged. In the sample, the needles were hand knitted all the way back to nonworking position. The stitches nonetheless tend to tighten after being worked, puckering the surface of the fabric.

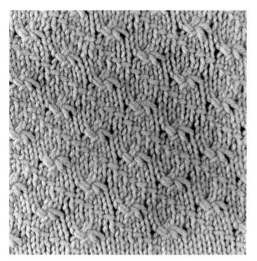

42. CHINESE KNOTS.

To work: Insert latch tool behind 4th ST & in front of 3rd ST. Grab 2nd ST with hook of tool, release it from its NDL & pull it through. Move 3rd & 4th STS over by 1 NDL & place (2nd) ST from tool into 4th NDL. Insert latch tool behind 3rd ST, in front of 2nd ST and grab 1st ST with hook. Place it and pull it through 2nd and 3rd STS. Move 2nd & 3rd STS over by 1 NDL & place (1st) ST from tool into 3rd NDL.

If you're comfortable with double latch tool, you can work process all in 1 step by inserting tool as shown in the drawing at right. Then release 1st & 2nd STS from NDLS onto tool to pull them past 3rd & 4th STS. Use a transfer tool to move 3rd & 4th STS onto empty 1st & 2nd NDLS, then place STS from latch tool onto 3rd & 4th NDLS.

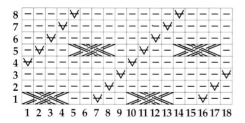

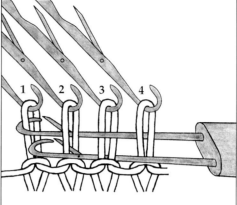

1. Weave double latch tool through a pair of stitches to hook on two adjacent stitches at left.

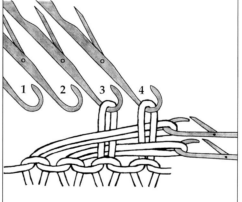

2. Remove stitches 1 and 2 from their needles and pull them past stitches 3 and 4.

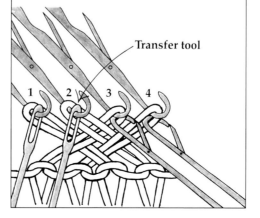

3. With a transfer tool, remove two stitches on needles 3 and 4 and deposit them on needles 1 and 2. Then deposit stitches in latch tool on needles 3 and 4.

Transfer tool

USING DOUBLE LATCH TOOL TO WEAVE STITCHES AROUND STITCHES.

Weaving stitches through stitches.
Another way of weaving stitches with stitches is to pull them through, rather than around, one another. You can pull a single stitch through one or several stitches, and you can also pull a pair of stitches through one or more stitches. In fact, the number of stitches that can be pulled through other stitches is limited only by the size of the stitches, the yarn's stretch and the amount of distortion it introduces into the fabric. Three stitches pulled through three other stitches is probably a reasonable limit.

In order to pull one stitch through another adjacent stitch, you need to coordinate using a transfer tool with a latch tool. To do this, insert the latch tool into the front of the stitch on the right and grab the left stitch with the tool's hook. Release the left stitch from its needle and pull it through the right stitch. Hold the latch tool toward the right as you use the transfer tool to remove the right stitch from its needle. Then move this stitch over to the left needle, and deposit the left stitch on the right needle (Swatch 43).

To pull one stitch through two stitches (Swatch 44), you will again need to coordinate the use of the latch and transfer tools. This time you'll need to use a double transfer tool, as shown in the middle and bottom photos on the facing page.

43. WOVEN DESIGN WITH ONE STITCH PULLED THROUGH AN ADJACENT STITCH.

One stitch pulled through another produces a low, subtle texture.

To work: Note that when line of design slants RT, latch tool should be inserted through RT ST to grab L ST. When line slants L, insert tool through L ST to grab RT ST. If you prefer opposite slant, reverse procedure, but be consistent.

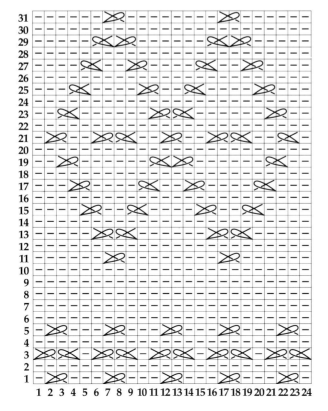

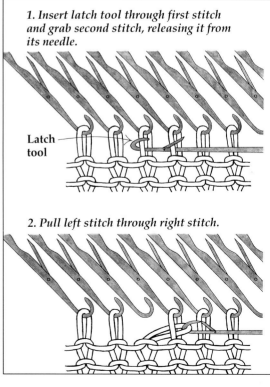

1. Insert latch tool through first stitch and grab second stitch, releasing it from its needle.

Latch tool

2. Pull left stitch through right stitch.

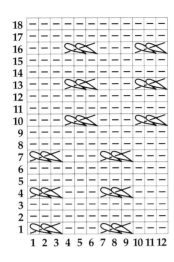

44. WOVEN DESIGN WITH ONE STITCH PULLED THROUGH TWO STITCHES.

When one stitch is pulled through two, texture is defined by double dashes on surface.

USING LATCH AND TRANSFER TOOLS TO PULL ONE STITCH THROUGH TWO.

Insert latch tool through 1st 2 STS & catch 3rd ST in tool's hook (left).

Release 3rd ST from its NDL, & pull it through other 2 STS. Remove 1st 2 STS on a tr tool & move them 1 NDL to L (below left). Replace ST from latch tool on empty NDL.

PULLING ONE STITCH THROUGH ANOTHER WITH LATCH AND TRANSFER TOOLS.

3. Insert transfer tool into right stitch, remove it from its needle and replace it on left needle, producing woven effect shown below.

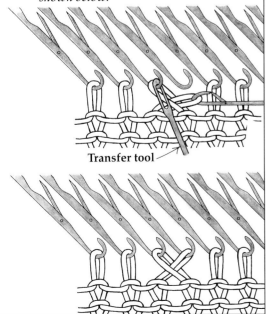

Transfer tool

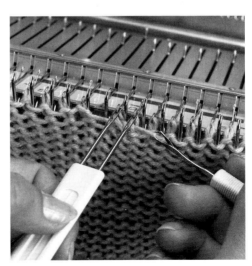

Knit-weaving with fabric strips

You may have thought about knitting with fabric strips to coordinate a sweater with a lightweight skirt fabric. While it's easier to knit fabric stips by hand, it can be done on a knitting machine. However, unless the strips are very narrow, they tend to rip and catch in the needle hooks. Yet when the strips are too narrow, they fray badly and fall apart. Lightweight polyesters are easier to handle than cotton and work fairly well when you knit on every other needle, with adequate weights and patience. Lightweight wools such as challis or Viyella do not work as well for knit-weaving as polyester

or cotton because they tend to fray badly, unless the fabrics are of very fine quality and hence expensive.

One simple solution to the potential problems of fraying is to use fabric strips for knit-weaving. Fabric strips weave beautifully, and, if the fabric itself seems a little weighty, the background fabric can be knit on every other needle to lighten it. The strips should be cut about ½ in. wide and should be continuous. To make them continuous, cut them on the bias or in a spiral, as shown in the drawing below. The fastest way to strip a lot of fabric is to run it through a serger and let the serger's knife do the cutting for you. When doing this, remove the serger's needle or needles to avoid damaging or dulling them.

One yard of 45-in. fabric usually yields about 75 yards of ½-in. bias-cut strip. To machine knit a medium-size vest with strips, you would need approximately 450 to 500 yards. The quantities needed for occasional, decorative weaving obviously vary from project to project. Hence, you should make a swatch and do some calculations based on it to figure out how many yards of fabric strips you'll need for your design. (If you are unfamiliar with swatching and calculating the amount of yarn needed, refer to one of the basic knitting books listed in the bibliography at the back of the book.)

45. KNIT-WOVEN FABRIC STRIPS.

Strips are woven under 1 & over 3 NDLS to produce well-secured floats, which highlight fabric's texture. By shifting interlacement 1 NDL to L on each R, fabric acquires a diagonal, twilled look.

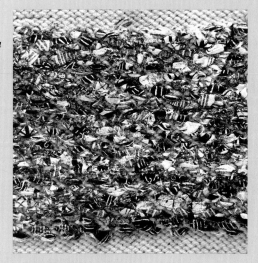

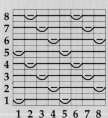

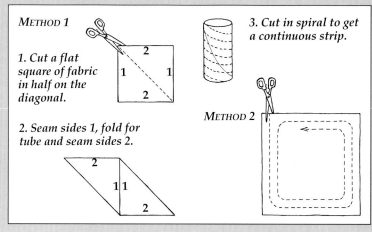

METHOD 1

1. Cut a flat square of fabric in half on the diagonal.

2. Seam sides 1, fold for tube and seam sides 2.

3. Cut in spiral to get a continuous strip.

METHOD 2

TWO METHODS OF CUTTING FABRIC STRIPS.

If you've sufficiently lengthened the stitches, it is possible to pull one stitch through three stitches. Swatch 46 is a very stable, yet open fabric, which creates a diagonal, nonbiased grid.

The best way to pull two stitches through one or more stitches is to use a double latch tool. To pull two stitches through one, reach through the first stitch to grab the second and third, one in each hook of the tool. Pull them through the first stitch and replace them on their needles without ever moving the first stitch. Because the first stitch never leaves its needle, it simply encases the other two, and the surface effect is one of horizontal dashes of texture.

If you don't have a double latch tool, you can try using a transer tool alone to remove the stitches. Keep the stitches far back on the tool as you insert it through the front of the first stitch to replace the stitches on the same needles they were removed from. You must be sure that the loop of the first stitch is clear of the needles and actually cages or surrounds the other two stitches. Whichever tool you decide to use, be prepared for the fact that this is not a speedy technique and that the manipulation is always apt to be rather clumsy. If you want to work this effect in several steps or are willing to improvise tools, that is, hold several latch or transfer tools together in your hand, you can probably manage to pull groups of stitches through a single stitch if you lengthen them enough.

Pulling two stitches through another pair of stitches again involves the double latch tool. The process, explained in the caption for Swatch 47 on p. 116, produces lacy, open spaces, which are permanent and stable. These spaces do not close up when the fabric is washed, nor do they shift with wear.

When pulling stitches through stitches, as with many other techniques, the direction you work from—whether left to right, right to left or a combination of directions—affects the textural ridges of the pattern. If you want a ridge to slant to the right, insert the tool from the right, and vice versa.

46. WOVEN DESIGN WITH ONE STITCH PULLED THROUGH THREE STITCHES.

To work: Use drop ST to enlarge all STS in EOR. Set MB carr to K in both directions, & RB carr to K L to RT & slip RT to L. Set both carr for same SS. Begin with STS on MB only, with RB NDLS empty but in WP, as for FNR.

COL & K 1 R. Drop RB loops & pull down on K to enlarge MB STS. [Insert latch tool through STS 2, 3 & 4 from RT to catch ST 1 with hook. Release ST 1 from NDL & pull it through other 3 STS. Hold latch tool to RT. Use 3-pronged transfer tool to move STS 2, 3 & 4 to L to NDLS 1, 2 & 3. Ret ST from latch tool to NDL 4.] Repeat [directions] for every 4 STS across entire R. K 1 R from RT to L (MB only will K). Rep from * to *, following chart for exact STS to use for each R.

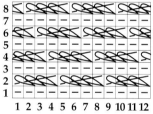

USING A TWO-PRONGED TRANSFER TOOL TO PULL TWO STITCHES THROUGH ONE STITCH.

In this alternative to using double-latch tool, remove 2nd & 3rd STS of 3 STS with tr tool. Then, keeping STS back on prongs, insert tool through 1st ST, as shown. Replace 2nd & 3rd STS on their NDLS without catching 1st ST, which will encircle other 2 STS.

47. WOVEN DESIGN WITH TWO STITCHES PULLED THROUGH ANOTHER PAIR OF STITCHES.

To work: Use double latch tool to reach through 4th & then 3rd STS with both hooks to catch 2nd ST in 1 hook & 1st ST in other hook. Release these STS from their NDLS & pull them through other 2 STS. Use double tr tool to move 3rd & 4th STS onto empty 1st & 2nd NDLS. Ret STS from latch tool to 3rd & 4th NDLS.

Chart shows bottom of sample. To knit variation at top, work all rows from the right.

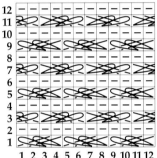

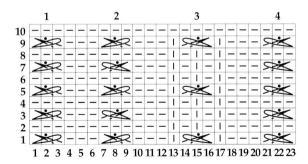

48. WOVEN DESIGNS WITH TWO STITCHES PULLED THROUGH ONE AND REHUNG ON A SINGLE NEEDLE.

To work: Designs 1, 2 & 4 are worked by pulling STS 2 & 3 through ST 1 with single-latch tool, EOR. Hold tool to L & use tr tool to move ST 1 onto NDL 3. Place STS 2 & 3 on NDL 1. NDL 2 is empty & in WP, so it will C/O & K with next pass of carr. For Design 1, tool is inserted from L; for Design 4, from RT; and for Design 2, alt from L and RT.

Design 3 is worked by by first latching up 1st & EOS, then pulling 2nd & 3rd STS through 4th ST. Then move 4th ST onto 2nd NDL & place both STS from latch tool into empty 4th NDL. Leave empty 3rd NDL in WP so it can C/O, & K with next pass of carr.

Swatch 48 shows an interesting variation on pulling stitches through stitches, in which two stitches are pulled through one, but both of them are hung on a single needle. The pattern on the far right was consistently worked from the left; the one on the far left, from the right. The second one from the right alternates left and right. All three of these designs were worked every other row. The cable-like motif is worked over five stitches, every five rows.

For a similar cable-like effect developed by Nihon Vogue, a separate strand can be carried up the back of the work from one repeat to the next. The result differs only slightly from Swatch 48, in that the gathering stitch slants to the left or right, rather than being horizontal, as with the separate-strand method. This factor alone would not be enough to make you choose one method over the other. Yet you must decide whether you want to work with two tools and no extra yarns or one tool and carry the separate strand. This is a good example of how one effect can be achieved by two different methods. Both methods, incidentally, can be worked diagonally as well as horizontally.

By combining the stitches-pulled-through-stitches technique with other basic moves, you can create smocked or gathered-rib designs (Swatch 49) by reforming some

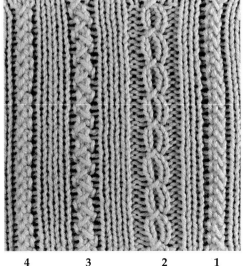

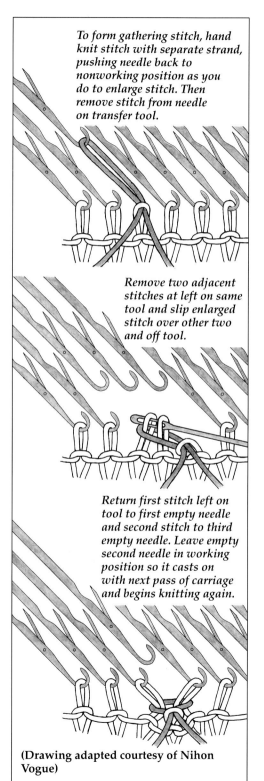

To form gathering stitch, hand knit stitch with separate strand, pushing needle back to nonworking position as you do to enlarge stitch. Then remove stitch from needle on transfer tool.

Remove two adjacent stitches at left on same tool and slip enlarged stitch over other two and off tool.

Return first stitch left on tool to first empty needle and second stitch to third empty needle. Leave empty second needle in working position so it casts on with next pass of carriage and begins knitting again.

(Drawing adapted courtesy of Nihon Vogue)

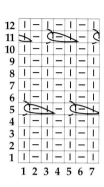

	12	I	—	I	—	I	—	I
	11							
	10	I		I		I		I
	9	I	—	I	—	I	—	I
	8	I	—	I	—	I	—	I
	7	I	—	I	—	I	—	I
	6	I		I		I		I
	5							
	4	I	—	I	—	I	—	I
	3	I	—	I	—	I	—	I
	2	I	—	I	—	I	—	I
	1	I	—	I	—	I	—	I
		1	2	3	4	5	6	7

49. GATHERED RIB.

To work: Latch up EON for rib, every 6/Rs. Then, 2 Rs down, insert latch tool under 1 side of 3rd ST, catching 1st ST with hook, as shown in the drawing below. Release 1st ST from its NDL, pull it through 3rd ST, then latch it back up & replace it on its NDL. You don't need to use tr tool because 3rd ST stays where it was & 1st ST ret to same NDL. Example was K by alt placement of gather, L & RT, every 6/Rs.

GATHERING RIBS BY PULLING STITCHES THROUGH STITCHES.

After inserting latch tool, as shown, through two knit stitches of rib, release Stitch 1 from its needle (it will drop and form a float). Then pull stitch on hook through Stitch 3, reach back to left and latch up float, and then return reformed stitch to Needle 1.

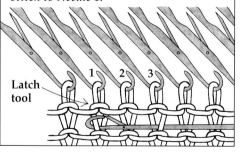

Latch tool

GATHERING STITCHES WITH SEPARATE STRAND.

stitches and pulling others through them. This swatch uses reformed stitches to create a rib texture, which is then smocked by pulling one knit stitch of the rib through the next knit stitch. This pattern is a single-tool (latch-tool) technique since one of the stitches remains on its needle throughout the process.

You can easily bead the smocked-rib pattern by placing a bead onto the latch tool (or on a beading tool) before reforming each stitch. Then proceed as for plain smocking, slipping the bead onto the first stitch after it is pulled through the third stitch and before it is reformed.

You can also smock double-bed ribbing if you drop the ribber bed by one notch to make room to manage the tool. (Since this is not a working position for the ribber, make sure you return it to the proper position before you resume knitting.) Double-bed and single-bed smocking are done in the same way, except that for double-bed work, the rib stitches you are working with are on the ribber bed, while the plain background stitches are on the main bed (or vice versa, if you prefer). To smock the ribbing, begin working in the last row of stitches, that is, the one in the needle hooks. If possible, leave the needles in holding position when you have finished the smocking, and let the carriage knit them back to ease any strain.

Wrapping methods

Wrapping is another means of adding texture and decoration to the surface of a fabric. Both needles and stitches can be wrapped, and additionally stitches themselves can be wrapped around each other. Yarn can be wound around a needle or stitch once or several times, and it can be wrapped in more complex ways as well. The effects produced by wrapping usually appear on the purl side of the fabric (but can be placed on the knit side with an extra step), and range from subtle ridges to extreme textures.

The simplest form of wrapping is the E-wrap cast-on. In addition to casting on stitches, E-wrapping can also be used on needles already holding stitches to create additional surface texture. The depth of this texture varies, depending on the number, order and spacing of the needles wrapped; the direction and number of times each stitch or row of stitches is wrapped; and the kind of yarn used for wrapping. If, instead of working a simple E-wrap, the yarn is wound several times around the shafts of the needles, the texture can be further increased. And, in addition to wrapping yarn around needles and stitches, the stitches themselves can be wrapped around each other.

The purl-side "puffs" that appear in Swatch 50 were made by wrapping the yarn around the same two or three needles several times, and then knit-weaving or hand knitting the stitches in between. The puffs in the first two borders of Swatch 51 can also be placed on the knit face of the fabric if stitches are removed from their needles before they are wrapped.

To wrap one or more needles or stitches with the main yarn rather than a contrast yarn, begin by putting needles into holding position at the point where you want to place the wrapped effect. Then knit the row, interrupting the carriage's movement to remove the stitches in question from their needles and wrap the stitches or the empty needles with the free yarn. When stitches, rather than needles, are wrapped, the effect is the same, but the actual knitting goes more smoothly and is easier to handle.

The bottom edge of Swatch 51 shows an interesting E-wrap cast-on variation in which three needles are wrapped, figure-8 style, after every two E-wraps. The figure-8 wrap, back and forth on the same needles, is worked five times. Because the figure-8 puts a lot of extra yarn on each needle, it's a good idea to hand knit the next row to

50. PURL-SIDE WRAPPED PUFFS.

To work: 1. Contrast yarn is wound around 3 adj NDLS, 3x & manually woven over & under 5 NDL shafts between each puff.

2. Contrast yarn is wound around 3 NDLS, 3x, but is manually K from 1 puff to next.

3. Contrast yarn is manually K between the figure-8 wrapped puffs.

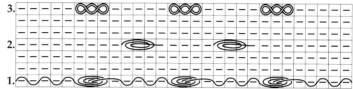

51. KNIT-SIDE WRAPPED EFFECTS.

All wrapping is done on empty NDLS to make effect show on K side of fabric. Remove stitches from needles before wrapping, then return them to needles to continue knitting.

To work: 1. This C/O edge combines figure-8 wrapping (back & forth 5x) on 3 NDLS with E-wrapping on next 2 NDLS.

2. Contrast yarn is wound around 3 NDLS, 3x, & manually woven over & under 5 NDL shafts before next group of 3 NDLS.

3. Groups of 3 NDLS wrapped figure-8 style alternate with groups of 5 NDLS wrapped over & under.

4. In this simple latch-tool B/O, 1 ST is drawn through the next. After latching 2 STS, remove and hold next 3 STS on tr tool. Wind free yarn around empty NDLS 3x & replace STS on top of winding. Continue latching off, being careful as you latch STS off 3 NDLS just wrapped.

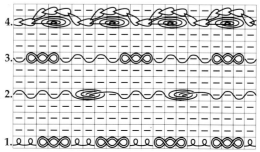

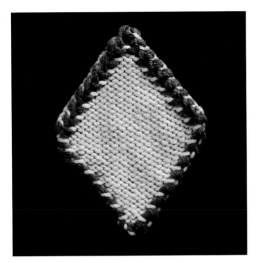

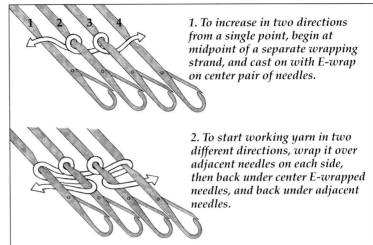

1. To increase in two directions from a single point, begin at midpoint of a separate wrapping strand, and cast on with E-wrap on center pair of needles.

2. To start working yarn in two different directions, wrap it over adjacent needles on each side, then back under center E-wrapped needles, and back under adjacent needles.

52 WRAPPED INCREASES AND DECREASES.

To work: Chart indicates incs with an X, & decs as FF decs. Edge pairs of NDLS are wrapped 3x to add texture & contrast to surface. C/O is a fancy E-wrap (adapted with permission of the Silver Knitting Institute), as shown in the drawing at right. By wrapping with middle of strand, STS are established on both NDLS, leaving a free end to wrap each side.

CASTING ON FROM A CENTRAL POINT.

WRAPPED INCREASING AND DECREASING.

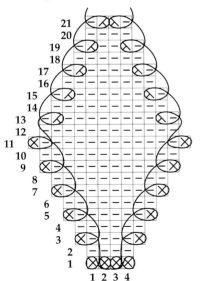

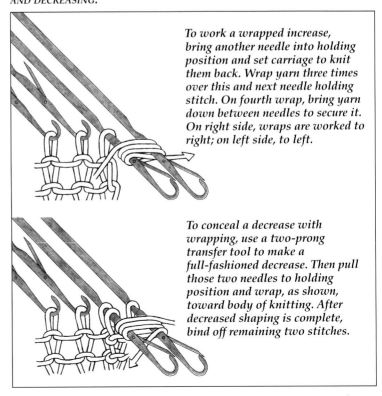

To work a wrapped increase, bring another needle into holding position and set carriage to knit them back. Wrap yarn three times over this and next needle holding stitch. On fourth wrap, bring yarn down between needles to secure it. On right side, wraps are worked to right; on left side, to left.

To conceal a decrease with wrapping, use a two-prong transfer tool to make a full-fashioned decrease. Then pull those two needles to holding position and wrap, as shown, toward body of knitting. After decreased shaping is complete, bind off remaining two stitches.

ensure that the extra yarn clears the needle latches. Similarly, casting on initially with scrap yarn and ravel cord makes the wrapping-and-knitting process easier because you can weight the work. If you use ribbon to work figure-8 wraps over four needles and let the cut ends of the ribbon hang down in the middle, the effect will look like bows on the surface.

The top edge of Swatch 51 on p. 119 is a fancy, latch-tool bind-off. To work this bind-off, begin by latching one stitch through the next adjacent stitch until you reach the point at which you want to form one of these wrapped puffs. At this point, leave the last bound-off stitch in the hook of its needle and use a transfer tool to remove the stitches from the three needles to be wrapped. Wind the yarn around the needles as many times as you want, then return the stitches to them. Continue

latching off as usual, paying close attention to each wrapped needle so that you don't split the yarn or miss any of the strands.

Wrapping can be used to form increases at the edges of a fabric and to conceal decreases, as it was in Swatch 52. In this swatch, the increases are worked from a single point, requiring a special two-needle cast-on, as shown in the drawing on the facing page. Wrapped increases and decreases could also be worked on the edges of a wide piece, which would require no special cast-on.

For wrapped increases and decreases, use a separate, doubled strand to wrap the two edge needles, every other row, on the side being narrowed or widened, making one wrap around both needles. Wrap toward the edge when increasing, and away from the edge when decreasing. There is a slight

Wrapping fringes and tassels

Wrapping is a decorative way to gather fringes, attach feathers and add shape to tassels. The simplest method for gathering fringes is to wrap tightly around the core strands, catching the beginning tail of the wrapping yarn in the wraps. At the end, thread the yarn through a tapestry needle and pull the yarn tail under and through the wrapping, clipping it close (see the top drawing at left). You can also start by wrapping over the (empty) tapestry needle right from the start by holding it with the core strands. This technique saves having to force the needle through a tight wrap, but you may need to use pliers to grab and pull it out of the wrapped cluster.

The second method of wrapping requires no needle. Begin by forming a long loop, as shown in the top drawing at right, and wrap it along with the core. When the wrapping is

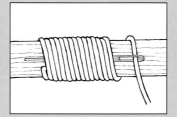

WRAPPING FRINGE WITH A TAPESTRY NEEDLE.

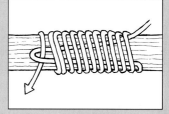

WRAPPING FRINGE WITHOUT A NEEDLE.

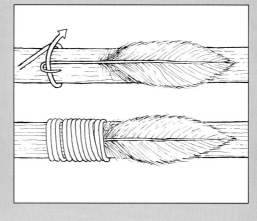

WRAPPING A FEATHER INTO FRINGE.

MAKING A SMALL TASSEL.

MAKING A LARGE TASSEL.

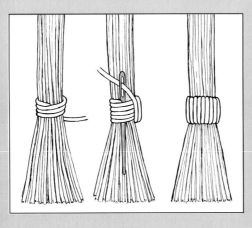

EMBROIDERED WRAPPING WITH BEADED EFFECT.

complete, insert the wrapping end through the loop and pull on the beginning end. As the loop closes and disappears under the wrapping, it will pull the end down inside the wrap, locking itself. Clip all ends close. Wrap more length than you really want to cover because pulling the ends to the inside tends to shorten the wrapping.

To attach a feather by wrapping, begin by wrapping over the shaft, as shown in the bottom drawing on p. 121. Then fold the shaft back on itself so that it can be covered by the rest of the wrapping.

To form a small tassel, wrap yarn around a piece of cardboard ½ in. to 1 in. longer than the desired length of the finished tassel, as shown in the top drawing at left. Wrap enough yarn around the cardboard to make a nice, thick tassel; then tightly tie a cord through the top of the wraps. Cut the strands at the bottom of the cardboard, and wrap the neck of the tassel by one of the above methods.

Large tassels can be formed over a knot or bead in a heavy cord by gathering and securing the tassel fringe with a cord just above the knot. Be sure to position the fringe at its midpoint around the knot before securing it with a short length of cord. Then smooth all the fringe downward, and wrap the neck of the tassel by one of the above methods (see the middle drawing at left).

"Beaded," or embroidered, wrapping looks great alone or combined with the other methods (see the bottom drawing at left). Wrap the contrast yarn around the core of the fringe or tassel. Wrap thickly, but not too tightly. Thread the yarn through a tapestry needle and stitch over the horizontal wraps, as shown. Now let the yarn hang down with the rest of the tassel or make a few extra stitches through the core and clip the tail close. This creates a round, beaded effect in the yarn itself. Of course, you can thread the needle though an actual bead and add that effect to the wrapping as well.

difference in the way the wrap appears along increased and decreased edges, due to the direction of the wrap. To increase, bring one empty needle to working position at the edge of the fabric, wrapping this and the original edge needle together. To decrease, make a full-fashioned decrease (see pp. 184-189); then wrap to conceal it.

Wrapping can be used to create floats the full width of the knitting that weave through both faces of the fabric. Floats normally fall on the purl side of the fabric, but by removing stitches and replacing them in front of the floats, you can cause the floats to appear on the knit side (Swatch 53).

You can also manipulate stitches so that they wrap around each other. Individual stitches, removed from their needles, can be wrapped around adjacent stitches and then returned to their same needles to create a sort of twisted texture on the knit side.

To wrap a stitch around another stitch, use a latch tool to reach behind the first stitch to grab, then release, the second stitch from its needle. Pull the tool so that the stitch passes behind the first stitch and then replace it on its needle. The second stitch wraps around the first, as shown in the drawing below.

53. KNIT-SIDE FLOAT MOTIF.

To work: Yarn is wound back & forth between end NDLS, 6x. With last 2 wraps, end NDLS are manually K back to WP to secure giant floats. Specific groups of STS are removed with a tr tool & replaced on same NDLS after floats are nudged to K side. 2 Rs are K between each band of floats, with each edge NDL in HP to compensate for extra STS formed on them when they are manually K back to secure floats.

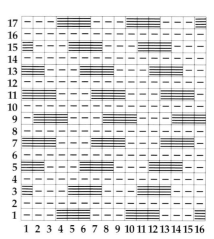

WRAPPING ONE STITCH AROUND ANOTHER.

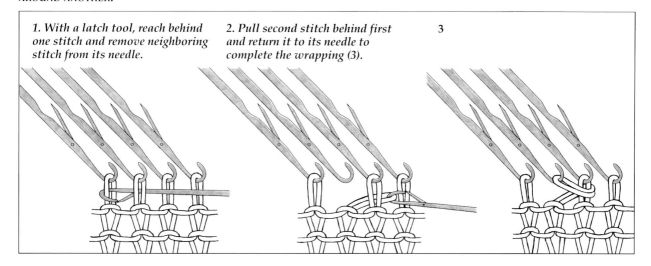

1. With a latch tool, reach behind one stitch and remove neighboring stitch from its needle.

2. Pull second stitch behind first and return it to its needle to complete the wrapping (3).

3

54. WRAPPED AND BEADED EFFECTS.

In this swatch, 3 STS holding each bead (indicated on the chart by the bead-like symbol) have been enlarged by K them back to NWP to avoid gathering or distorting fabric.

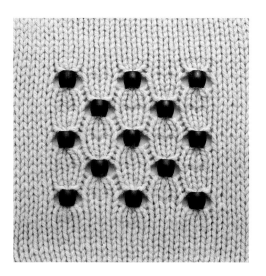

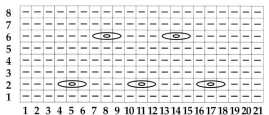

To produce diagonal lines of texture, you must wrap the stitch by entering the tool from the same direction the line is moving. That is, if the texture is slanting toward the right, insert the tool into the stitch from the right and wrap from right to left. For vertical lines, the direction of the wrap doesn't matter at all. You should be consistent, however.

You can also reach behind two stitches to wrap them with a third stitch. To produce a softer texture or to work with larger groups of four or more stitches or more elaborate combinations, you'll probably need to enlarge some of the stitches (see pp. 67-68).

By alternately wrapping needles on the main bed and your fingers, a rigid gauge or the sinker posts of the ribber bed, you can create looped fringes. You can use a separate, contrasting yarn or work with the free yarn as an extension of knit-weave or hand knitting rows of stitches. The procedure for using the free yarn is similar to that for starting the French knots in Chapter 3 (see pp. 93-94).

To create looped fringes using the ribber-bed sinker posts, first put the beds in half-pitch and then wrap the yarn from the main-bed needles to alternate ribber sinker posts. The number of needles wrapped determines the density of the fringe. If you want to wrap every main-bed needle, the fringe will be more secure if you wrap every other needle and alternate sinker posts from left to right (or vice versa), and then wrap the alternate needles and sinker posts from right to left.

Textured, fuzzy yarns form a much more stable fringe than do smooth yarns, and you may want to double the yarn for an especially thick, full fringe. Looped fringes tend to catch and pull, and can be cut to eliminate these problems. Fringes that will be cut should be made long enough to prevent the strands from working loose. And, although knitting with a reduced stitch size will help secure the fringe, you also need to E-wrap or knit back the main-bed needles as they're wrapped.

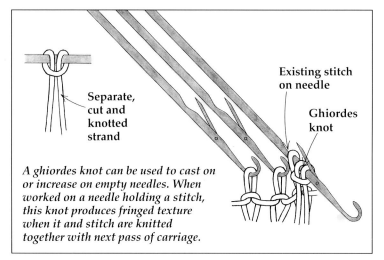

Existing stitch on needle

Ghiordes knot

Separate, cut and knotted strand

A ghiordes knot can be used to cast on or increase on empty needles. When worked on a needle holding a stitch, this knot produces fringed texture when it and stitch are knitted together with next pass of carriage.

GHIORDES, OR LARK'S HEAD, KNOT.

The longer the pile you create with the fringe, the more rows of plain knitting you can knit between looping without it being seen—and hence the faster the overall fabric can be worked. With too few rows knitted in between, the fabric will become stiff because of the extra bulk of the knots.

The best method for securing cut fringes is to attach precut lengths of yarn with the ghiordes, or lark's head, knot (see the drawing on the facing page). This is one of the knots used for Scandinavian and Persian rugs, which attests to its durability. You can use this knot both on needles with existing stitches and on empty needles to begin or increase a piece of knitting. Be careful when forming this knot not to over-tighten it since then it would not be able to slide over the needle latch.

Finally, although not wrapping in the strictest sense of the word, groups of stitches can also be bound together by beading. In Swatch 54, alternating groups of three stitches were enlarged by knitting them back to nonworking position. The enlarged stitches were pulled through the bead together and individually rehung on their needles.

Loop-through-loop seaming

Loop-through-loop seaming is an easy way to seam garments and probably one of the fastest methods for joining afghan sections. To work seams in this fashion, knit both sections to be joined, and, just before binding off, drop the first two stitches on the right edge of one section and the left edge of the other section. Run a ravel cord through the loops in each piece to gather them together temporarily while you steam them. Pull slightly on the ravel cord so the loops extend their full length from the edge of the fabric. The steam will set them so they are untwisted, open and easy to see. Then, using a large crochet hook, alternately chain three loops from one piece through three loops of the other for the length of the entire seam (Swatch 55). Secure the top loops with a short piece of yarn.

When you cast on to knit pieces that will be joined by this method, do not include the two stitches that will be dropped in the initial cast-on. Add them after the first row by increasing so that, when these stitches are later dropped, it will not affect the cast-on edge. Also, if you will be joining garment pieces that need to be increased or decreased, make sure that you use full-fashioned methods that will place the increases and decreases inside the two edge (dropped) stitches. You can make the joining even more decorative by crossing cables on the four stitches adjacent to the two stitches that will be dropped.

55. LOOP-THROUGH-LOOP SEAMING.

This lacy seam is created by crocheting 3 edge loops of 1 piece through 3 edge loops of other piece.

CHAPTER 5

Lifted
Stitches

If you lift stitches from previously knitted rows and hang them anew on the needles, the next pass of the carriage will secure the lifted stitches to the fabric and cause it to pucker, pleat or gather. You can lift individual stitches and groups of stitches as well as sinker loops, floats and ladders. The needles on which the lifted stitches are hung can be either empty or filled by another stitch, and they can be directly above the lifted stitches or off to one side.

Lifted stitches create a wide variety of effects, depending on where and how often they are lifted and whether extra rows have been knitted specifically for lifting. When extra rows are not knitted, lifted stitches pucker the base fabric, producing ruched and honeycomb designs. When extra rows are knitted, the protrusions form popcorns (if the rows are worked on individual stitches) or pleats (if entire rows are worked) and leave the base fabric undisturbed.

LIFTING STITCHES, SINKER LOOPS AND FLOATS.

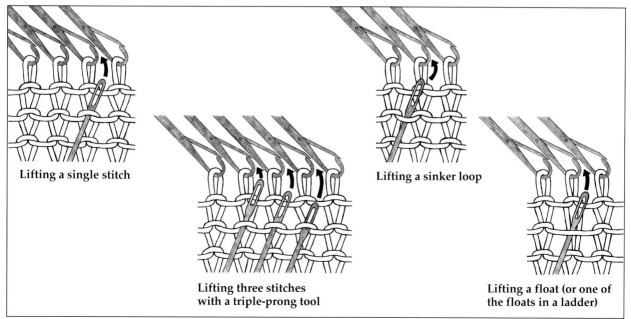

Lifting a single stitch

Lifting three stitches with a triple-prong tool

Lifting a sinker loop

Lifting a float (or one of the floats in a ladder)

*LIFTED-STITCH
SYMBOLS (SEE
ALSO PP. 25-26).*

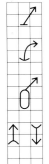

Lifted stitch

Lifted sinker loop

Lifted group of stitches or sinker loops

Purl loops lifted from one bed to another

Generally speaking, the more rows knitted between a stitch and the row to which it is lifted, or the more stitches lifted, the more extreme the resulting texture. And when there are fewer stitches lifted or the stitches are spaced farther apart, the texture tends to soften and drape more easily. Swatches 56 and 57 are basically the same pattern with variations in the number of stitches lifted and/or the number of rows knitted between the original stitches and the point of lifting.

Lifting stitches is a single-bed technique that produces both knit-side and purl-side textures. Some of the fabrics are interesting on both sides, and many patterns take on a whole new personality when knitted in two or more colors, textures or yarn sizes (Swatch 58). The many patterns that involve lifting floats offer interesting possibilities for working with two yarns, with the yarn floating across the surface a perfect candidate for ribbon, a metallic or another textural splendor. Since the very nature of the lifting process tends to create somewhat heavier, less drapable fabrics

*56. SMALL-SCALE
RUCHED PATTERN.*

For this pat, pairs of STS are alt lifted to L or RT every 5/Rs.

*57. LARGE-SCALE
RUCHED PATTERN.*

This is an exaggerated version of Swatch 56, in which same groups of 3 STS are picked up every 10/Rs & alt hung 5 NDLS to L or RT.

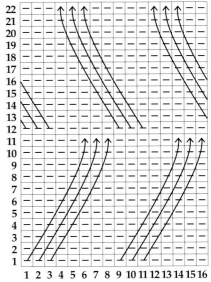

than usual, the choice of yarns is important for both aesthetic and practical reasons. In fact, many of the swatches pictured in this chapter would drape better and be far more interesting in lighter-weight yarns, but these finer yarns would not have photographed as clearly.

Although some lifted effects are similar to those created by holding stitches, the techniques are actually very different. When a needle is placed in hold, it collects a float every time the carriage passes. When that needle eventually knits again, all of the floats are knitted together into a new tuck stitch. When a stitch is lifted from a previous row, however, only the lifted stitch knits with the stitch on the needle. Since rows have been knitted between the stitch being lifted and the point to which it's lifted, the fabric has meanwhile grown in length and consequently puckers when the stitch is lifted. While both tuck and lifted stitches pucker the knitting, tuck-stitch fabrics have a less prominently raised surface than lifted-stitch fabrics.

Repeating lifted-stitch patterns may cause distortion in the fabric unless you stagger the position of the lifted stitches to balance one another out or take advantage of the fact that knit, tuck and slip stitches all have different rates of take-up. That is to say, a tuck-stitch swatch worked with the same stitch size and same number of stitches and rows as a knit swatch would be shorter and wider than the knit swatch, while a slip-stitch swatch would be taller and narrower than the knit one. In some cases, combining or alternating blocks of stockinette and tuck stitches can be used to solve distortion problems. For example, when blocks of stockinette alternate with blocks of tuck stitch in the same fabric, the stockinette sections are longer than the adjacent tucked areas. Some of this difference can be evened out by lifting stitches to shorten the knit sections (Swatch 59 on p. 130). In less extreme cases of distortion, you can achieve a sort

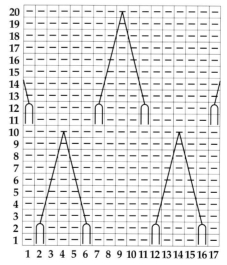

58. RUCHED DIAMONDS.

Bottom half of swatch shows a 1-color, softly ruched fabric with alt, 10-row pattern. Top half shows same pattern from K side. To work this pat with 2 colors, K 1st 2 Rs of each rep (same 2 Rs in which marker tucks are formed) in a CC.

59. *RUCHED HEART CABLE AND TRIM.*

To work: For heart cable at L, charts are provided for 12-ST, 24-ST & 30-ST pattern formats for chunky & standard punchcards & electronics. K all versions with cam lever set for tuck. At end of each rep, lift isolated pairs of tuck STS in rows 1 & 2 of each rep (indicated by an * below them) onto NDLS marked with ** above them. On an electronic machine, you can inc or dec size of tucked "seed-stitch" area (shown at L of chart) as desired for garment placement, & you can program machine to buzz every 16/Rs to indicate when to lift marker STS (at RT of chart). When working on a chunky machine, lift marker STS every 12/Rs. (Pattern courtesy of Silver Knitting Institute.)

Heart trim at center is a 9-ST variation on basic heart cable at L. When knitting R 1, pull NDLS 2 & 8 to HP to form tuck-ST markers. Lift STS 2 & 8 every 12/Rs to center NDL.

Heart trim at RT is a variation on its neighbor, with a more exaggerated texture. This version inc number of plain Rs K between each rep, pulls NDLS 2 & 8 to HP in R 1 to form marker tucks, & lifts STS 2 & 8 to NDLS 4 & 6 every 12/Rs.

STS are lifted for all versions as follows: Before K last, plain R of each rep, insert a single-prong tr tool under 1 set of marker STS in, for example, R 1, catching any tucks with K ST & hanging them tog on center pair of marker tucks at top of repeat. Then hang other set of R 1 marker tucks. You can hang either L or RT set first. Bring NDLS holding marker tucks to HP and let carriage knit them back on next row. Note that trim variations have 2 & 4 plain Rs, respectively, at end of each rep.

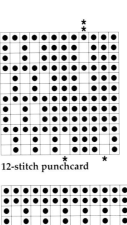

12-stitch punchcard

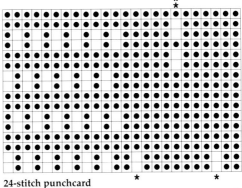

24-stitch punchcard

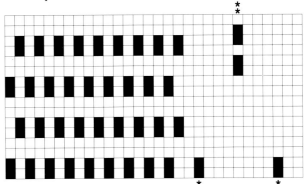

30-stitch electronic card

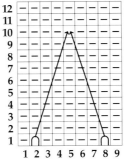

LIFTING CHART, CENTER TRIM.

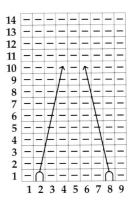

LIFTING CHART, RIGHT TRIM.

of seersucker effect by not lifting the knit section, which would ripple and pucker slightly between the tuck sections.

You can usually ease minor distortion into the seams (Swatch 60), and even the more extreme textures are suitable for garments with basic shapes and simple lines. If there's considerable distortion at the fabric's edges that cannot be incorporated into the design, you'll probably need to use cut-and-sew construction methods for all or part of the garment. Swatch 61 is a good example of irregular edges that would make an interesting jacket front, but would require either a zigzag, interlocking design or cut-and-sew side seams.

60. RUCHED CABLE EFFECT.

This is 1 rep of a lifting sequence in which same 3 STS are hung L or RT every 8/Rs. Side edges of fabric are slightly longer than center portion, but excess can be eased into seams.

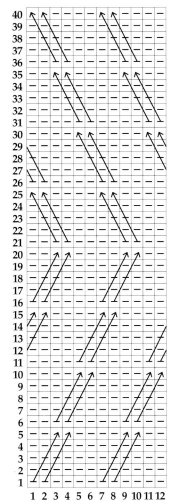

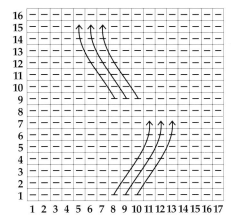

61. GIANT RUCHING.

To work: Lift 2 STS 2 NDLS to RT every 5/R. On next 3 reps, move lifted STS again 2 STS to RT. For next 4 reps, shift lifting sequence to L.

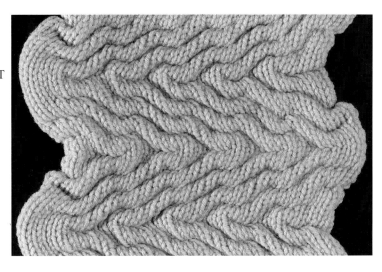

LIFTING A STITCH.
After inserting tr tool through ST, ST is lifted & deposited in hook of NDL above, whether directly above or to L or RT.

How to lift stitches

A basic transfer tool (single, double or triple eyelet) is all that's needed to lift most stitches. If you are working with very tight stitches, you will find the point of the Unicorn tool (see p. 242 for the address of a supplier) extremely helpful for picking up these stitches.

PLACING LIFTED EFFECT ON PURL SIDE OF FABRIC.
After removing STS from NDLS with tr tool, tip tool down behind fabric & reinsert it into fabric, catching STS to be lifted (right).
Tip tool back toward you (below right) so that you can hook it onto empty NDLS & place lower STS & then upper STS onto NDLS, causing effect to bulge & show on P side.

To lift a stitch, insert the transfer tool or Unicorn tool through the stitch, as shown in the top photo at left. Then lift the tool upward and deposit the stitch on a needle, which will cause the knit side of the fabric to pucker.

To produce the same texture on the purl side of the fabric, first remove the stitch (or stitches) currently in the needle(s) with the transfer tool (the middle and bottom photos at left illustrate the process with two stitches being lifted on a double-prong tool). Push these stitches back on the tool's shaft and tilt the tool down toward the knit side of the fabric. Insert the prongs on the knit side of the fabric into the stitches to be lifted and rotate the tool upward, tilting the handle toward you so that the lifted stitches can be placed in the needle hooks. Then deposit the first stitches on the transfer tool into the needle hooks along with the lifted stitches. This technique is generally used to place popcorns on the purl surface and has limited application elsewhere.

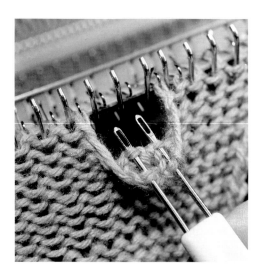

When stitches are lifted, a single needle usually holds two stitches before they are knitted off in the next row. Sometimes several stitches are lifted to a single needle. If you find it difficult to knit the next row, bring the needles holding the lifted stitches out to holding position and let the carriage knit them back on the next pass (see pp. 49-60 for a full discussion of holding). Make sure you push all stitches as far back on the held needle shafts as possible and that your weights are always under working stitches, where they will prevent split or dropped stitches.

Sometimes when you're knitting a single-color fabric, it's difficult to locate the stitches to be lifted for your pattern. To eliminate any confusion, knit in markers as you work to identify these stitches or the rows they're in. You can hang tags or hand-knitting stitch markers on stitches as you knit, or you can knit marker stripes of a different color, texture or size. These stripes are easy to see, but they do become a permanent part of the design. Alternatively, you can knit-weave a marker, which can be removed later (see p. 102 for information on knit-weaving markers). Choose a smooth, strong weaving yarn that can be pulled out without breaking or leaving a fuzzy residue.

If your machine is capable of automatic patterning, you may want to rely on a pattern of slip, tuck or Fair Isle stitches to indicate which stitches to lift for a pattern sequence. The pattern needn't become part of the fabric design. It can be small or subtle enough simply to indicate which stitches to lift. On manual machines you can create markers by periodically reforming stitches or collecting tucks on needles in holding position. These two techniques help locate the stitches to be lifted in your pattern, and they usually do not show after the lifting is completed (see Swatch 59 on p.130). If you're working with an electronic machine, program it to buzz at the end of every repeat or whenever it's time to stop knitting and lift stitches. If you don't have an automatic buzzer to remind you, keep an eye on your row counter.

Lifting single stitches and small groups of stitches

There are three basic effects created by lifting individual stitches or small groups of stitches: ruching, honeycombs and popcorns. Ruched fabrics, like those pictured in Swatch 58 on p. 129, have a strongly puckered knit surface. Honeycomb effects (Swatch 62) are similar on their knit face to ruched fabric, but it is their purl-side indentations that are the real source of interest. Popcorns, or

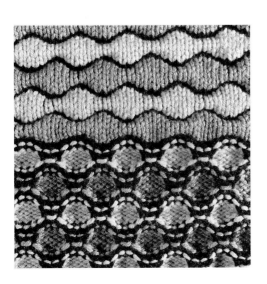

62. HONEYCOMB DESIGN.

These honeycomb cells are all outlined by same color but use 2 alt pat colors for added interest. Note that top portion of swatch shows K side of fabric.

To work: *K 2 Rs in MC, then 6 Rs in CC1 (or CC2); lift 2 STS from 2nd R of MC & hang on NDLS directly above.* Rep from * to *.

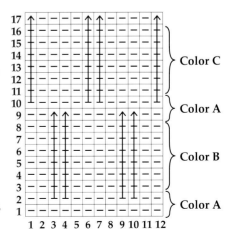

63. FIVE-STITCH POPCORNS.

All these popcorns are K with incs & decs to shape them. Those in bottom R are worked with a separate strand & made like 3-ST version, inc from 1 central ST. Those in top R are worked with continuous method, inc 4 STS to L of a base ST, which makes them rounder & more even than those in bottom R.

BASIC METHOD OF FORMING A TWO-STITCH POPCORN.

1. Knit five or six extra rows on two needles.

2. Insert a two-prong transfer tool into original stitches that were on the needles and hang them atop last two popcorn stitches.

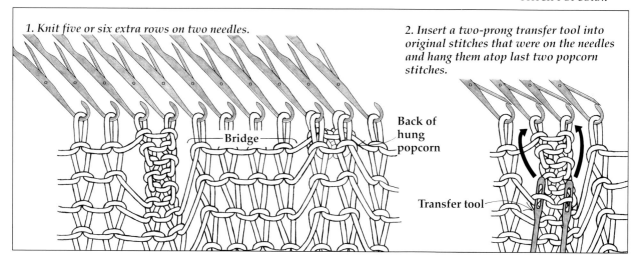

Bridge

Back of hung popcorn

Transfer tool

64. BASIC POPCORNS.

Popcorns in bottom R are worked 2 STS wide & 5 Rs long, with no inc. Those in top R are inc to 3 STS. Both rows are K with separate strand of yarn.

bobbles (Swatch 63) are quite different from ruched or honeycomb effects because, although the surface protrudes in tight little bumps, there is no distortion of the underlying fabric. This is because extra rows are knitted specifically for creating and lifting each popcorn or bobble (see the drawing on the facing page).

The ruched and honeycomb examples in this chapter illustrate a variety of effects that depend on the spacing and number of stitches lifted, the number of rows between lifts, the direction the stitches are lifted and how much they are pulled or distorted in the process. Apart from introducing color changes or automatic patterning, the general method for lifting is the same for all of these fabrics: After knitting a given number of rows, stitches in an earlier row are picked up and lifted onto the needles so that the next pass of the carriage forms a new stitch joining the separate points on the fabric surface. Remember, when working from the stitch charts, to lift the stitches *before* knitting the row in which the lifted stitches are called for.

Popcorns (bobbles)

Popcorns (also called bobbles) are simply raised bumps on the surface of a fabric. Long a mainstay of traditional Irish fisherman sweaters, popcorn textures can add a decidedly handmade look to machine knits.

Popcorns can be formed with as few as two stitches or as many as five or six. There are two methods for sizing and shaping popcorns; for clarity's sake I'll call them methods A and B. The simple approach (Method A) uses a consistent number of needles and stitches throughout (usually just two). The more complex approach (Method B) requires additional stitches and two more steps for increasing and decreasing. Method B is needed only for popcorns worked on four or more stitches. Either method can be worked with a separate strand of yarn or with the same yarn used for the main knitting.

If you look at Swatch 64, I think you'll find that there's very little difference between the basic two-stitch popcorns in the bottom row and the three-stitch popcorns in the top row, which were worked with Method B. I question whether Method B justifies the time and effort it requires, and for most small popcorns I favor Method A.

Method A involves hand knitting five or six rows of stitches on two adjacent needles to create a short tab of fabric. When lifted, this tab forms a rounded bump on the knit side of the fabric (with an extra step or two, the popcorn can be placed on the purl side, as explained below). To lift the tab after it's knitted, a transfer tool is inserted into the stitches originally held on the two needles, and these stitches are rehung on their needles—as if none of the extra rows had been knitted.

If you were to work Method A on more than two needles or knit more than five or six rows, the resulting tabs would be too wide or too long to appear rounded like a popcorn when lifted. There may be times when you can use an effect like that, so it is certainly not wrong, but it is just a tab, not a true popcorn.

Method B involves the added steps of increasing and decreasing. There are two ways to work Method B, with the difference based on the location of the needle used for the increases and decreases. If you study Swatch 63 you'll see that Method B, used for the popcorns in the top row, produces a much rounder, more perfect, giant popcorn.

Whichever method you use, you'll first need to empty some needles by removing their stitches to adjacent needles (opposite needles, if you're working with a ribber bed) or stitch holders. To create a three-needle popcorn with Method B, transfer the stitches on the first and third of three needles to adjacent needles, as shown in

*INCREASE METHOD
FOR WORKING A THREE-
STITCH POPCORN.*

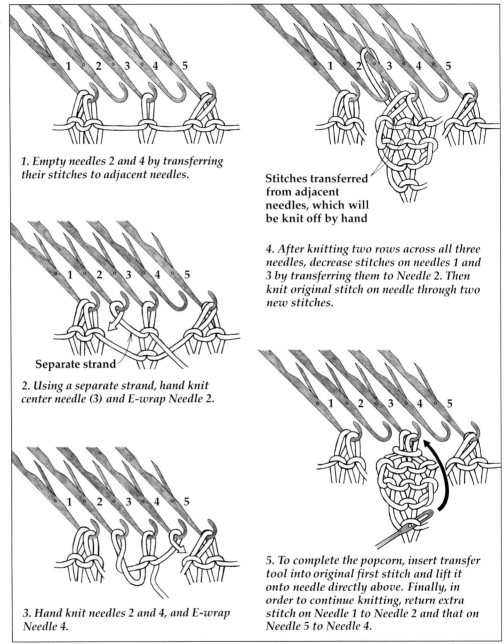

1. *Empty needles 2 and 4 by transferring their stitches to adjacent needles.*

Separate strand

2. *Using a separate strand, hand knit center needle (3) and E-wrap Needle 2.*

3. *Hand knit needles 2 and 4, and E-wrap Needle 4.*

Stitches transferred from adjacent needles, which will be knit off by hand

4. *After knitting two rows across all three needles, decrease stitches on needles 1 and 3 by transferring them to Needle 2. Then knit original stitch on needle through two new stitches.*

5. *To complete the popcorn, insert transfer tool into original first stitch and lift it onto needle directly above. Finally, in order to continue knitting, return extra stitch on Needle 1 to Needle 2 and that on Needle 5 to Needle 4.*

the drawing on the facing page. Then, using a separate strand of yarn, hand knit the center needle, E-wrap the first needle, knit the center needle and E-wrap the third needle. Knit two rows across all three needles, and then decrease back to one stitch by transferring the first and third stitches to the center needle. Push the center needle's butt forward so that its stitch slides behind the latch, and then push the needle back so that the other two stitches are knitted through this stitch. Lift the original center stitch onto the center needle, which will cause the extra rows to bulge out on the knit side, and return the original first and third stitches to their needles. The triangular, three-stitch popcorns that accent Swatch 65 were simply not decreased.

Large, five-needle popcorns must be made with Method B, but you'll need to empty two needles rather than one on each side of the center needle. Transfer these stitches across to the ribber bed or place them on a stitch holder. It's unlikely that you'll be able to move these stitches to adjacent needles on the same bed without producing considerable distortion in the fabric.

To work this large popcorn, hand knit the center needle and then increase out to the full five stitches by E-wrapping two

stitches on one side, knitting back across those three stitches, and E-wrapping the remaining two needles on the other side. Once you have established stitches on all five needles, knit two or three rows. Then decrease one stitch at each edge by transferring the stitch to the adjacent needle toward the center of the popcorn, knit one row and complete the popcorn, as you would for the three-needle version. Hang the original center stitch back on its needle, and return all the displaced stitches to their original needles.

It will be easier eventually to hang the center stitch if at the outset, when you remove the other four stitches to the holder, you allow the center stitch to be caught by, but not removed on, the holder. That is, the center stitch will be held by both its needle and the holder. When it's time to rehang the original center stitch on the needle, this stitch will be easy to find.

To work a rounder five-stitch popcorn with an alternative method, you would increase four stitches directly to the left (or right) of what's called the base stitch, rather than increasing on either side of a center stitch. This base stitch marks the position the popcorn will eventually occupy. To begin a five-stitch popcorn, transfer the four needles to the left of the fifth base needle onto a stitch holder, as

65. THREE-STITCH TRIANGULAR POPCORN.
Lamb's body is K in Fair Isle, while its head is an inc 3-ST popcorn that has not been dec back to 1 ST. With crocheted detail for ears or embroidery for eyes, this seemingly abstract shape takes on a new personality. You can also try K more Rs to make longer heads or not lifting 1st R, which causes shape to hang downward from fabric.

To make head: Placement of head is indicated by triangle on punchcard. Begin working inc 3-ST popcorn, inc to 3 STS & K 3 Rs across the 3 NDLS. Return original STS 1 & 3 to NDLS 1 & 3, placing them on top of popcorn STS. Lift & hang center popcorn ST.

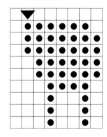

PUNCHCARD (1 REPEAT).

shown in the drawing below. Knit the base needle, then use the free yarn to chain or E-wrap the four empty needles. Knit three rows over all five needles, then decrease one stitch at each edge. Knit one more row and decrease to one central stitch. Hang the first and fifth stitches from the first hand-knitted row on top of this single stitch, and move all three stitches to the base needle at the right to complete the popcorn. Return the four stitches from the holder to their original needles. If you lift only one stitch from the first hand-knitted row instead of two, the popcorn does not quite close and creates a flower-like shape, as you can see in Swatch 66.

Separate-strand vs. continuous method. In additon to the two different methods of sizing popcorns, there are also two distinct ways of working with the yarn, the so-called separate-strand and the continuous-strand methods. As its name suggests, in the separate-strand method you use a strand of yarn separate from the main yarn, hand knitting and carrying it across the purl surface of the fabric from one popcorn to the next. The continuous method works with the main knitting yarn, using holding position to allow the carriage to knit bridges from one popcorn to the next and to knit the popcorns themselves.

WORKING A FIVE-STITCH POPCORN.

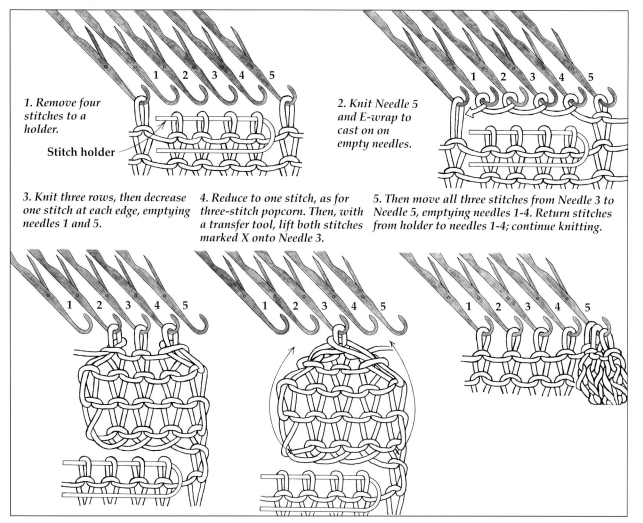

1. Remove four stitches to a holder.

Stitch holder

2. Knit Needle 5 and E-wrap to cast on on empty needles.

3. Knit three rows, then decrease one stitch at each edge, emptying needles 1 and 5.

4. Reduce to one stitch, as for three-stitch popcorn. Then, with a transfer tool, lift both stitches marked X onto Needle 3.

5. Then move all three stitches from Needle 3 to Needle 5, emptying needles 1-4. Return stitches from holder to needles 1-4; continue knitting.

The separate-strand method is simple, fast and flexible; it allows you to vary the yarn color, texture and size for the popcorn. This method, however, is suitable only for placing popcorns on the knit face of the fabric because the separate strand is carried across the purl side.

The continuous method is also fast and is quite automatic since the carriage carries the yarn and knits all the stitches. However, this method limits the design choices to the yarn used in the the body of the fabric. Another consideration is whether you're already using holding position for patterning or shaping. If so, this may prevent you from using the continuous method, which depends on holding position. Thus, if you're knitting a pattern that requires the carriage to be set to knit needles in holding position, you cannot use the continuous method.

In the separate-strand method, the stitches are all hand knitted by manipulating the needles. The popcorn stitches must be well weighted to knit cleanly, which means that you must move your weights often. I extend a finger to pull down on the stitches as I knit them, or I hang a paper clip and fishing weights under the actual popcorn stitches. You can carry the same strand across a row from one popcorn to the next, and you can carry it up the back of the work from one row to the next. If you carry a contrast yarn from row to row, you might want to use vertical weaving to cage the yarn against the back of the fabric, since just hooking it over a needle to carry it from row to row may cause it to show through on the knit side (see pp. 104-108 for a discussion of vertical weaving). When working with heavy yarns, you can avoid adding extra bulk by using a finer-weight yarn or even sewing thread to cage the separate strand.

To work a bobble with the separate-strand method, leave enough of a yarn tail on the strand to finish it off later. Manually push

SEPARATE-STRAND VS. CONTINUOUS METHOD.

66. SWEET PEAS.

These are K with Method B for making 5-ST popcorns, inc to 1 side of a base ST, but only 5th ST in R 1 is lifted. This procedure forms an open flower, instead of a closed popcorn. Knit stem by holding & hand knitting 1 NDL with a separate strand, E/R. Flowers are formed to L or RT of stem, or base, stitch, to which lifted ST & last dec ST always return.

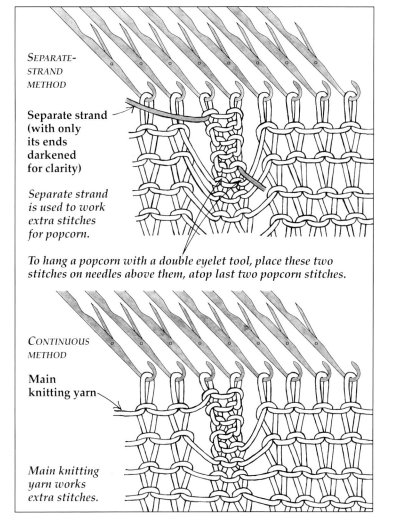

SEPARATE-STRAND METHOD

Separate strand (with only its ends darkened for clarity)

Separate strand is used to work extra stitches for popcorn.

To hang a popcorn with a double eyelet tool, place these two stitches on needles above them, atop last two popcorn stitches.

CONTINUOUS METHOD

Main knitting yarn

Main knitting yarn works extra stitches.

the butts of the popcorn needles forward, then lay the strand across the open hooks from right to left before knitting the needles back. To knit the next row of the popcorn, lay the yarn across the hooks from left to right. Continue manually knitting these narrow rows alternately to the right and left. After five or six rows, carry the strand across the surface of the fabric to the location of the next popcorn and repeat the procedure. If you have no more popcorns to knit in a particular row, the strand can be carried up the back of the work to the next row with popcorns by catching it over a needle hook every three or four rows.

67. SLIP-STITCH POPCORN.

This is fastest, most automatic method for K popcorns. Bobbles (at bottom), however, tend to be flatter than when made by all other methods, & floats on back of fabric (at top) make fabric especially heavy & without stretch. To work this method, set cam lever to slip & use punchcard for pat. After 4/Rs of slip floats, lift stitches to form bobble. Two plain Rs will automatically follow.

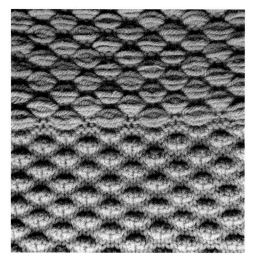

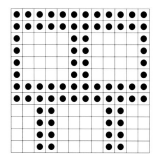

PUNCHCARD
(1 REPEAT).

In order to work a popcorn with the continuous method, set the carriage to hold needles in holding position. To clarify the directions for this method, let's assume that you're working two-stitch popcorns with a six-needle bridge between them and the carriage starting on the right. Place all needles except the first eight at the right edge (the needles for the first bridge and first popcorn) into holding position. Knit one row to the left and then place the bridge needles at the right edge into hold as well. *Now you'll be working with only the two needles that form the popcorn. Knit four more rows across these needles, ending with the carriage on the right. Place the bridge needles at the left of this popcorn and the two needles for the next popcorn into upper working position, and knit one more row to the left.* This pass of the carriage completes the fifth and last row of the first popcorn, and knits one row across the bridge and the first row of the second popcorn as well. Lift the first popcorn and then place its needles and those of its bridge into holding position so that only the next two popcorn needles are working. Repeat from * to *, lifting each popcorn immediately after it is knitted.

You can, of course, hang these popcorns on the purl side of the fabric because the knitted bridges eliminate any floats from one popcorn to the next. Remember to turn off the row counter before you begin a row of popcorns by the continuous method, then advance it by one number when the row is complete to account for the one row knitted across each of the bridges. When the entire row of popcorns and bridges has been knitted, you can return the needles to working position manually or with the carriage controls, depending on your machine and whether any other patterning is involved.

For machines with automatic needle selection, there is another continuous method based on slip stitch that's even faster and which does enable you to use a contrast yarn for the popcorns. Prepare a punchcard or electronic card for a slip-stitch pattern that will, for example, alternately knit two stitches and slip the next four, for five or six rows. Follow this patterning with two or more rows punched for stockinette, then repeat the selected rows or stagger them, as you like. You can knit as many rows of stockinette between rows of popcorns as you please. Set the carriage for slip, knit the pattern rows, then hang all the popcorns formed by the last row of the slip pattern. Instead of knitting bridges or carrying a separate strand from one popcorn to the next, you'll have five or six floats of yarn between all the popcorns since they're simultaneously produced by the carriage. While this is definitely the fastest way to knit an allover popcorn texture, it does produce a typical slip-stitch fabric with limited stretch and increased bulk (Swatch 67).

You can either individually knit and lift each popcorn in a row, or you can wait to lift them all at once if you're placing them on the knit side of the fabric. If you want the popcorns on the purl side of the fabric, you must lift each one immediately after it is knitted because the needles need to be placed in holding position to continue knitting the bridge to the next popcorn and the popcorn itself. Also, unless it interferes with some other patterning or shaping function, you can usually bring the needles that hold the lifted stitches to holding position to help the carriage knit them back more easily.

With either the separate-strand or continuous method, you can place popcorns wherever you want, combine them with lace and cable techniques (see Chapters 7 and 8) or add a bit of whimsy to a garment, as shown in swatches 65 on p. 137 and 66 on p. 139. The separate-strand and continuous slip-stitch methods allow you to knit popcorns in a different yarn from the body of the fabric. You can also use your main yarn doubled or stuff popcorns with polyester batting to make them stand out even more. If you want to combine the popcorns with ribbed effects, the number of ribs involved determines whether it's more practical to latch up the

ribs or work them with a second bed of needles (Swatch 68). The ribber bed, however, makes it harder to knit and lift each popcorn on the main bed since there's very little hand room between the beds when they are dropped.

It's also possible, of course, to hand crochet popcorns and apply them to the surface of the fabric. You can even use the continuous method to produce them by crocheting the free yarn with a crochet hook each time the carriage is interrupted. Crocheted popcorns and picots can be positioned on either side of the fabric before the carriage knits the next group of stitches.

68. POPCORN RIBBING.
These 3-ST inc popcorns are worked on center ST of rib, using continuous method. The continuous method is easiest to manage for latched-up SB ribs (like this one) & DB arrangements, where handling a separate strand between beds would be a bother.

To work: Bring empty NDLS to WP & C/O, inc from 1 ST to 3 STS. After K several Rs on all 3 NDLS, dec to 1 ST & ret empty NDLS to NWP. Hang popcorns, drop STS marked X, & latch them back up as knits. They will absorb some slack created by NWP NDLS & make a softer ribbed effect & more prominent popcorns.

NEEDLE DIAGRAM.

69. PIN-TUCKED DIAMOND.

All NDLS are placed in HP, except those that continue K to form tucks. These NDLS, indicated by Xs on chart, K an extra 4 Rs, then 1st R of STS is lifted to complete tuck.

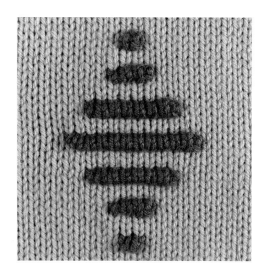

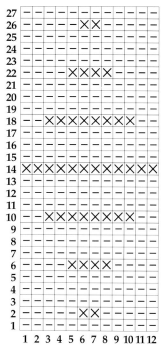

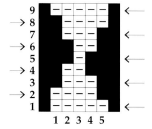

Short-row heel-shaping

Lifting chart (first row)

70. 3-D TRIANGLES.

These triangles are knitted exactly like tiny sock heels, using HP to inc and dec number of NDLS working. Knitted by continuous method, these triangles are 5 NDLS wide, with 1-ST bridges and 3 Rs between staggered placements. You can space them as desired.

To work: Start with COR and set to hold NDLS in HP. Put 1st 6 NDLS on RT in WP and all others in HP. K 1R to L. *Place single bridge NDL at RT and 1st NDL at L into HP. K 1 R to RT. Hold 1 NDL on carr side each R until 1 NDL rem. Return 1 NDL to UWP, E/R until 5 NDLS are working, ending with COR. Lift 5 STS from R 1 to close shape. Bring next (bridge) NDL and group of 5 NDLS at L into UWP, and K 1 R to L. Place bridge NDL and NDLS for completed shape into HP so that only 5 NDLS are working.* Rep from * to *.

71. FIVE-STITCH DOUBLE TRIANGLES.

Knitted like the 3-D triangles in Swatch 70, these triangles have 3 STS between them & 1 plain R separating identical reps. Steamed apart, the puckered-lip effect becomes that of raised diamonds on surface.

When you knit popcorns on more than five stitches, the effect is more horizontal than rounded, forming pin tucks rather than bobbles (Swatch 69). The arrangement and spacing of these pin tucks creates patterns in raised ridges. When the number of stitches is shaped by short-row knitting (see the Glossary on p. 238) or the number of rows in each popcorn increases to produce a lengthy tab, it opens up a whole new set of possibilities for creating highly dimensional appendages to the fabric (swatches 70 and 71).

Lifting entire rows of stitches

Lifting an entire row of stitches creates a pleat in the fabric (Swatch 72). Pleats are formed exactly like the basic hems that most beginning machine knitters learn to do, that is, by knitting twice as many rows as the depth of the pleat requires, then lifting all the stitches or every other stitch in the first row to the needles above. Because pleats and hems tend to be bulky and heavy, many variations are based on an effort to reduce bulk or make a sharper crease in the pleat.

Lifting every other stitch or sinker loop is often adequate for closing a pleat and additionally can be done in half the time and with less chance of the stitches showing on the face of the fabric. However, be careful when working such pleats to pick up the edge stitch or loop, which will keep the end of the pleat from drooping. And if you start with waste yarn, be sure to pick up the sinker loops, not the stitches, of the first row of the main knitting, lifting all of them, not just every other one. If you do not pick up the stitches, you may find the pleat is separate from the fabric when you remove the waste.

There are a number of techniques for working crisp, flat pleats. First, when pleating across the middle of the fabric (rather than the lower edge), use stripes or marker stitches (either reformed or slipped) to ensure that you lift the right stitches and keep the pleats straight. To get a sharper crease on the lower edge of a pleat, knit the turning (middle) row with a larger stitch size or a row of garter stitch, or otherwise differentiate it from the previous and following rows.

72. PLEAT AND HEM VARIATIONS.

To work: All pleats are K with 5 Rs for underside, 1 turning R (see below), 6 Rs for top side & 10 Rs between pleats. After hanging 1st R on NDLS to form pleat, bring all NDLS to HP & set carr to K them back. K next R with 1 SS larger.

Each turning R in swatch (numbered 1-5, starting from bottom) is worked differently:

1. K with largest SS (10).
2. Form picots by transferring EON & leaving empty NDLS in WP.
3. Produce garter-stitch ridge by turning fabric twice with GB (see pp. 78-79) or reforming all STS in R.
4. Form tucked scallops by placing every 5/ST in HP for 1st 5 & last 6 Rs. All NDLS K turning R with SS 10.
5. Create crocheted ridge by bringing all NDLS to HP, sliding fabric forward & working 1 R of crochet on shafts of NDLS. K turning R with SS 10.

Pleats generally lie flatter when the underside of the pleat has one to four fewer rows than the top side or is knitted with a stitch one to two sizes smaller than the top side. When working with heavy yarns, you can reduce the bulk of the fabric by knitting the underside of the hem on every other needle, bringing the empty needles to working position at the turning row and then finishing the knitting and hanging the hem. If you pick up the loops to fill the empty needles, the lower edge will be solid. If you allow the empty needles to cast on, they will form a picot edge (as on the second pleat from the bottom in Swatch 72 on p. 143).

A pleat will fall a little more softly when the row closing it is knitted with an increased stitch size. Usually one to two stitch sizes larger is sufficient to join the layers with stitches that do not bind or show on the face of the fabric.

Pleats knitted with only a few rows become pin tucks. Because pin tucks hug the fabric more closely than wider pleats, they stand up better and usually need no turning row. Individual pin tucks can be used to accent buttonholes, slits or pocket openings and to outline intarsia detail (Swatch 73).

When outlining short-row intarsia shapes, the pin tucks can be knitted across all of the needles that comprise the outline of an area or shape, regardless of whether they were working in the previous rows. Because, as with pleats, the first row of each pin tuck is lifted back onto the needles, the base fabric remains unaffected, as though the extra rows never happened. Even though it appears to break some of the rules for short-row knitting (see pp. 49-53), you can knit one row with the main color across all the needles in holding position before making the pin tuck, which will knit the stitches and wraps together. Then use the contrast yarn to knit the required number of rows for the pin tuck. Lift the first row of the pin tuck onto the needles and knit one row with the main yarn, or change colors as desired. Return the needles to holding position before knitting the pin tuck, and continue with the short-row intarsia method to produce the next shaped area.

 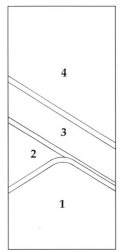

73. PIN-TUCK-OUTLINED, SHORT-ROW INTARSIA DESIGN.   *KNITTING SEQUENCE.*

To work: K Section 1, as shown in the drawing above, moving NDLS in & out of HP, A/R. K 6 Rs across all NDLS, hang pleat & ret NDLS to HP.

To K Section 2: With COL, begin Section 2 by ret NDLS at L to UWP on A/R until shape is at widest point. Dec shape by placing NDLS at RT of it into HP. K 6 Rs across all NDLS, hang pleat & ret all NDLS to HP.

With COR, begin Section 3 by ret NDLS to UWP on A/R until enough NDLS are working to K stripe of desired width. Continue K stripe by inc at L of stripe (placing NDLS in WP) & dec at RT (placing NDLS in HP). Follow this shape with a 6-R pin tuck, as for sections 1 & 2.

K Section 4, beginning with COR, placing NDLS in UWP, A/R until all NDLS are K.

Pleating always shows on the knit side of the fabric. You can, of course, place pleats on the purl side if you're willing to go to some trouble. After knitting all the rows needed for the depth of the pleat, use a garter bar to remove all the stitches from the machine. Then use a transfer tool to pick up, lift and hang on the needles the right side of the stitches in an earlier row. Finally, rehang the stitches from the garter bar on the needles, which will pleat the fabric on the purl side (see Chapter 6 for information on rehanging).

Lifting sinker loops, ladders and floats

The sinker loops that form between stitches can be lifted just as easily as stitches. In fact, sinker loops are easier to lift than tightly formed stitches, and the resulting lifted effects often join the base fabric more smoothly and easily than lifted-stitch effects since the loops are a little looser than stitches. Sinker loops are also faster to locate for lifting than stitches.

The ladders that are formed when needles are left in nonworking position are really just columns of enlarged sinker loops, and they too can be lifted. In fact, ladders are even easier to manipulate than ordinary sinker loops, and, when lifted, yield even more ease to the fabric than lifted sinker loops.

The floats formed as a by-product of slip stitches, Fair Isle knitting, knit-weaving and thread lace can be lifted. They too are faster and easier to lift than stitches since they lie on the fabric's surface and generally offer no resistance. When lifted often, floats produce simple surface textures. When lifted less frequently, they create ruched effects. Both types of lifted effects appear on the knit side of the fabric, but I often find the float patterns on the purl side more interesting.

In many patterns, it doesn't really matter whether you lift a stitch or a sinker loop, but be consistent in your choice from one lifted effect to the next. While lifting sinker loops, ladders and floats offers a little more ease to the fabric, lifting stitches creates a slightly sharper join between the two layers of fabric. However, when sinker loops earmarked for lifting adjoin ladders formed by out-of-work needles, they absorb extra length from the ladder bars and can be lifted further without strain.

If the ladder is formed by a single nonworking needle or if the adjoining sinker loop is lifted often enough, the ladder may close enough to be barely noticeable in the finished fabric. Swatch 74 is a simple lifted float pattern that illustrates this point well.

74. ZIGZAG RUCHING.

To work: After C/O, tr every 6/ST to adj NDL, leaving empty NDLS in WP. *K 5 Rs. Drop STS formed on every 6/NDL to form ladders. Leave empty NDLS in WP for next rep. P/U sinker loops between 4th & 5th STS from 1st 2 Rs & place them on 1st NDL. K 5Rs & continue as before, but P/U sinker loops between 1st & 2nd STS & place them on 5th NDL.* Rep from * to *. (Pattern courtesy of Silver Knitting Institute.)

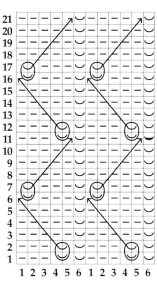

Swatches 75, 76 and 77, all variations on lifting ladders, rely on needle arrangements to form very wide ladders, which are lifted to create open faggoting effects. Swatch 78 also lifts ladder floats but combines this technique with a twist at the edge of the fabric (see the drawing on p. 148), producing an interesting edging for scarves or shawls that doesn't roll. An open-cable effect can be produced when this edge is paired with a second identical edge and joined on the machine while the second piece is being knitted (see pp. 162-165 for a discussion of the seam-as-you-knit method).

75. FAGGOTED LADDERS.

To work: C/O 6 NDLS in WP & 6 adj NDLS in NWP. K 8 Rs. P/U 1st 4 bars from ladder & hang them on 1st NDL to their L, as shown in the drawing on the facing page. K 4 Rs, P/U next 4 bars from ladder & hang them on 1st NDL to their RT. Continue K 4 Rs & hanging lowest 4 bars to L or RT. Plain K will be slightly distorted by take-up. Fabric could be embellished with lace, cables, popcorns, etc. (Pattern courtesy of Silver Knitting Institute.)

76. TUCK-STITCH VARIATION OF FAGGOTED LADDERS.

In this variation of Swatch 75, tucking absorbs surface distortion. Note odd number of NDLS in each section (7 WP & 5 NWP) & their location on bed. If punchcard pat rep is not coordinated with WP & NWP NDLS, it will not K correctly.

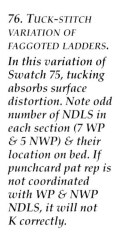

77. FAIR ISLE FAGGOTING.

This pattern uses same punchcard & NDL diagram as Swatch 76. Lifting sequence for Fair Isle differs in that working with 2 colors of yarn always makes 2 sets of bars to deal with. Every 4/R, both sets of bars (MC & CC) are lifted one group to the left and the other to the right, alt. sides 4/R. Also, there is no 4-R overlap.

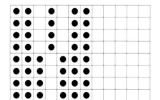

PUNCHCARD (1 REPEAT).

NEEDLE DIAGRAM.

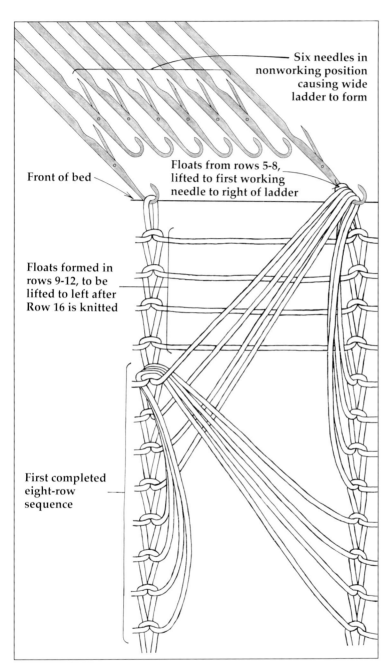

Six needles in nonworking position causing wide ladder to form

Front of bed

Floats from rows 5-8, lifted to first working needle to right of ladder

Floats formed in rows 9-12, to be lifted to left after Row 16 is knitted

First completed eight-row sequence

FAGGOTED LADDERS.

78. SPIRAL EDGING.

To work: C/O, leaving 4th & 5th NDL from edge in NWP to form a ladder. Every 6/R, insert latch tool from back of fabric, over 1st 5 bars of ladder. Catch 6th bar in hook, as shown in the drawing on p. 148, & pull it down & through to back of fabric. then place it in hook of 3rd NDL.

To join 2 pieces of fabric with mock-cable ladder-seam using this edging, K 1st piece with spiral edging above & B/O. *K 4 Rs of 2nd piece & make eyelet seam through openwork edging of 1st piece. K 2 Rs, twist ladder bars of 2nd piece, as for the 1st*. Rep from * to *, alt making seams & twisting edging of 2nd piece (see also p. 164). (Pattern courtesy of Silver Knitting Institute.)

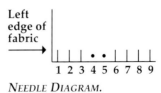

Left edge of fabric →

1 2 3 4 5 6 7 8 9

NEEDLE DIAGRAM.

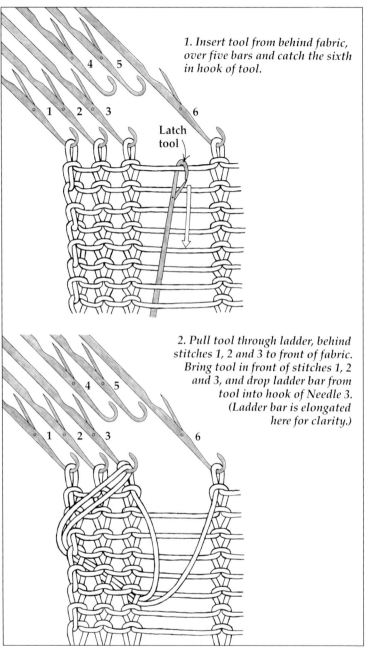

1. *Insert tool from behind fabric, over five bars and catch the sixth in hook of tool.*

Latch tool

2. *Pull tool through ladder, behind stitches 1, 2 and 3 to front of fabric. Bring tool in front of stitches 1, 2 and 3, and drop ladder bar from tool into hook of Needle 3. (Ladder bar is elongated here for clarity.)*

SPIRAL EDGING.

LIFTING TWO FLOATS TOGETHER.

The floats produced by Fair Isle, slip, weaving and thread-lace patterns can be lifted individually or in groups, and they can also be twisted or latched up before being lifted.

Lifted-float patterns are best worked on an automatic machine. Yet, even if your machine is manual, you can still create patterns of floats by hand selecting patterns that produce floats. Hand selecting, of course, takes more time because you'll probably have to make a new selection every row. The fabric shown in Swatch 79 is interesting on both sides. Wide floats are created by holding needles, and then those floats are periodically lifted to form a purl-side crisscross pattern. The polka dots on the knit side are formed wherever the contrast yarn knits the needles between floats.

In Fair Isle, automatic knit-weaving and thread lace, the fabric is knitted with two yarns held simultaneously in the carriage. In Fair Isle patterns, both the main and accent yarns produce a set of floats, while in weaving only the accent yarn creates floats, and in thread lace, only the main yarn. In slip-stitch patterns, knitted with a single yarn in the carriage, there's only one set of floats to deal with at any one time. (You can, of course, change colors in slip-stitch patterns, but there's still only a single set of floats at any given time.)

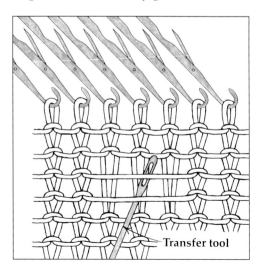

Transfer tool

Having only one set of floats makes it very easy to design slip-stitch patterns because what you see is really what you get. With Fair Isle, weaving and thread lace, there are always suprises, depending on whether the yarns are the same or contrast in size, color or texture. Swatches 80 and 81 are both variations on the same punchcard pattern, knitted as lifted Fair Isle and thread lace.

Whenever you bring a needle holding lifted floats to holding position to knit the next row, the needle in hold will knit on the next pass of the carriage. Whether this adds to the pattern effect may depend on color changes and the placement of the

80. LIFTED FAIR ISLE.

To work: Use punchcard below & set cams for Fair Isle. Every 4/R, lift all floats to center NDL directly above. If you bring center NDL to HP, it will K CC even in MC areas & change design by securing the floats with opposite color.

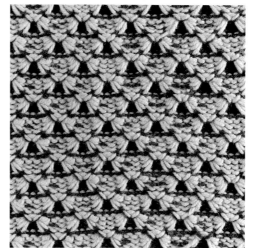

81. LIFTED THREAD LACE.

This pat and Swatch 80 use punchcard below, but this one requires cams to be set for thread lace. Knitted as thread lace, pat forms floats only with MC. Do not bring center NDLS to HP after lifting floats since color shift changes design.

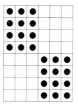

PUNCHCARD (1 REPEAT).

79. REVERSIBLE LIFTED FLOATS/POLKA DOTS.

To work: Set carr to hold NDLS in HP. Follow chart, bringing groups of 5 NDLS to HP, alt with groups of 3 NDLS in WP. With CC, K 4 Rs. Set carr to K NDLS from HP & K 6 Rs with MC. Lift 4 floats (CC) & hang them on center NDL (indicated on chart by star). Rep entire sequence, staggering placement, as shown.

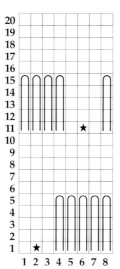

82. LIFTED SLIP STITCH.

To work: Use punchcard below & set carr to slip. K 5 Rs & lift each float onto center NDL above (only 1 with a K ST in that R, with all others slipped). *K 4 Rs & hang floats.* Rep from * to *.

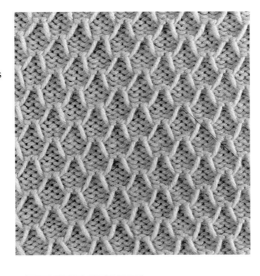

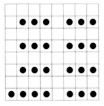

PUNCHCARD (1 REPEAT).

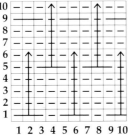

next group of floats. Sometimes you may want to add one plain knitted row between pattern repeats. As always, be consistent.

Swatch 82 shows a one-color slip-stitch pattern, which, especially when knitted on finer-gauge machines, has a smocked look to it. You can also knit the slip row with elastic thread to produce a stronger smocked effect. Swatch 83 is a much firmer, more intricate fabric than Swatch 82 because the slip-stitch floats have been latched up and lifted over a number of plain rows.

Sinker-post looping can be used to create extra-long floats for large-scale honeycombs and overlay effects (Swatch 84). The easiest way to create large, consistent floats is to wrap yarn from the main bed to the ribber, using the needles on the main bed and the sinker posts on the ribber to space the wrapping evenly (see the bottom photo on p. 69). After knitting a specified number of rows, the floats are lifted off the sinker posts onto the opposite needles. When many rows are knitted before lifting the floats, it causes the background fabric to pucker and gather. It's important to knit only enough rows so that the lifted floats lie flat on the surface of the fabric.

83. LATCHED-UP, LIFTED SLIP STITCH.

To work: Use punchcard at right & set carr to slip. K 7 Rs. Latch up floats in first 3 Rs & lift onto NDLS above. *K 4 Rs, latch & lift bottom group of 3 floats.* Rep from * to *.

PUNCHCARD (1 REPEAT).

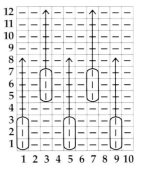

So-called "Volume Knitting" is an interesting variation on lifting floats. It is presented in the Brother International knitting books as a technique for applying very heavy yarns to the purl surface of a fabric. Instead of lifting the entire float into the hook of the needle, this technique calls for inserting the transfer tool into the yarn to split its plies and hang only part of the strand's thickness. The entire strand, however, is effectively caught, and the resulting fabric is much like other lifted-stitch fabrics. This is also an interesting way to apply surface embroidery to a fabric, using yarns that are far too heavy for vertical weaving or other embroidery methods.

Swatches 85 on p. 152 and Swatch 86 on p. 154 present a hybrid technique of lifting and embroidery, which decorates the purl side of the fabric. These effects are different from the other lifted examples in this chapter because they are not part of the structure of the fabric, but rather an addition to the surface. Both of the following techniques combine reforming and lifting by working through ladders, eyelets, sinker loops or actual stitches to form simple loops, chained stitches or a combination of the two. Unlike true embroidery, these effects are applied as the fabric is knitted. The embroidery yarn should be about three times as long as the distance to be embroidered. When in doubt, remember that having too much yarn is better than running short.

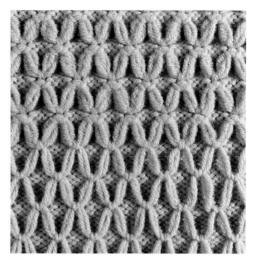

84. SINKER-POST-LOOPING HONEYCOMB.

To work: Bottom half is K using free yarn to *form loops on every 4/NDL & alternating 4/sinker post, working over & back to carr 1x. Top half is looped over & back 2x to form heavier loops. For both pats, K 6 Rs & lift loops off sinker posts & onto NDL directly opposite.* For bottom pat, immediately rep from * to *; for top, K 1 R & rep. Note division in top, produced between reps. Alt placement from 1 rep to next, as shown. A separate, contrasting yarn can substitute for free yarn.

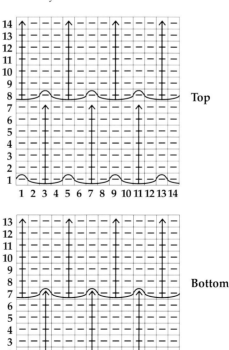

85. FENCE KNITTING.

Work with embroidery yarn held on K side & pulled through to P side to form loops that create decorative effects.

To work border at bottom: K at least 4 Rs, lay embroidery yarn behind fabric, *insert latch tool into 1st ST in 4th R down below NDLS & pull loop through to P side. Insert tool into a ST 2 Rs above, pull another loop of yarn through ST already on tool & lift it onto NDL 2 Rs directly above. Rep for EOS across R.* K 4 Rs & rep from * to *, working on alt STS.

To work flower, stems & leaves: K 5 Rs. Insert latch tool in 6th ST, in R 1 of 5 Rs just K to pull through a loop. Insert tool in 6th ST in 4th R to pull another loop through fabric & through loop already on tool. Continue pulling loops through fabric & each other to form a chain of STS on surface, lifting last loop on 6th NDL to complete center stem.

To chain leaves, reinsert tool in 6th ST in 5th R & pull a loop through. Move over to 5th ST, then 4th & so on, as you chain, ending by lifting loop onto 1st NDL. Rep for other leaf.

Lower half of flower is made of simple unchained loops. K 5 Rs. Following diagram, pull loops through fabric & lift each 1 onto center NDL. Move down by 1 R & in by 1 ST as you work from L to center; then move out by 1 ST and up by 1 R as you work towards RT. Center NDL of each flower holds 9 loops; bring center NDLS to HP & set carr to hold NDLS in HP. K 1 R. Manually K back each of center NDLS, using loop of yarn that passed over each NDL as R was knitted.

To begin upper half of flower, K 3 Rs. *In sinker space to RT of center ST, 3 Rs below, pull a loop through & lift onto 9th NDL. In space to L of center ST, pull a loop through & lift onto 3rd NDL.* K 1 R. Rep from * to *, working through same spaces (now 4 Rs below), lifting loops onto 8th & 4th NDLS. K 1 R. Rep from * to *, working through same spaces (now 5 Rs below), lifting loops onto 7th & 5th NDLS. K 1 R. Pull last loop through center ST, 6 Rs below & lift onto 6th NDL.

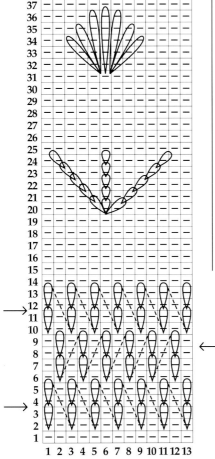

(Dotted lines indicate yarn on underside of fabric. Arrows indicate direction from which chaining begins.)

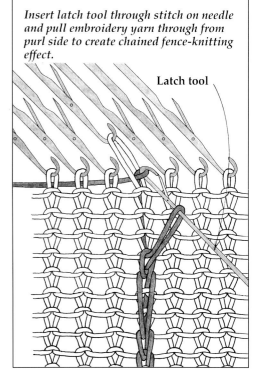

Insert latch tool through stitch on needle and pull embroidery yarn through from purl side to create chained fence-knitting effect.

Latch tool

FENCE KNITTING.

The first hybrid technique is one that Nihon Vogue calls "fence knitting" (Swatch 85). One or several contrast yarns are carried underneath, on the knit face of the fabric as it's worked. The technique can be awkward to do, but I position the embroidery yarn exactly where I need it (close to the bed, just below the needles) by passing it behind the fabric and weaving it through a few sinker posts on the opposite side of the bed. This provides enough tension to catch the yarn easily with the hook of the latch tool when it's inserted from the purl side to pull a loop of embroidery yarn through a stitch. This motion can be repeated across a fabric to produce surface chaining (as it is in the stems and leaves of the flowers of Swatch 85). The tool can also be inserted through a live stitch in the top row of knitting in order to pull a final loop of embroidery yarn through that stitch and the previously embroidered loop. This final loop is deposited in the needle hook with the stitch to complete this column of fence knitting. This is the way the border at the bottom of Swatch 85 was knitted. The flowers themselves are just simple loops pulled through the fabric at several places and then lifted to the same needle. Alternatively, these loops can be pulled through adjacent spaces and lifted to different needles, as shown in the drawing at top right.

If the stitch in question is dropped from the needle onto the latch tool first, it creates an open, crocheted effect rather than surface embroidery when the embroidery yarn is pulled through and deposited alone in the needle hook (see the drawing at right). To keep the fabric soft and pliable, be sure to work with a very large stitch size.

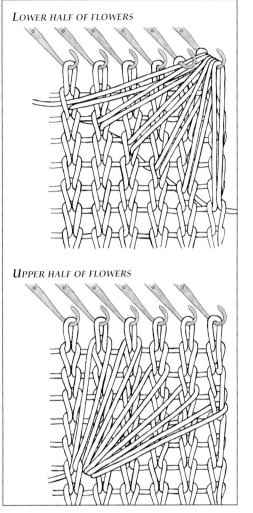

LOWER HALF OF FLOWERS

UPPER HALF OF FLOWERS

FORMING FLOWERS IN SWATCH 85.

FENCE-KNITTING VARIATION FOR OPEN CROCHETED EFFECT.

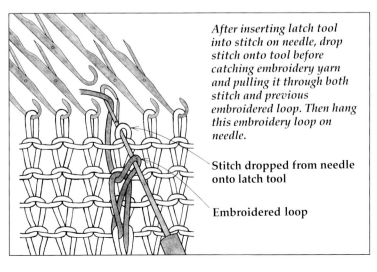

After inserting latch tool into stitch on needle, drop stitch onto tool before catching embroidery yarn and pulling it through both stitch and previous embroidered loop. Then hang this embroidery loop on needle.

Stitch dropped from needle onto latch tool

Embroidered loop

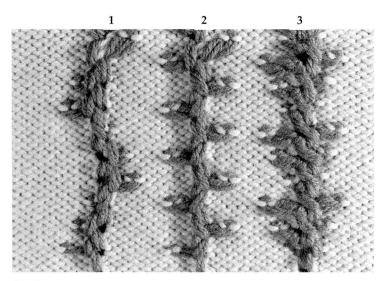

86. EMBOSSED EMBROIDERY STITCHES.

All 3 designs are worked L & RT of a ladder formed by tr 1 ST to an adj NDL & leaving empty NDL in NWP, with 3 Rs between each embossed ST. Bottom half of each design is worked with free yarn caught under loops. Top half is worked with free yarn on top of loops.

To work: Begin each design with strand of embroidery yarn twice length you need. Fold strand in half to double it & catch looped end to begin. Follow chart, noting Design 1 is worked 3x to L of ladder & then 3x to RT, moving in by 1 NDL each time. Design 2 alt to 3rd NDL L & RT, & Design 3 works both sides of ladder at once, moving out by 1 NDL each time.

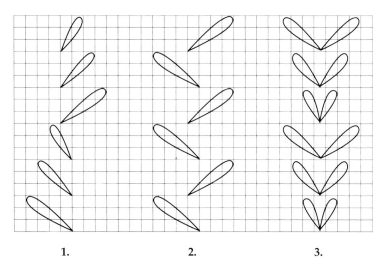

I learned an interesting variation of this technique from Lin Higgins, a talented teacher from Chattanooga, Tenn. She carries the yarn on the purl side of the fabric to form what she calls "embossed embroidery stitches" (Swatch 86) This technique differs from fence knitting in that it is always worked through ladders or eyelets and the loops are not chained. Instead, they are simply pulled through the fabric and lifted to a needle at the left or right of the ladder.

To work this technique, insert the latch tool under several bars at the top of a ladder where it catches the embroidery yarn (as shown in the drawing on the facing page) and pull out a loop long enough to reach a needle above. Because the embroidery yarn is carried on the purl side of the fabric, pay careful attention to whether it lies below or on top of the loop lifted to the needle. Both positions are correct, but each produces very different effects.

To keep the free (embroidery) yarn on top of a loop as it's lifted to a needle on the right, hold the yarn to the left. To lift the loop to the left, hold the yarn to the right. To trap the free yarn under a loop, hold it to the side to which you are lifting. That is, if you're lifting a loop to the right, hold the free yarn to the right first and then lift the loop to its needle.

All the designs on the bottom half of Swatch 86 were knitted with the free yarn caught under the loop; those on the top of the sample were knitted with the yarn on top. The bottom half of Swatch 85 on p. 152 was also knitted with entire rows of these embossed stitches. The bottom left half of that example was knitted with the yarn on top; the right half, with yarn below.

WORKING EMBOSSED EMBROIDERY STITCHES.

1. *Knit three rows. Insert latch tool under ladder bars of these rows and catch embroidery yarn in hook of tool. (For first repeat, catch loop at end of strand doubled to begin.)*

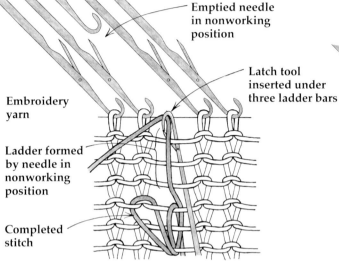

Emptied needle in nonworking position

Latch tool inserted under three ladder bars

Embroidery yarn

Ladder formed by needle in nonworking position

Completed stitch

2. *Pull latch tool down behind ladder bars and out to surface, bringing through a large enough loop of yarn to hang on a needle above.*

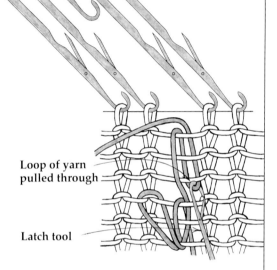

Loop of yarn pulled through

Latch tool

3. *Next, you can either catch yarn tail under loop or keep it free of loop. To catch tail under loop, lift loop from tool to a needle at left or right of ladder, trapping embroidery yarn under loop. When hanging loop to a needle at left, hold embroidery yarn to left; when hanging loop on needle at right, hold yarn to right before hanging loop.*

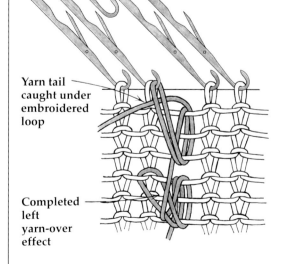

Yarn tail caught under embroidered loop

Completed left yarn-over effect

To keep yarn free of loop, lift loop from tool to a needle at left or right of ladder, clearing embroidery yarn. When hanging loop to a needle at left, hold yarn to right. When hanging to needle at right, hold yarn to left to keep it free of loop.

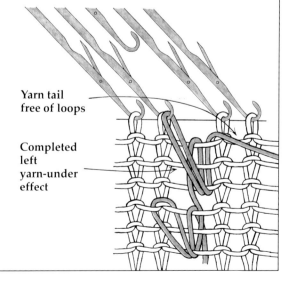

Yarn tail free of loops

Completed left yarn-under effect

CHAPTER 6

Rehung Stitches

Rehanging stitches is similar to lifting stitches, but there's an important distinction between the two techniques. Stitches that are lifted are part of a fabric still in progress on the machine (see Chapter 5). Stitches that are rehung are part of a fabric earlier completed or temporarily held on some form of stitch holder and removed from the machine. Thus, when stitches are lifted from one point in a fabric and hung anew on the needles, the fabric puckers, gathers or pleats. When stitches of one piece of knitting are rehung on needles holding another piece, the two fabrics are joined with the next pass of the carriage. Rehanging is most often used to add surface decoration to a fabric, but it can also be used to relocate a piece of knitting on the bed, reverse the work to the knit side or alter its width by spacing increasing, decreasing, pleating and gathering.

Stitches can be rehung from the edge or from within the body of a piece of knitting. These stitches can be either live or bound off, and they can be rehung horizontally or vertically. And they can be rehung gradually or all at once.

If you don't want to bind off the fabric before rehanging it, you can remove live stitches from the machine on a garter bar, a stitch holder (which looks like a wide transfer tool) or scrap knitting. Stitches removed on a garter bar or stitch holder are rehung by catching the needle hooks in the eyes of the tool and tipping the tool, causing the stitches to slide off the prongs and back onto the needles. While the stitch holder is simply handled like a transfer tool, the prongs of the garter bar do not fit between the sinker posts. Thus you need to remove or replace stitches on needles a little differently. To do this, bring the needles to holding position, then hook the garter bar onto them. You'll need to tug a bit on the fabric to help the stitches slide over the latches, off the needles and past the notches or necks of the individual prongs of the garter bar. These notches keep the stitches from sliding forward on the prongs and falling off when you handle the tool. They also make it easier to knit and stack several pieces on the same bar by pushing each one as far back on the prongs as possible before adding the next. For extra protection when I plan to set the filled garter bar aside for several days, I usually cap it with a plastic spine from the stationary store. If the spine is at all loose, I secure it with rubber bands on each end.

REHANGING WITH
SCRAP KNITTING.

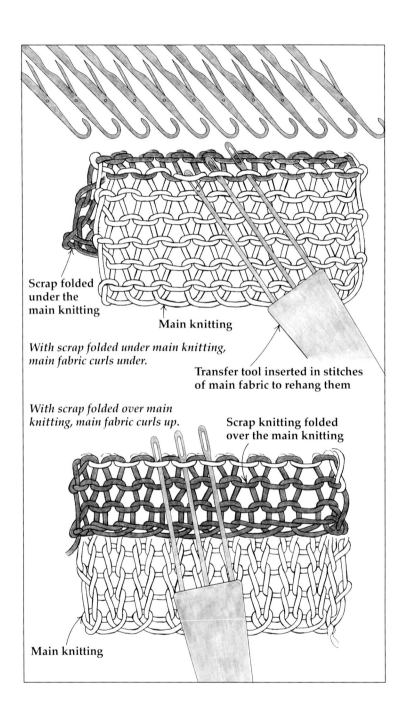

Scrap folded
under the
main knitting

Main knitting

With scrap folded under main knitting,
main fabric curls under.

Transfer tool inserted in stitches
of main fabric to rehang them

With scrap folded over main
knitting, main fabric curls up.

Scrap knitting folded
over the main knitting

Main knitting

If you're using multiple rows of scrap knitting to preserve live stitches at the edge of a fabric, rehanging these stitches is as easy, though not as fast, as rehanging fabric held on stitch holders or the garter bar. While slower, rehanging with scrap knitting offers some advantages. You're not limited by the width of a given tool, the number of tools you have available, or your skill in handling a particular tool. You can scrap off as large a piece or as many pieces as you want, storing them in a basket until you're ready to rehang. And if you leave the scrap in place until all the knitting is complete, you'll be able to retrieve mistakes easily, rather than having to reknit work that cannot be corrected (if you remove the scrap, you'll have no way to rehang the last row of open stitches). Gradual rehanging is also easier to do with scrap than with other stitch holders because the scrap is flexible and doesn't get in the way. Vertical rehanging is easier to work with scrap because you don't need to hold onto a tool while you work.

Although the edges of the scrap knitting tend to curl, steaming helps control this and also sets the stitches so they are less likely to run if they've not been bound off. You can, of course, bind off the scrap if the piece will be handled a lot before or during rehanging.

To rehang a piece held on scrap knitting, first fold the scrap out of the way. Then insert a transfer tool into each stitch in the first row of the main fabric, hook the tool onto a needle and tip it to transfer the stitch to the needle. You can use a single-pronged or multi-pronged transfer tool to return stitches one at a time or in groups, but make sure each stitch is picked up to prevent it from running when the scrap is removed.

Pay attention to how you fold the scrap back to rehang the fabric for applied surface trim. Small pieces of knitting held on scrap always curl toward the scrap. If you fold the scrap back so that it lies beneath the main knitting when the stitches are rehung, the main fabric will curl downward toward the scrap below. If you fold the scrap forward so that it lies on top of the main knitting when the stitches are rehung, the main fabric curls upward toward the scrap. The curling may not affect your design unless you're working with two contrasting colors. Then an upward-curling fabric could be used to advantage to create a sharper line and cover any two-tone stitches where the fabrics join.

Rehanging decorative trim

The simplest use of rehanging is to add a separate piece of trim to a completed fabric or garment piece. Usually it's the fabric or garment piece that's rehung on the needles holding the trim. However, the trim can, of course, be completed first, removed from the machine and returned to the needles holding the main portion of the knitting.

Wherever you have stitches, sinker loops or eyelets to work with, a fabric can be hung vertically or horizontally. You can add a preknit piece to the edge of another fabric and bind the two off together, or

PICKING UP STITCHES.

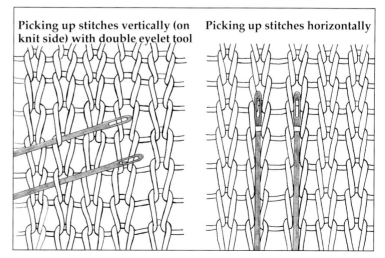

Picking up stitches vertically (on knit side) with double eyelet tool

Picking up stitches horizontally

87. VERTICAL STOCKINETTE CURLS.

This simple surface texture was added to base fabric after it was completely K. Vertical columns of STS in main fabric were P/U & hung horizontally on machine, K 5 or 6 Rs in stockinette & binding off. Trim pieces curl under naturally.

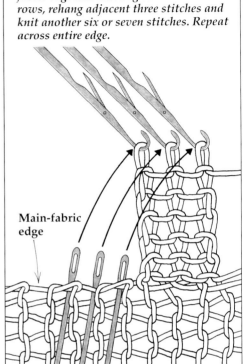

After rehanging three stitches on main-fabric edge and knitting six or seven rows, rehang adjacent three stitches and knit another six or seven stitches. Repeat across entire edge.

Main-fabric edge

KNITTED-ON THREE-STITCH EDGING.

88. RIPPLED TRIM.

Plain vertical seams join these dark & light fabrics. One of 2 pieces was K 1st & bound off. With wrong side facing, it was joined on A/R to edge NDL of 2nd piece by P/U every other edge ST, as shown in the drawing on p. 166, & knitting 2 Rs.

To work as an edging: With wrong side of base fabric facing you, hang 3 edge STS on NDLS. *K 6 or 8 Rs. Hang next adj group of 3 edge STS on same 3 NDLS.* Rep from * to * until entire edge is complete. The more rows K before rehanging next 3 edge STS, the more raised the edge becomes.

To decorate within body of fabric: Work with RT side of base fabric facing you. For vertical trim, P/U 3 STS, hang them on 3 adj NDLS & K 8 Rs. Then, 4 Rs higher on same vertical column of STS, P/U & hang 3 STS on same NDLS. For diagonal trim, beg as for vertical trim, & K 8 Rs before rehanging base STS 3 Rs above & 1 ST to RT on main fabric. Continue in this fashion diagonally across fabric.

you can rehang the preknit trim within the body of the fabric, joining the two by simply continuing the knitting (swatches 87 and 88). Rippled trim, like that in Swatch 88, is an old favorite, knitted onto a completed base fabric. In finer-weight yarns, this trim nicely decorates a neckline. In heavier-weight yarns, it makes a quick edging for afghans.

To appliqué preknit pieces as surface trim to another fabric while it's being knitted, it's easier to plan and join the pieces horizontally than vertically. Joining the work horizontally can often be done in a single step. The most straightforward method of joining the two fabrics is to hang stitches from one fabric onto the needles already holding the stitches of the other fabric and continue knitting. The two fabrics will be joined with the first pass of the carriage. This places the texture on the purl side of the fabric (Swatch 89) unless you remove specific stitches from the needles in order to apply the trim from behind to the knit side of the fabric (Swatch 90).

To add trims as horizontal and diagonal insertions within the body of a fabric, the fabric is removed from the machine at the point at which the trim is to be placed. If you're working with diagonal insertions, use short-row knitting to build up the

89. FLAPS AND FRINGES.

To work: All flaps & fringe strips are preknitted & stacked on GB. To make 6-ST wide flaps & 3-ST wide fringe, chain C/O & weave yarn over & under NDLS to avoid having to finish ends later. K 10 Rs & remove on GB or scrap. To turn flaps over & have K side facing up, remove flaps on GB with ridge side up. Apply flaps & fringe strips directly to P side of fabric every 3/R. (See also the sidebar on pp. 167-168.)

90. CORDED EDGING AND CRISSCROSSES.

To work: Rehang preknitted, 3-ST wide cord horizontally across empty NDLS for desired width of base fabric, eliminating need for special C/O to beg base fabric. Seam edging to vertical edge of base fabric on A/R as fabric is K.

Three-ST, crossed strips of stockinette are K 10 Rs long & S/O. They are attached to K face of base fabric as it is K by removing only 3 base-fabric STS from NDLS with tr tool before rehanging strips, which are manipulated from behind fabric. Base fabric is K for another 8 Rs, & strips are crossed & rehung to complete Xs.

slant, then remove all of the stitches at once with the garter bar or scrap knitting. The edge of the trim is then hung on the needles with the right side facing up, and the fabric is returned to the needles with the wrong, or purl, side facing up (that is, with the right sides of the two pieces facing one another). The next pass of the carriage joins the fabric and trim, placing the insertion on the knit side of the fabric (swatches 91 and 92). If you want the purl side of the fabric to become the right side of the fabric, you would rehang the main fabric with the right side facing up so that the right and wrong sides faced each other.

In order to insert narrow cords (see the sidebar on pp. 167-168), lace, ruffles and commercial lace and trims, work the trims as regular insertions (as explained above) and continue knitting. In order to insert wide, flat bands or trims, you must first bind off the two fabrics together to join them, then remove them from the machine and rehang the other edge of the band before you can continue knitting. Wide insertions are used to connect garment sections (for example, a sweater yoke and body) or to use horizontal effects that were created vertically (for example, horizontally placed cables). For diagonal insertions, once the second edge of the band or trim has been rehung, return the needles to holding position and use short-row knitting to increase and fill in the shape above the insertion.

Vertical joins usually attach only one or two stitches every few rows and can be used to add textural accents to a surface or to seam garment pieces together as they are knitted. In addition to its decorative applications, seam-as-you-knit construction is also a speedy alternative to hand seaming and conventionally finishing a garment. However, it leaves you at a distinct disadvantage if you make a seaming mistake because, in order to correct the problem, you must ravel the second piece back to the point where the two fabrics are incorrectly joined (swatches 93 and 94).

Plain, nondecorative, vertical seaming is usually done by picking up a half-stitch every second row from the edge of the first completed piece of knitting and hanging it on the edge needle of the second piece, as in Swatch 88 on p. 160. Some people prefer working vertical seams with the inner half of the edge stitch; others prefer the tight little nub on the outer half of the stitch. The difference is slight, but a half-stitch is preferable since it makes the seam less bulky and visible than picking up the entire edge stitch. Whatever choice you make, be consistent so that the seam line will be sharp and clean.

91. PLAIN AND CABLED HORIZONTAL INSERTIONS.

92. CORDED INSERTION.
Cord dividing this short-rowed stockinette & reverse-stockinette fabric was rehung on empty NDLS after removing completed 1st section of main fabric on GB. Fabric was then hung on top of cord, & short-row K continued.

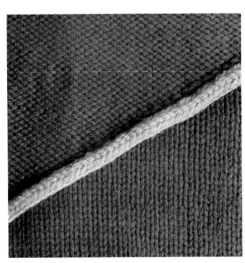

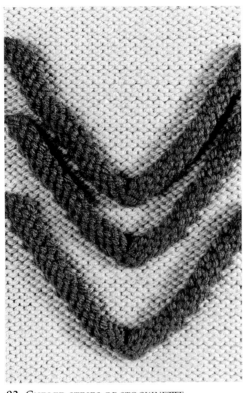

94. INTERLACED CORDING.

Intricate-looking, applied grids are a simple alternative to true cables or tr-ST designs. This design was created by rehanging 4 separate cords (see the sidebar on pp. 167-168) every 2/R, according to chart. (Solid line in chart indicates 1 cord crossing over other without being attached to the base fabric.)

93. CURLED STRIPS OF STOCKINETTE.

The 6-R wide pieces of stockinette were preknitted & S/O. As base fabric was K, a few stitches of strip's S/O edge were rehung every 2/Rs. Because scrap was folded on top of strip as STS were rehung, trim curls upward, covering actual joining STS.

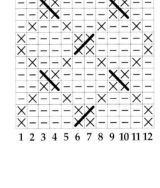

1 2 3 4 5 6 7 8 9 10 11 12

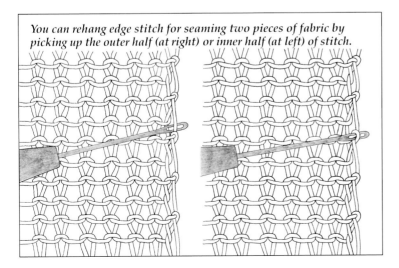

You can rehang edge stitch for seaming two pieces of fabric by picking up the outer half (at right) or inner half (at left) of stitch.

REHANGING EDGE STITCHES.

Joining fabrics with eyelet seams.

To join 2 pieces of fabric with an eyelet seam, you need 1 completed piece worked with eyelets every 4/Rs at edge & removed from KM, and 2nd piece without eyelets still being K on KM.

To work, top right: Begin seam by inserting tr tool through eyelet on 1st piece (at L). Then hook tool onto NDLS to remove 2 edge STS of 2nd piece (at RT).

To work, middle right: Slip eyelet over 2 STS & off prongs of tool so that STS emerge from center of eyelet.

To work, bottom right: Place 2 STS from tr tool back on their NDLS.

As an alternative to joining two pieces of knitting with edge stitches, you could work eyelets or ladders along the edge of one of the two pieces as it's being knitted and then join them with this series of eyelets, as shown in the three photos at left.

The eyelets can be made by manually transferring stitches (one or two stitches in from the edge) and leaving the empty needles in working position to cast on in the next row; or they can be formed automatically if your machine has a lace carriage (swatches 95 and 96). Swatch 97 has ladder joinings where the second stitch from the edge of each main piece has been

95. Vertical eyelet seam.

To work: K 1st piece (black fabric in photo), making an eyelet every 4/R on 2nd NDL from R edge. Remove 1st piece from KM, & K 1st 4 Rs of 2nd piece. With wrong side of 1st piece facing you, insert 2-prong tr tool through 1st eyelet. On same tool, remove 1st 2 STS on L edge of 2nd fabric from NDLS. Lift eyelet over STS, as shown in the three photos at left & replace STS on their NDLS. Rep every 4/R. (Pattern courtesy of Nihon Vogue.)

dropped to form a ladder, and a separate, narrow strip is used between each of these sections to connect them. The ladders do not show in the completed fabric but provide the necessary slack to join the two pieces. This joining can also be worked diagonally, as explained in the caption for Swatch 97.

Eyelet seams can also be used to insert simple shapes like diamonds and triangles. This is done by first knitting the shapes with eyelets along all vertical or diagonal edges. The main fabric will need to be knitted by the short-row method to produce the slanted edges needed to match and join the diamond or triangle.

96. DIAGONAL EYELET SEAM.

Diagonal eyelet seams are worked exactly like vertical eyelet seams, except that the fabrics themselves require some extra attention. Note in chart at right alt methods of dec to slant edge & form eyelets.

To work: Eyelets are formed in 1st (white) piece every 4/R as part of 2-step dec. To work dec, *1st make simple edge dec, then use 2-prong tool to form eyelet & create ff detailing along joining. K 2 Rs. Use 3-prong tool to make regular ff inc. K 2 Rs.* Rep from * to *.

Assuming that L edge of 1st piece is dec, RT edge of 2nd piece must be inc to match it. To work inc, C/O 3 STS & K 4 Rs. Make 1st eyelet joining (as in Swatch 95). Bring 1 NDL into WP next to eyelet joining & K 2 Rs. Inc 1 ST & K 2 Rs. Continue inc 1 ST, A/R &, at same time, making eyelet joinings every 4/R. (Pattern courtesy of Nihon Vogue)

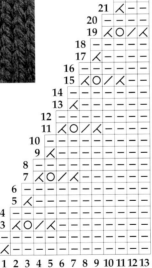

97. VERTICAL LADDER SEAM.

To work: K all main (white) sections same length & drop 2nd ST from each edge before B/O. C/O 5 STS for joining strip. Opposite edges of strip will be attached to 2 main sections at same time, on opposite edges. *K 5 Rs & make eyelet-type seam on side opposite carr by inserting 2-prong tool under 1st 4 bars of ladder. K 1 R & make eyelet seam at other side.* Rep from * to * until both main sections have been joined to entire length of center strip.

To work a diagonal ladder seam: Center strip is joined to 2 adj fabrics, as for vertical ladder above, but triangular shapes must be dec by ff method to drop 2nd ST safely from slanted edge to form ladder (see Swatch 96 caption for more dec information). C/O enough STS for widest part of piece & dec 1 ST, A/R, using 3-prong tool. Drop 2nd ST from edge before B/O. K 2nd triangle exactly same & turn it upside down when joining to center strip.

WORKING TWISTED INSERTION.

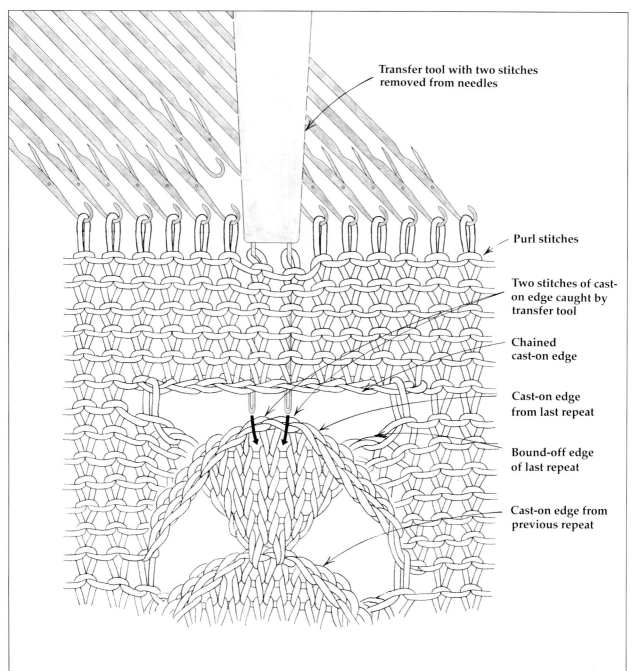

Transfer tool with two stitches removed from needles

Purl stitches

Two stitches of cast-on edge caught by transfer tool

Chained cast-on edge

Cast-on edge from last repeat

Bound-off edge of last repeat

Cast-on edge from previous repeat

1. Remove center two stitches from needles on transfer tool.

2. Tip tool down behind last section knitted to catch center two stitches of previous cast-on edge, twisting section so cast-on edge is above bind-off edge.

3. Tip tool toward needle bed and rotate it upward to replace stitches removed in steps 1 and 2 on needles. Bind off central group of stitches to complete repeat.

In the insertion shown in Swatch 98 the open work was created by binding off, casting on and rehanging specific stitches from one section with the next. This insertion could be rehung either horizontally or vertically.

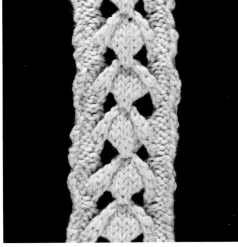

98. TWISTED INSERTION.

To work: C/O 16 STS & K 6 Rs, ending with COR. Set carr to hold NDLS in HP.

To work B/O R for this & all reps, put all NDLS into HP except 3 NDLS on carr side. K 1 R to L, place NDLS just K into HP & ret carr to RT side. Place center 10 NDLS in UWP & set carr for largest SS. K 1 R to L, place these center NDLS into HP & ret carr to RT side. Reset carr for original SS & K last 3 NDLS by placing them in UWP. B/O center 10 STS by chain/crochet method, working from RT to L & placing last ST on 3rd NDL from L edge.

Place 3 NDLS at left in UWP and K 1 R to right. With free yarn, *chain C/O 10 empty NDLS in center, using HP to interrupt carr for next R. Set carr to K all NDLS & K 6 Rs. Use 2-prong tool to remove & hold center 2 STS. Tip tool down behind 6 Rs just K & in front of Rs previously K to P/U center 2 STS of C/O edge of previous section (turn edge upward to connect with tool). Rehang both pairs of STS from tool, & K next B/O row. * Rep from * to *. (Pattern courtesy of Nihon Vogue.)

Most of us remember knitting yards of tubular cords on spool knitters as children — and then trying to think of ways to use the cords. These cords make great additions to knitted garments either knitted on or laced through the piece, and they're much faster to produce on a knitting machine than on the old wooden spool with nails.

Although the cords are circular, they're knitted on a single-bed machine. To work a narrow cord, simply cast on three stitches and set your carriage to knit in one direction and slip (free pass) in the other. Using a stitch size or two smaller than you would for stockinette, knit a few rows and hang a weight on the knitting. The knit stitches will absorb the slack left by the short float when the carriage slips every other row, and the gap will close entirely (see Swatch 99 on p. 168). With this method, you can knit cords up to about six needles wide. With wider cords, you'll find the slip-gap doesn't always close. You can, of course, latch up the floats, or use the wider cords (which tend to be flatter) as insertions, with the gap facing inside the garment. If you knit cords longer than needed and begin hanging them from the cast-on end, you can always ravel any excess at the other end.

There's no end to the variation you can add to the basic cords. In addition to changing the number of needles you use to knit a cord, you can hold some stitches and allow others to continue knitting in order to add appendages and tucked textures. Within the body of the cord, you can work cables, twist stitches and add beads. If you create ladders in a cord, they provide ease and at the same time open effects, which can be left as they are or manipulated by twisting, lifting and reforming.

Equally endless are the uses for cords. They can serve as cast-on substitutes,

Cords and Curled Stockinette

edge bindings (see Swatch 90 on p. 161), neckline edgings and ties, button loops, and weaving yarns. You can use them to lace garment sections together or create mock cable effects (see p. 229). You can employ them to enhance appliqués and pattern stitches, divide textures or accent seams. And you can braid, twist, weave or drape them across a fabric.

You'll also find that narrow strips of flat stockinette (three stitches wide) tend to curl tightly enough to be used in most of the same ways. Although they're not quite so rounded as tubular cords, they're lots faster to produce when you need quantities of cording. Wider pieces of stockinette will curl somewhat, but can be used for flaps and other flat applications; (In Swatch 89 on p. 161, the curling is less noticeable as the pieces get larger.) If you have a double-bed machine, you might also try knitting some wide tubes for braiding, stuffing or attaching to surfaces where you want more weight or edge definition.

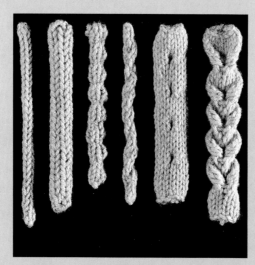

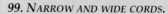

99. NARROW AND WIDE CORDS.

All cords were K with carr set to K from RT to L & slip from L to RT.

To work samples (numbered from L to RT):
1. Make a basic 3-NDL cord.
2. Make a basic 6-NDL cord.
3. For 3-NDL scalloped cord, K basic 3-NDL cord, lifting slip floats every 5/R onto 3rd NDL.
4. For 3-NDL corkscrew cord, C/O 1st 3 NDLS on L end of bed. K basic 3-NDL cord, every 4/R removing 1st & 2nd STS on L from their NDLS & placing them on next 2 empty NDLS to RT. When you come to RT end of bed, remove all 3 STS on tr tool & move them to extreme L of bed to continue.
5. For 9-NDL buttonhole cord, chain C/O 9 NDLS & K for basic cord. Every 6/R (for example), latch up slip floats & hang on center NDL. K 1 R. Move center ST to adj NDL; leave empty NDL in WP to C/O & form eyelet. Rep, spacing buttonholes as desired. For plain cardigan band, leave out buttonholes, but latch up slip floats.
6. For 9-NDL inside-out cord, K as for buttonhole band, spacing buttonholes every 6/R for desired length. Pull B/O end of band entirely through last buttonhole from back to front, then through each buttonhole in turn.

KNITTING SINGLE-BED CORDS.

Narrow cords are worked on 3 STS, K in 1 direction & slipping in other. In photo, carr has just K from L to RT. Note float from preceding slip R & how earlier floats have disappeared into adj STS.

Swatch 100 illustrates elaborate combinations of holding and rehanging stitches. Although fairly slow to produce, fabrics like this are not especially difficult to work. And in my opinion, the results are dramatic enough to justify the effort.

Other uses for rehanging

Rehanging can also be used to reverse the face of a fabric on the machine, place lots of texture on the fabric's knit side, alter its width and pleat or gather it. Reversing the face of a fabric involves using the garter bar, scrap knitting or a stitch holder to remove live stitches from the machine and turn the knitting over before rehanging the stitches. (The one stitch holder that does not allow you to turn the fabric over before rehanging is a multipronged holder, whose prongs have no grooves.) By reversing the face of the fabric, you can create garter-stitch ridges, or alternate stockinette and reverse stockinette effects (see also pp. 42-43).

The garter bar is also the most efficient tool for placing lots of texture on the knit side of a fabric. It enables you to remove all the stitches in order to gain quick access to an empty bed to wrap and embellish the needle shafts before returning the stitches to the needles. Stitch holders are useful for narrow pieces, but they are limited by their width. Garter bars, on the other hand, can accommodate all needles on the bed at once.

The garter bar is certainly the easiest tool to use to alter the width of a piece of knitting and to pleat or gather it. The width of a fabric is changed by increasing or decreasing at regular intervals across it, rather than at its edges. Pleats are formed by folding the fabric back on itself (like the

100. FISH SCALES.

To work: Use small stitch holder to empty groups of NDLS while each scale is K & rem NDLS are placed in HP. Bridges between scales should be 2 or 3 NDLS wide.

COR & set to hold NDLS in HP. Do not wrap. Bridge NDLS on RT are in WP. *Remove next 5 STS to holder & place these NDLS in NWP. All NDLS to L of these 5 are in HP. COR. K 1 R across bridge, then place NDLS for bridge in HP. COL. Bring 5 empty NDLS to WP & E-wrap them from RT to L, leave these 5 NDLS in UWP to K. K 1 R to RT.

Place 1st & 2nd NDLS at L of group of 5 in HP. K 1 R to L. Place 4th & 5th NDLS of group into HP. Ret 2nd NDL to UWP, & K 1 R to RT. Move 4th NDL to UWP, & K 1 R to L. Move 1st NDL to UWP, & K to RT. Move 5th NDL & NDLS for next bridge into UWP, & K 1 R to L. Ret 5 STS from holder & place the 5 NDLS & those for bridge at L just K, into UWP.* Rep from * to *, staggering placement from 1 row of scales to next. In example, only 1 R was K back to RT between Rs of scales. More Rs can be K plain between reps, as desired. Odd numbers of Rs let you work all scales from R to L; even numbers of Rs force you to work alt reps from L to RT. Scales curl but will lie flat when steamed.

STITCHES ARRANGED ON PRONGS OF STITCH HOLDER FOR BOX PLEATING.

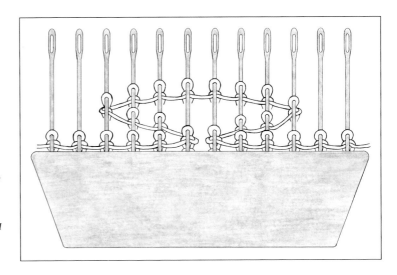

101. CABLED YOKE SECTION.

To work: P STS highlighting cables are latched up, rather than K on RB since GB cannot be used with DB work. All dec are made in spaces between cables &, because direction of dec slant is important, dec are made before fabric is removed on GB. Then, as STS are ret to NDLS, they are moved in to fill empty spaces. Cables are crossed every 8/R, & dec are made every alt 8/R to avoid having to move crossed STS.

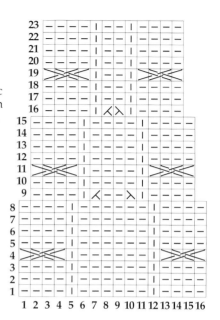

102. FAIR ISLE YOKE SECTION.

All decreases are made in 2 plain Rs separating each band of pat. Because dec itself does not contribute to pat, STS are doubled when replaced on NDLS.

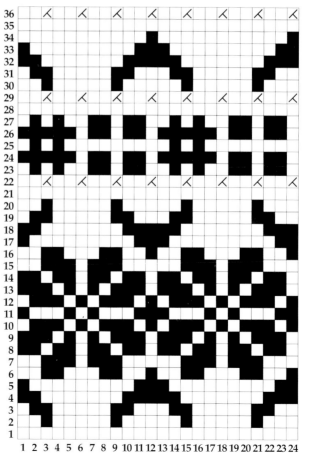

letter Z) as it is rehung, so that three stitches are replaced on each needle forming the pleat. Gathers are made by working many adjacent decreases, doubling or tripling stitches.

Increasing, decreasing, pleating and gathering all rely on doubling stitches as they are rehung, which means that the entire fabric has to be removed from the machine and rehung to fill the resulting empty needles. The cabled and Fair Isle yokes in swatches 101 and 102 were both decreased in width as they were worked. The decreases in the cabled yoke are easier to see than those in the Fair Isle swatch, where they are hidden in the plain rows between pattern borders (see the sidebar on pp. 172-173).

Interior decreasing is much more common than interior increasing, pleating or gathering, but all these techniques are useful for managing extra stitches (Swatch 103). These effects are created as part of the base fabric by interrupting the knitting, then removing and rehanging the fabric before continuing. The two examples at the top of the photo illustrate "tulips" produced by interior decreasing. The bottom example was shaped by short-row knitting and, like the second example, was rehung to reduce the lower edge.

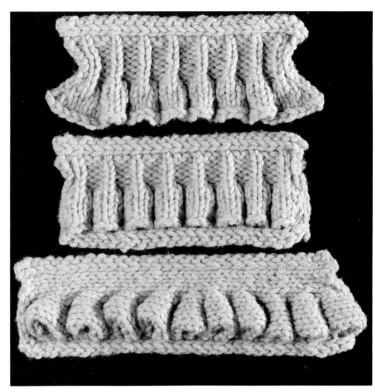

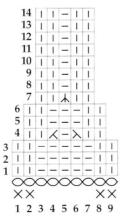

TULIP BORDER AND INSERTION.

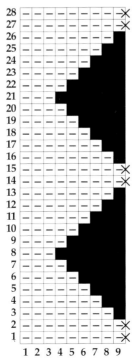

SEASHELL INSERTION.

103. TULIP BORDER AND INSERTIONS.

To work tulip border (top): Chain C/O multiple of 7 STS plus 2 to balance ends & K 3 Rs. Reform 1st 2 STS and then every 6th & 7th ST. Make dec as shown on chart (R 4) & use GB to remove & rehang fabric. (Note on chart, X indicates STS to rehang later to define lower edge of insertion at center, below tulip.) K 3 Rs, & reform same STS. Make dec as shown on chart (R 7); remove & rehang with GB. Continue K for desired length, latching up same STS. Each pat rep reduces from 7 to 3 STS. Before B/O, work 1 R of crochet across NDLS from behind fabric; then work chain B/O.

To work tulip insertion (center): Lower edge of above border was rehung to pleat & form tulip shapes that stand out from background fabric. For insertion, before rehanging lower edge, work 1 R of crochet across NDLS, allowing 3 NDLS for each tulip so border conforms to overall width of fabric. Rehang only latched-up STS (marked X), skipping every 3rd NDL.

To work seashell insertion (bottom): Work short-rowed gores on a narrow strip. Gores are redefined when completed strip is turned & rehung sideways, P/U only edges of straight Rs between gores. (On chart, X shows STS to be rehung between gores on Rs 1, 2, 14, 15, etc.)

Increasing and Decreasing with a Garter Bar

In order to space decreases or increases evenly across the width of a fabric, you have to remove the stitches from the needles and then shift them all toward or away from each other to accommodate the decreases or increases. If you tried to use a regular transfer tool, you would be able to move only a few stitches at a time. With a garter bar, you can move an entire row of stitches at once.

The first step in increasing and decreasing with a garter bar is to remove all the stitches on the bar. To do this, bring the needles to holding position, making sure the stitches are behind the latches and that all of the latches are open so that you will be able to hook the bar onto the needles. Run your finger under all of the needle shafts to make sure each one has been caught by a prong of the tool. The needles that have not been caught will pop up and identify themselves.

It's a good idea always to hook the bar onto the needles with the ridged side up. It is crucial to use the tool this way when you plan on turning the fabric over to knit garter stitch. In this case, the grooves in the prongs will enable you to return the reversed stitches to the needles (see also pp. 77-79).

Then, starting at one end of the bed, pull the fabric toward you so that the stitches slide over the latches, off the needles and onto the prongs of the tool. Continue across in the same direction. If you work from side to side, you are certain to split some of the stitches in the hooks of the needles. You will then have to use a transfer tool or crochet hook to lift the stitches onto the prongs of the garter bar, thereby adding another step to the process and slowing things down. When all the stitches have been moved to the garter bar, remove the garter bar from the needles, leaving them in holding position with their latches open.

In order to decrease, for example, every fourth stitch, hang the bar onto the needle hooks and, with your index finger, nudge the first three stitches at the left onto the needles, keeping the other stitches back at the neck of the prongs. Lift the tool just enough to release it from the hooks of the needles and move it one needle to the left. Rehang the tool so that the third needle of the last group becomes the first needle of the next and holds two stitches. When all of the stitches have been rehung, every third needle will hold two stitches, and you'll have to push empty, unused needles back to nonworking position. All of the decreases will slant in the same direction, in this case, from right to left.

When the decreases will show as part of the design (for example, as in Swatch 101 on p. 170) and the direction of the slant changes from one decrease to the next, you need to make the decreases first, using a transfer tool, and then remove all the stitches on the garter bar. Some of the prongs will hold doubled stitches and some will be empty, but you will not need to make any further overlaps when replacing the stitches on the machine. You will still have to shift the tool, however, to fill in the gaps left by the empty needles. If you don't mind handling doubled stitches, you may even prefer using this method for all garter-bar decreasing.

To increase with the garter bar, for example, every third stitch, hang the bar onto the hooks of the needles and manually nudge the first three stitches at the left onto the needles, keeping all other stitches back at the neck of the prongs. Lift the tool just enough to release it from the needles and move it to the right, skipping the fourth needle entirely. Now rehang the tool so that the next three stitches will be nudged onto the fifth, sixth and seventh needles. When all of the stitches have been rehung, every fourth needle will be empty. To prevent forming holes, pick up the purl bars from the adjacent stitches and hang them on the empty needles.

You will always need to figure the spacing of increases and decreases before working them. Because it's easiest to work with the fabric centered on the bed, try to eliminate or add needles evenly at both edges of the fabric before rehanging the bar.

To figure spacing for decreases, begin by subtracting the number of stitches you want to end up with (for example, 80) from the number you now have (for example, 100) to find out how many decreases to make (20). Then divide to find out how often to make the decreases: 100 ÷ 20 = 5. That is, every fifth stitch should be doubled.

To figure spacing for increases, subtract the number of stitches you have (for example, 40) from the number you want to end up with (for example, 50) to determine how many stitches you need to increase (10). Then divide: 40 ÷ 10 = 4. That is, you need to increase one stitch after every fourth stitch.

The numbers do not always work out as evenly as in these examples, but you can usually take care of any discrepancies near the edges of the row by adding or eliminating an extra increase or decrease. Most knitters split the very first group so they don't end up with an increase or decrease at the very edge of the row. In other words, instead of placing a decrease after the first four stitches on the left and ending up with one decrease on the last needle on the right, make the first decrease after the second stitch from the left edge. You'll then end up with two plain stitches following the last decrease on the right.

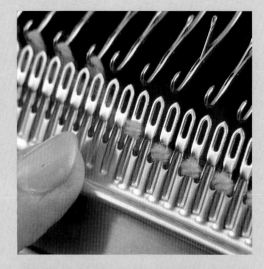

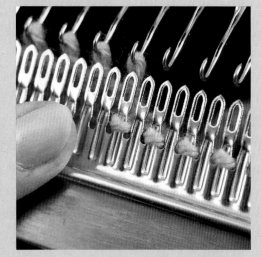

INCREASING AND DECREASING WITH THE GARTER BAR.

Top left: In order to inc, GB is shifted 2 NDLS to RT, so that leftmost ST on GB is deposited on 2nd empty NDL to RT of working NDLS. Empty NDL will be filled by picking up P bar from adj ST.

Bottom left: In order to dec, GB is shifted 1 NDL (in this case) to L, and leftmost ST on GB will be deposited on 1st NDL holding a ST. That NDL then holds 2 STS, thus decreasing 1 ST.

Chapter 7

Transferred Stitches

As their name suggests, transferred stitches are stitches that are moved from one set of needles to another. A single stitch or many stitches can be transferred in the same move, either at the edge or within the body of a fabric. These stitches can be transferred to adjacent or nonadjacent needles on the same bed, or, if double beds are being used, from one bed to the other. The needles to which the stitches are transferred can be empty or already filled with one or more stitches.

Lateral transfers (stitches moved to adjacent or nonadjacent needles on the same bed) are commonly used for increasing or decreasing and thus shaping the edge of a fabric or garment section. These transfers are also the basis for a variety of lace eyelet designs. Crossed transfers (stitches moved to nonadjacent needles on the same bed without moving any stitches in between) are decorative transfers that pucker and gather the fabric. And cross-bed transfers (stitches moved from one bed to the other) change the structure of a fabric by producing either full-fledged double-knits or a combination of double-knits and single-knits, which often yields a simple knit-purl stitch pattern. Regardless of whether the transfer is made at the edge or in the middle of a fabric, transferred stitches are live stitches taken from the row currently in the needle hooks, rather than completed stitches lifted from earlier rows.

When a single stitch is transferred to an adjacent needle, there are two possible effects, depending on where the stitch is located in the fabric. When a stitch at the edge of a fabric is transferred to its adjacent needle, the two stitches knit together with the next pass of the carriage, and the fabric is narrowed, or decreased, by one stitch. When a stitch elsewhere in the fabric is transferred to an adjacent needle, the fabric's width remains the same. And if the empty needle produced by the transfer remains in working position, it will cast back on with the next pass of the carriage, forming an eyelet on that row and knitting regular stitches on all following rows. If that empty needle is returned to nonworking position, a ladder will form. It's possible to prevent eyelets and ladders from forming by picking up the purl bar from an adjacent stitch (or, if you're working on double beds, from an opposite stitch) in order to fill the empty needle before it knits again, as shown in the drawing at the bottom of p. 176. For lack of another name, I call the patterns produced by this motion "closed-eyelet" patterns.

Reading charted transfer patterns

TRANSFER SYMBOLS (SEE ALSO PP. 26-29).

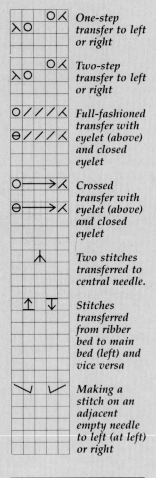

One-step transfer to left or right

Two-step transfer to left or right

Full-fashioned transfer with eyelet (above) and closed eyelet

Crossed transfer with eyelet (above) and closed eyelet

Two stitches transferred to central needle.

Stitches transferred from ribber bed to main bed (left) and vice versa

Making a stitch on an adjacent empty needle to left (at left) or right

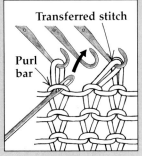

Transferred stitch

Purl bar

FORMING A CLOSED EYELET BY PICKING UP PURL BAR OF ADJACENT STITCH TO PREVENT EYELET FROM FORMING ON EMPTY NEEDLE.

Although some transfers can be explained clearly with words, diagrams and charts are extremely important when knitting transfer patterns because there is so much information involved. A single diagram can indicate exactly which stitches to move, where to move them, the total number of stitches and needles in a repeat, whether an eyelet is formed or closed (see the drawing below), which stitch shows on the face of the fabric and how many plain rows to knit between transfers. The text for a particular pattern usually provides any additional information to clarify the charts and diagrams. For example, if it's important for a particular stitch to lie on the face of the fabric, it may take verbal directions to indicate which stitch to placed on the needle first.

Pay attention to row numbers when reading charts and when knitting because most lace patterns call for transfers only on alternate rows, and very often the charts do not show the plain rows in between. And, as with all machine-knitting charts, be sure to perform the operation indicated before knitting the row. That is, if a transfer is shown on the chart for Row 2, make the transfer after knitting Row 1 and then knit Row 2.

The transfer process

On a single-bed machine, transfers are generally done by using an eyelet transfer tool to remove the stitch from one needle and place it on another. All knitting-machine manuals describe this transfer process as a basic decrease. You can also work single-bed transfers with a transfer tool that handles multiple stitches or one that has prongs arranged for every other needle. In some cases, you can also use a garter bar to make several decreases at once or to manage a fancy decrease like that in Swatch 117 on p. 188.

Whichever tool you use, it's important to hold it perfectly straight when catching it on the needle hook, as if it is an extension of the needle, in order to prevent dropping or splitting stitches. Use one hand to hold the fabric taut against the bed and let the other manipulate the tool as you pull the needle forward. This movement causes the stitch to open the latch and slide over it onto the shaft of the needle. Then, as the tool guides the needle back in its slot, the stitch closes and slides over the latch, onto the shaft of the transfer tool. As you move the tool over to the new needle on which you want to place the stitch, hold the tool vertically so that the stitch stays near the base of the prong, where it is less likely to drop off. Then hook the eye of the tool onto the needle and pivot the tool (as if it were hinged to the needle) so the stitch slides down its shaft and into the needle hook. Do not lift the tool away from the needle until you're sure the stitch has been caught by the needle, and avoid lifting the fabric where it can catch on the sinker posts or adjacent needles.

When using multiple transfer tools to move several stitches at once, you'll find that not all the stitches slide off the tool and into the needle hooks at the same time. Thus you'll drop stitches if you remove the tool too quickly. If you do not have a single tool wide enough to handle a particular transfer, you can pair two smaller tools, holding them side by side to span more needles, or you can make the transfer in several steps.

For double-bed transfers, a number of tools can be used. The simplest and most common is the bodkin, a straight metal shaft with an eyelet at each end. After removing a stitch with one end of the tool, the bodkin tilts so that the stitch slides to the other end and can be replaced on the opposite bed.

You can also use a pair of transfer tools to move stitches from one bed to the other. Do this by removing the stitches with one tool and then holding this tool horizontally and stretching the stitches upward enough to insert a second tool from the opposite direction. The second tool should be inserted so that the eyes of the two tools face each other (see p. 89 for photos showing this method up to the point at which the first tool is pulled away). Pull away the first tool, and use the second to replace the stitches on the opposite bed. Once you get the knack of this, you can easily transfer groups of stitches with a pair of multi-eyelet tools. This is one reason I always buy transfer tools in pairs whenever I find a new one with an unusual number or arrangement of prongs. The "shadow lace" tool, available for Singer and Studio standard-gauge machines, is a hinged version of a pair of transfer tools.

When I need to transfer stitches that are particularly tight or difficult to see, I use the bodkin because it's the easiest (if not the fastest) tool to work with in this case. Otherwise I use one single-prong transfer tool. To work the transfer with one single-prong tool, remove the stitch with the tool and hold it horizontally above the needle

bed with enough upward tension to keep the stitch stretched open. With your free hand, push the needle on the opposite bed forward so that it passes through the extended stitch, and then remove the tool to deposit the stitch on the needle. Because the eye of the single-prong tool points away from the hook of the receiving needle, you won't make eye-to-hook contact.

To speed things up with the single-prong tool, I usually push out to holding position all the needles holding stitches to be transferred. That way I only have to push these needles back with the tool as I slip the opposite needle through the stitch. You can use a multi-prong tool to transfer several stitches at once. Toyota makes a 15-stitch, standard-gauge transfer tool with bent prongs that reduce the probability of dropping stitches, making it easier to handle a group of stitches by this method.

PAIRING TRANSFER TOOLS TO MOVE STITCHES FROM ONE BED TO OTHER.

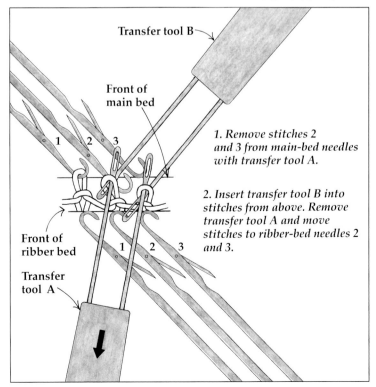

Transfer tool B

Front of main bed

1 2 3

Front of ribber bed

Transfer tool A

1. Remove stitches 2 and 3 from main-bed needles with transfer tool A.

2. Insert transfer tool B into stitches from above. Remove transfer tool A and move stitches to ribber-bed needles 2 and 3.

1 2 3

In addition to the manual transfer tools, automatic transfer carriages are also available for some machines. For single-bed lace and closed-eyelet patterns, there's an automatic lace carriage for Japanese standard-gauge knitting machines, which automatically transfers stitches to adjacent needles and also enables you to combine lace with various other hand-manipulated techniques.

One unique feature of the Brother and Knitking lace carriages is their ability to make what amounts to a "half-transfer" in order to knit fine lace. In a half-transfer, the carriage transfers a given stitch to an adjacent needle without removing it from its original needle. The stitch is thus spread over two adjacent needles, preventing an eyelet from forming since neither needle is ever empty. Instead, the stitch opens slightly as it spans both needles, creating a subtle, lacy pattern. Transfers of this type would produce more modest lace designs on a chunky machine, on which the eyelets tend to be very open.

Some lace-transfer maneuvers, however, like crossed transfers and the final step of all closed-eyelet stitches, are too involved to be produced by a lace carriage and still must be worked by hand. Similarly, since no bulky-gauge machines have lace carriages, hand transfer remains the only method for producing all chunky-gauge lace and transfer patterns. Thus the half-transfers necessary for fine laces would be no more difficult to manage than any other transfer.

If you own a standard-gauge machine, you might want to use what's called a rib-transfer carriage for occasional cross-bed transfers. However, all rib-transfer carriages are somewhat limited, and they're seldom practical for elaborate cross-bed transfer patterns. Also, while they're fast and automatic, not all of them can be used on both beds. Perhaps most important, except for the fully selective Passap transfer carriage, these carriages usually remove all of the stitches from one bed and place them on the other. In deciding whether to use one for a particular project, consider the kind of yarn you're using, the distribution of weights, and whether you're using holding position or any other patterning that may interfere with the function of the transfer carriage. More important, can your carriage transfer specific stitches, or must it transfer every stitch on the bed? Finally, does it transfer from either bed to the other, or only from the ribber to the main bed?

Whether you're working with a bodkin or a sophisticated transfer carriage, stitches are easiest to manipulate when the fabric is properly weighted. If there is not enough weight, the stitches tend to split when they pass over the needle latches. If there is too much weight, the stitches are tight, difficult to handle and run quickly when dropped.

Single-bed transfers

Any stitch transferred on a single bed is referred to as a lateral transfer. A single-stitch, adjacent transfer is called a basic transfer. And a single-stitch, nonadjacent transfer in which no intervening stitches are moved is called a crossed transfer.

Single-stitch transfers are used to decrease stitches, shape edges and create eyelets for simple lace designs and small buttonholes within a fabric. Basic transfers are also used to move several stitches to a single needle for patterning, to reposition stitches to alter the shape or width of a ladder, and to fashion simple flowers (swatches 104, 105, 106, 107 and 108).

Decreasing the edge of a garment section with a single decrease can be done in one of two ways, the first producing an irregular edge and the second creating a consistent edge. By simply transferring the first stitch onto the second needle, the edge stitch of the fabric changes with every decrease, producing an irregular

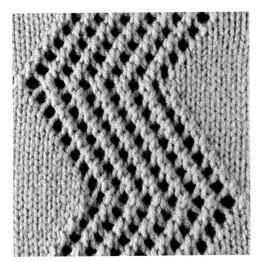

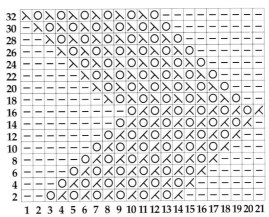

Chart 104 (rows read bottom to top, columns 1–21):

	1	2	3	4	5	6	7	8	9	10	11	12	13	14	15	16	17	18	19	20	21
32	\	O	\	O	\	O	\	O	\	O	\	O	–	–	–	–	–	–	–	–	–
30	–	\	O	\	O	\	O	\	O	\	O	\	O	–	–	–	–	–	–	–	–
28	–	–	\	O	\	O	\	O	\	O	\	O	\	O	–	–	–	–	–	–	–
26	–	–	–	\	O	\	O	\	O	\	O	\	O	\	O	–	–	–	–	–	–
24	–	–	–	–	\	O	\	O	\	O	\	O	\	O	\	O	–	–	–	–	–
22	–	–	–	–	–	\	O	\	O	\	O	\	O	\	O	\	O	–	–	–	–
20	–	–	–	–	–	–	\	O	\	O	\	O	\	O	\	O	\	O	–	–	–
18	–	–	–	–	–	–	–	\	O	\	O	\	O	\	O	\	O	\	O	–	–
16	–	–	–	–	–	–	–	–	O	/	O	/	O	/	O	/	O	/	O	/	
14	–	–	–	–	–	–	–	O	/	O	/	O	/	O	/	O	/	O	/	–	
12	–	–	–	–	–	–	O	/	O	/	O	/	O	/	O	/	O	/	–	–	
10	–	–	–	–	–	O	/	O	/	O	/	O	/	O	/	O	/	–	–	–	
8	–	–	–	–	O	/	O	/	O	/	O	/	O	/	O	/	–	–	–	–	
6	–	–	–	O	/	O	/	O	/	O	/	O	/	O	/	–	–	–	–	–	
4	–	–	O	/	O	/	O	/	O	/	O	/	O	/	–	–	–	–	–	–	
2	–	O	/	O	/	O	/	O	/	O	/	O	/	–	–	–	–	–	–	–	

104. ZIGZAG LACE.

Same group of 6 STS was moved EOR, 8 times to RT, then 8 times to L, to form this zigzag pat of eyelets. Mesh designs of this type are fastest to K when trs are made with a multiple-tr tool, so that all trs in each R can be made in 1 motion.

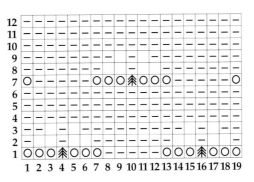

Chart 105 (rows read bottom to top, columns 1–19):

	1	2	3	4	5	6	7	8	9	10	11	12	13	14	15	16	17	18	19
12	–	–	–	–	–	–	–	–	–	–	–	–	–	–	–	–	–	–	–
11	–	–	–	–	–	–	–	–	–	–	–	–	–	–	–	–	–	–	–
10	–	–	–	–	–	–	–	–	–	–	–	–	–	–	–	–	–	–	–
9	–	–	–	–	–	–	–	–	–	–	–	–	–	–	–	–	–	–	–
8	–	–	–	–	–	–	–	–	–	–	–	–	–	–	–	–	–	–	–
7	O	–	–	–	–	–	O	O	O	⋀	O	O	O	–	–	–	–	–	O
6	–	–	–	–	–	–	–	–	–	–	–	–	–	–	–	–	–	–	–
5	–	–	–	–	–	–	–	–	–	–	–	–	–	–	–	–	–	–	–
4	–	–	–	–	–	–	–	–	–	–	–	–	–	–	–	–	–	–	–
3	–	–	–	–	–	–	–	–	–	–	–	–	–	–	–	–	–	–	–
2	–	–	–	–	–	–	–	–	–	–	–	–	–	–	–	–	–	–	–
1	O	O	O	⋀	O	O	O	–	–	–	–	–	O	O	O	⋀	O	O	O

105. PEACOCK TAILS.

Decreasing 6 STS to a central NDL all at once makes this lace pattern particularly dimensional.

To work: Be sure to bring center NDL to HP after all STS are tr. Let carr K it back on next R. K slowly because center NDL tends to float forward. Empty NDLS are brought back to WP before alt R is K, until all NDLS are working. They C/O automatically & resume K, shaping & narrowing ladders that create openings in fabric.

106. DIAMOND LADDERS.

Half the STS are stationary, while other half zigzag RT & L, forming pat in ladders. Alone, this fabric would be unstable, & ladders would shift & lose definition as fabric is handled, washed & worn. But by pulling STS through STS (as shown on every 8/R of chart) or crossing a cable, wrapping, weaving or twisting STS tog before reversing the traveling STS, ladders can be secured. To make STS to be pulled through other STS easier to manage, inc SS of entire R.

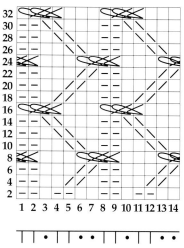

NEEDLE DIAGRAM.

107. GATHERED FLOWER.

To work: C/O a multiple of 5 STS (example has 40 STS), using EON C/O method so edge can be gathered later. Immediately put all NDLS except 1st 5 on carr side into HP. *K 5 Rs, then dec 1 ST each edge. (Return empty NDLS to NWP after all dec.) K 2 Rs, dec 1 ST each edge. K 1 R & tr rem 1 ST to 1st NDL in next group of 5. Place those 5 NDLS in UWP.* Rep from * to * for each group of 5 NDLS until only 1 ST rem on K/M. Pull yarn tail through to secure. Gather C/O edge by tightening beginning yarn tail.

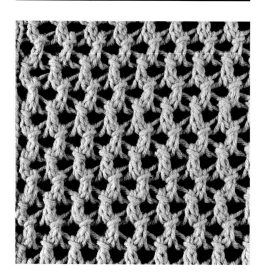

108. OPEN STITCH.

Crocheted effect is worked on 3 STS, transferring 2 adj STS to same NDL.

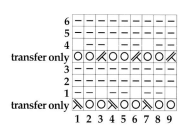

To work: (Note on chart that basic transfer symbol has been modified for this pat.) SS is several numbers larger than for stockinette. *Tr 2nd & 3rd STS to 1st NDL, & manually K them through to form 1 ST. 2nd NDL in WP; 3rd NDL in NWP. K 1 R, & ret 3rd NDL to WP. K 2 Rs. Tr 1st & 2nd STS to 3rd NDL, & K through to form 1 ST. 2nd NDL in WP; 1st NDL in NWP. K 1 R, & ret 1st NDL to WP. K 2 Rs.* Rep from * to *. Note that every 4/R in diagram indicates trs, but does not represent a K R because 1 of empty NDLS must first be ret to WP.

edge and sometimes making smooth seaming difficult. By adding a second step to the decrease process, a consistent edge can be maintained. To produce an even edge, begin by removing the stitch from the second needle from the edge and placing it on top of the edge stitch. Then move the two stitches from the first needle to the second needle and place the empty first needle in nonworking position. This method keeps the same stitch on the face of the fabric and creates a straighter edge for seaming and a sharper line that more clearly defines the edges of complex transfers.

Whenever a stitch is transferred and the emptied needle remains in working position, it casts on a stitch with the next pass of the carriage and creates an eyelet. An eyelet can result when a stitch is transferred to an adjacent or nonadjacent needle. Whenever an eyelet forms, there will be a doubled stitch somewhere in the same row as a result of the transfer. These eyelets are the basis for lace knitting and can also be used for a variety of other embellishments.

When their placement and spacing are carefully planned, a series of eyelets makes a simple casing for elastic or ribbon, a stable opening in a fabric through which to lace cord or strips of fabric for mock cables and decorative seaming (Swatch 109). Eyelets are easy to embellish with embroidery or beading, and they also serve as an interesting variation on seam-as-you-knit construction (see pp. 164-165). Transfer tools that are arranged for every other needle are invaluable for creating rows of eyelets and open-mesh designs like that in Swatch 104 on p. 179.

109. CORDS LACED THROUGH EYELETS.
While cords can be laced right through a K fabric, eyelets make it easier to space cords evenly, without distorting any STS. (Note that dotted arrows on chart indicate yarn traveling behind fabric.)

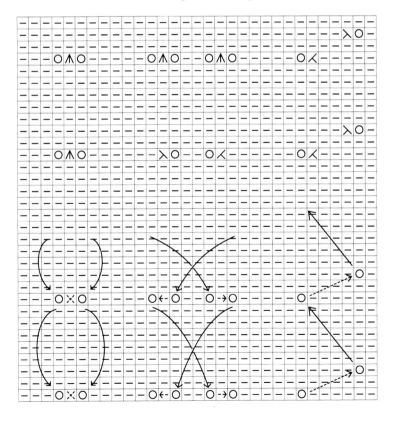

MAKING A CROSSED TRANSFER.

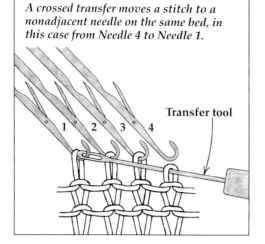

A crossed transfer moves a stitch to a nonadjacent needle on the same bed, in this case from Needle 4 to Needle 1.

Transfer tool

Like basic transfers, crossed transfers produce eyelets if the needles emptied by the transfer remain in working position and cast on with the next pass of the carriage. The lace fabric produced by crossed transfers has a texture that's more raised than that created by basic transfers.

111. REVERSIBLE LACE.

This texture is produced by combining crossed trs & latched-up STS. Both back & front of fabric are interesting.

To work: Pat calls for 6-ST/6-R reps. *K 3 Rs. Drop & latch up 1st & 5th STS in each rep, ret them afterward to 3rd NDL. Empty NDLS rem in WP. K 3 Rs. Drop & latch up 2nd & 4th STS in each rep, & ret them to 6th NDL. Empty NDLS rem in WP.* Rep from * to *. Note that STS on 3rd & 6th NDLS are never latched up or tr.

110. BRAIDED TEXTURES.

Both examples were formed by crossed trs with closed eyelets. The main difference between them is that eyelets in RT pat were filled by P/U P bars of nonadjacent STS (indicated on chart by curved arrows), while eyelets in L pat were filled with adj P bars.

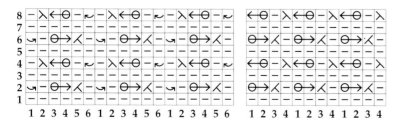

When the eyelets are closed by filling the empty needles, the fabric has a rich, braided texture, compared to the stockinette fabric produced by basic transfers (Swatch 110). Although the knit side of these crossed-transfer patterns is generally the right side, some have interesting purl sides as well (Swatch 111).

I tend to think of these crossed transfers as the horizontal equivalent of lifted stitches (see Chapter 4) because of the puckered textures they produce. However, unlike for lifted-stitch patterns, it may be necessary to enlarge the transfer stitch when it's to cross behind more than three stitches. When two tools are used to cross and move all of the stitches in the group, the process is akin to crossing cables. And if the crossing leaves empty needles, cables and lace are formed simultaneously (see also Chapter 8).

London-based fiber artist Judith Duffy has created a cabled edging that is an exaggerated and very interesting example of a crossed transfer. The deceptively complex-looking effect she produces is often used in her sculptural knits (Swatch 112).

112. JUDITH DUFFY'S CABLED EDGING.

This edging is K on 3-ST strips, which curl & look like cords.

To work: COR. Set car to hold NDLS in HP. Hang entire edge of fabric on NDLS & put all but needles 1, 2 & 3 in HP. *K 12 Rs on these 3 NDLS, ending with COR. Use 3-prong tr tool to remove STS from NDLS 1,2 & 3; pass tool under NDLS 4, 5 & 6 to rehang STS on following group of 3 NDLS (7, 8 & 9). Put 1st 3 NDLS now empty (1, 2 & 3) into NWP. NDLS 4, 5 & 6 are now 1st group on RT. Put these NDLS into UWP, so they K.* Rep from * to *. A short float will be concealed inside spiral. Altenatively, you can manually K NDLS 6, 5 & 4 back to WP to eliminate float as yarn ret to RT edge.

Needles in nonworking position
3 2 1

12 11 10 9 8 7 6 5 4

Needles in holding position

Yarn floats under needles 4, 5 and 6 to carriage.

First three-stitch strip is completed and crossed under needles 4, 5 and 6 and rehung on needles 7, 8 and 9. Needles 4, 5 and 6 are next placed in upper working position to knit next repeat.

Main-fabric stitches

JUDITH DUFFY'S CABLED EDGING.

113. FULL-FASHIONED LACE AND CLOSED-EYELET PATTERNS.

Unless otherwise stated, eyelets in these 2 pats are always closed by filling empty NDLS with P bars of adj STS.

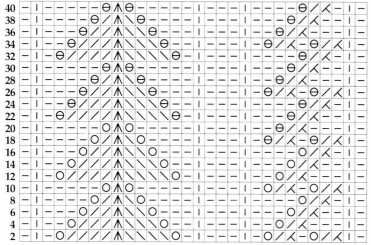

Single-bed, multiple-stitch transfers

Instead of transferring a single stitch on a single bed, you can, of course, transfer two or more stitches on the same bed. Just as when transferring a single stitch, multiple-stitch transfers can be made to adjacent or, less commonly, nonadjacent needles. Multiple-stitch transfers are generally worked either to decrease or increase (and thus shape) the edge of a garment piece and to create elaborate lace designs and biased stitches within a fabric.

If you transfer two or more stitches one needle inward, left or right, you'll produce what is called a full-fashioned transfer. When repeated regularly at the edge of a fabric, this transfer places a constant number of somewhat slanted stitches between the edge of the fabric and the doubled stitch that constitutes the decrease. For most decreasing, a three-prong tool is generally used, with the result that two plain stitches define the edge of the fabric and the third stitch in from the edge disappears behind the fourth stitch in the decrease. Full-fashioned transfers can be worked either by the one-step or two-step method explained in the single-stitch transfer discussion above, producing either an irregular decrease line or one that's sharp and even.

Most knitters are familiar with full-fashioned transfers used at the edges of a fabric for decreasing and increasing, but they are less conversant with the decorative application of these transfers within the body of a fabric. Full-fashioned transfers are, in fact, the basis for some very elaborate allover lace patterns. And if these patterns are worked with the needles emptied by the transfer being filled with adjacent purl bars to prevent eyelets from forming, the resulting fabric has an entirely different pattern of slanted stitches and closed eyelets. In fact, all full-fashioned lace patterns can be interpreted as closed-eyelet patterns (Swatch 113), including those that are knitted with a lace carriage.

Depending on whether the purl bar is picked up from the base of the stitch to the right or left of the empty needle, the closed eyelet creates a ridged effect and makes the edge of the design look a half-stitch wider or narrower. This half-stitch effect cannot be eliminated, but it will not be visually distracting if the purl bar is consistently taken from either the left or right stitch.

When working full-fashioned decreases as part of a design, it's important for the direction of the decreases to be the same as the direction of the slant. That is, if the line slants toward the left, all of the decreases should be made on needles to

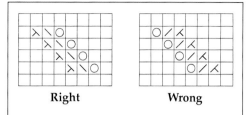

Right   **Wrong**

COORDINATING DIRECTION OF DECREASE AND EYELET SLANT.

Direction of transfers should repeat direction of slanted lines in design. Above, simple line of eyelets slants left, and transfers should likewise be made to left.

One-step, closed-eyelet increase method

ONE-STEP METHOD FOR SIMULTANEOUSLY TRANSFERRING STITCHES AND CLOSING AN EYELET.

The one-step method for making a full-fashioned increase and simultaneously picking up a purl bar to close the eyelet can save lots of time when you have many full-fashioned increases or internal diagonal moves to make. To work this method, you'll need a transfer tool with one more prong than the number of stitches being moved. The extra prong will pick up the purl loop of the first stitch adjacent to the transferred stitches.

Use the tool to remove the stitches to be transferred, allowing one prong to overlap the stitches not being transferred (to left in the drawing). As you push the needles back (for the stitches to slide over their latches and onto the prongs of the tool) the last, empty prong of the tool pushes through and picks up the purl bar of the adjacent stitch. When all the stitches are moved and replaced one needle to the right (for example), the purl bar is also deposited on a needle, closing the eyelet on the next pass of the carriage.

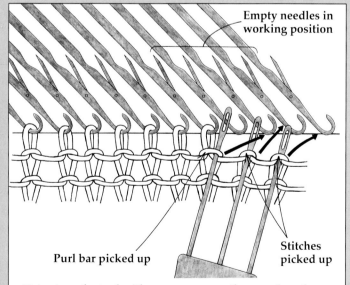

Empty needles in working position

Purl bar picked up

Stitches picked up

Using transfer tool with one more prong than number of stitches being transferred, slip stitches to be transferred onto prongs of transfer tool as needles are pushed in. In same motion, pick up adjacent purl bar on empty prong. Move stitches and pur bar together to designated needles.

the left of the eyelet position. Otherwise, the eyelets tend to pull in the opposite direction of the design and look rough and distorted. This is an important consideration when planning diamonds and other designs in which the direction of the transfers or slanting lines changes as the motif is worked (Swatch 114).

If you work a wide full-fashioned transfer, it's possible to create additional effects within the slightly angled plain-stitch area between the edge of the fabric and the decrease. If you drop one of the plain stitches, it will run at an angle, and if you transfer one of the plain stitches to an adjacent needle and leave the empty

needle in nonworking position, a diagonal ladder will form. These angled stitches can easily be decorated with lace eyelets, cables, popcorns and latch-ups to create decorative raglans (Swatch 115) and V-necklines (Swatch 116).

When you plan cables or other special effects as part of a wide decrease, remember to include enough stitches for any latched-up or plain border stitches and to allow for the fact that you'll lose one stitch to the decrease. For example, a four-stitch cable would require moving a group of at least seven stitches to include a latched-up stitch on each side of the cable and the decreased stitch at the leading

114. *LEAVES.*

Leaves at R were worked against a latched-up P background. Those at L were worked separately & appliquéed to K background. C/O 3 STS to start, inc & dec, as shown on chart.

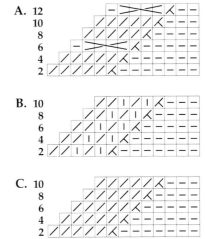

115. *RAGLAN DECREASES.*

In all 3 examples, 6 STS were moved 1 NDL EOR. STS within these edges lie at a distinct angle to fabric.

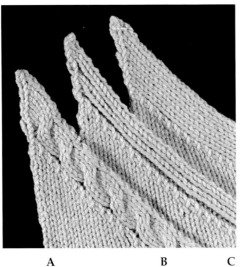

A   B   C

edge of the group. You can also choose between the one-step and two-step decrease methods, but this does not affect the total number of stitches with which you'll work.

Since the frequency of decreasing will probably not coincide with the spacing of the textural requirements, it's a good idea to make a list of the row numbers involved, indicating when to decrease, cross cables, make eyelets and so on. If a row requires both a decrease and a cable crossing, make the decrease first. Never try to transfer crossed stitches.

116. V-NECKLINE.

To work: Follow chart to keep track of dec (4/R) & cable crossings (6/R). Note that some cable crossings coincide with dec, in which case, dec 1st & then cross cable.

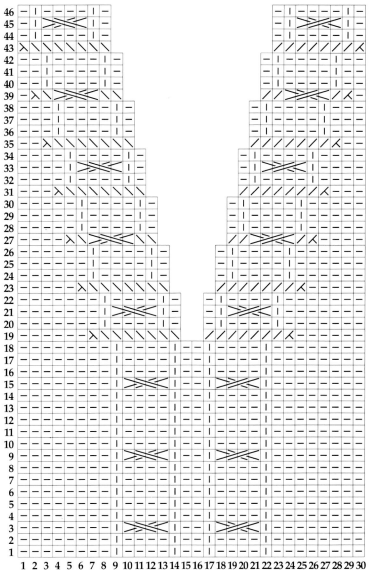

117. FANCY RAGLAN DECREASES.

Example A is a classic dec that can be applied to any pat calling for a 1-ST dec EOR. Example starts with 6-ST dec & works its way to a 2-ST dec, 5 Rs later. Example B is a smaller version of same effect, but instead of dec 1 ST EOR, pat dec 2 STS E 4/R. This dec is faster & more decorative than 1-ST dec & produces a firmer, less stretchy edge.

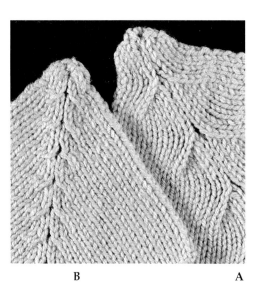

B   A

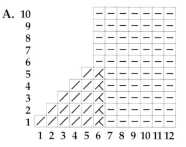

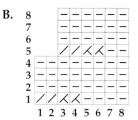

118. DIAGONAL TEXTURES.

Same 6 STS were moved EOR to same NDLS, closing all eyelets. When direction of tr is changed at regular intervals (every 10/R in example), column of STS produces zigzag effect.

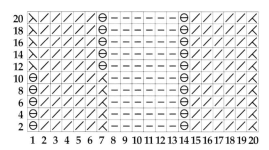

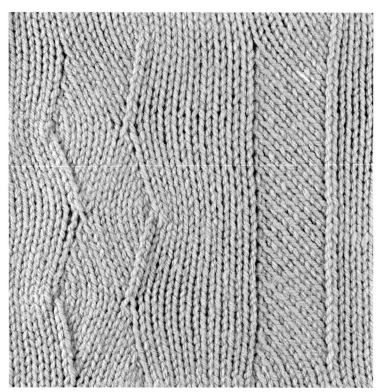

In addition to wide full-fashioned transfers, where consistent groups of stitches are transferred, you can vary the number of stitches moved in each transfer to produce decorative effects (Swatch 117). When these transfers are worked every row instead of on alternate rows, they are balanced out by knitting a number of plain rows between each total repeat sequence.

In addition to being worked at the edge of a fabric, full-fashioned transfers can also be used within the body of a fabric to provide biased stitches for textural contrast or to highlight diagonal cables and V-shaped yokes (swatches 118 and 119. These "diagonal moves" produce a group of stitches that lie at an angle to the base fabric by shifting the same group of stitches by one needle, usually every other row. Unlike decreasing for raglans or V-necks, however, you cannot allow the fabric to become narrower for these effects. Thus, every decrease must be balanced by an increase at the opposite edge of the transfer group. You can work the increase by letting the empty needle cast on and form an eyelet, or you can pick up the purl bar before knitting the next row to close the eyelet (Swatch 120). For electronic machines with full-width patterning capabilities, you can use a lace carriage to make these large-scale diagonal moves. Nonetheless, you'll still have to pick up the purl bars manually if you don't want the diagonal stitches outlined by eyelets on one edge.

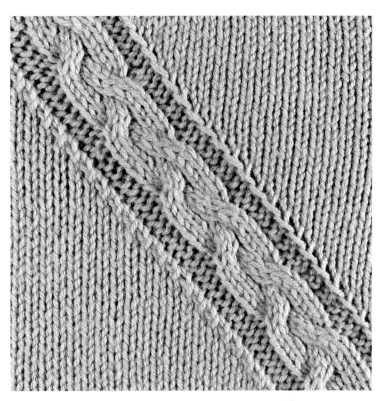

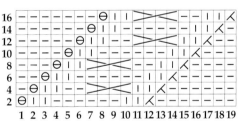

119. DIAGONAL CABLE.

The same 11 STS were tr 1 NDL to RT, EOR. Edge STS were latched up when cable was crossed (braided) every 4/R.

120. DIAGONAL MOVES.

These diagonals were all K by moving a group of 4 STS, EOR. Two-step dec edge (at L) would be wasted on a fuzzy, textured yarn, while eyelet-inc edge (RT) might enhance such a yarn. Center example is basic ff tr with closed eyelets. Pay attention to both yarn & design when deciding how to handle eyelets & dec edges.

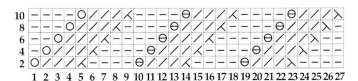

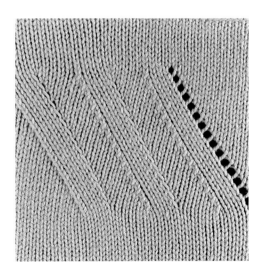

Double-bed transfers

Double-bed knitting makes possible a wider range of transfers than can be worked on a single bed. Double-bed transfers include lateral transfers, or those made on only one of the two beds; cross-bed transfers, those moved from one bed to the other; and combined transfers, involving both stitches transferred laterally and those moved cross-bed.

The fabric produced by double-bed transfers is either double-knit embossed, double-knit "debossed" or single-knit knit-purl. Embossed fabrics are worked with the beds in half-pitch, using all the needles on the main bed and only a few selected needles on the ribber. The main bed usually knits the background stitches, and the ribber works the pattern or motif, which appears as knit stitches embossed on the purl side of the main-bed fabric.

Debossed fabrics are also worked with the beds in half-pitch, using all needles on the main bed and most needles on the ribber bed. The few ribber needles that remain in nonworking position cause the pattern to knit only on the main-bed needles, producing a recessed, single-knit effect in the double-knit background.

Single-knit knit-purl fabrics—like the wide ribs familiar to all machine knitters—are worked with the beds in full pitch, so that working needles on both beds are always opposite nonworking needles. Rather than being embossed onto or recessed into one another, the knit surfaces produced on each bed are positioned side by side.

When the beds are in half-pitch to knit embossed or debossed fabrics, they will never have the same number of needles working, empty or opposite. Instead, one bed will always have one more working needle than the other. The simplest analogy is your hand, which has five fingers, but only four spaces between them. Similarly, if there are five needles working on the main bed, there must be either four or six needles working on the ribber. Because embossed and debossed fabrics tend to be thick, you may want to knit them in lightweight yarns. And when one bed has more needles working than the other, that bed should have a larger stitch size than the other.

Embossed-rib patterns are familiar to many knitters as swing, or racking, patterns in which the ribber bed is shifted one position every given number of rows. While this constitutes a lateral move in relation to the main-bed stitches, all the ribber stitches shift together in the same direction and by the same number of

121. EMBOSSED RIBS.
These pairs of rib STS travel across surface of base fabric by transferring 1 NDL to RT or L on RB, EOR. They cross like cables where they intersect.

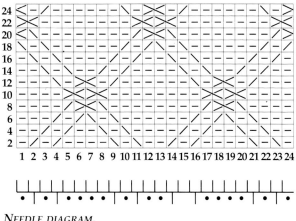

NEEDLE DIAGRAM.

needles to the left or right. This maneuver is a good way to emboss a diagonal cable across the purl surface of a sweater or to produce many parallel, diagonal ribs. By moving stitches manually, instead of shifting the ribber bed, it's possible to deal with individual stitches and groups of stitches without restriction and to

introduce nonparallel ribs and motifs that cross and change direction.

Patterns based on ribs (Swatch 121) are the simplest double-bed embossed motifs to deal with because once the stitches are established on the ribber needles, they usually just continue knitting straight or

Bias knitting

Bias-knit strips make lovely bindings for necklines and armholes, and wide bias bands make effective welts on the lower edge of sweaters that you don't want to rib. Simple edge increases at one end of a row and edge decreases at the other are usually sufficient to work the basic bias strip. However, if you work the edges with full-fashioned methods, you can create a more consistent edge for re-hanging or crocheting. Because of the simultaneous increasing and decreasing, bias knitting is a lot like making diagonal moves, except that there are no stitches on the machine other than the group being moved.

To work bias knitting, begin on the extreme left end of the bed, casting on as many needles as the width of the band requires. *Knit two rows. Increase one stitch on the right edge of the group. Decrease one stitch on the left edge of the group.* Repeat from * to * until you reach the right end of the bed. Remove all the stitches on a transfer tool, garter bar or scrap yarn, and replace them on the left end of the bed to continue knitting.

122. LATTICE RIBS.
All EOR RB trs were worked with pair of 6-pronged, EON tr tools. Where ribs cross, all cables were crossed at same time (see also p. 213).

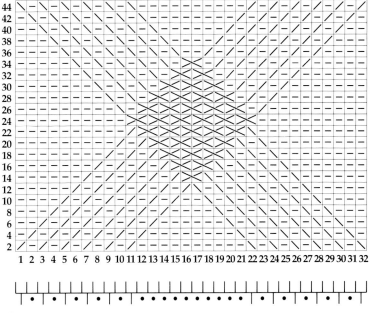

NEEDLE DIAGRAM.

123. EMBOSSED 1x1 RIB DESIGN.

Pat on L of this ff design has closed eyelets but barely differs from pat on RT, whose eyelets were allowed to form. Hence in this type of design, closing eyelets is unnecessary.

To work: All NDLS on MB K, but only EON on RB K, with specific STS tr laterally. Leave empty NDLS in WP after all trs so that NDLS resume K. Use EON tool to make tr.

moving laterally as traveling stitches. Most moves are made on alternate rows, and the charts indicate any cables, twisted stitches or stitches pulled through other stitches where ribs cross. If there are a lot of manipulations involved, you might want to make lateral transfers when the carriage is on the right and any other manipulations when it is on the left. You can move several parallel ribs with a multi-eyelet tool (Swatch 122 on p. 191) or treat them as smaller pattern repeats. Diamond motifs or trees like the ones in Swatch 124 require initiating new stitches and terminating old ones according to a chart. It isn't difficult to do as long as you follow the chart and check off each row as you knit it. This method of working provides all kinds of possibilities for Aran effects and double-bed twisted stitches (see Chapter 3).

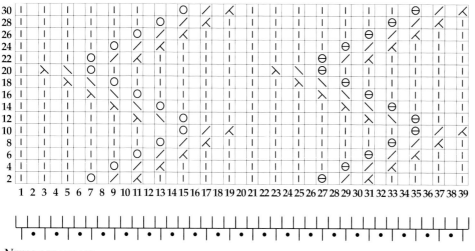

	1	2	3	4	5	6	7	8	9	10	11	12	13	14	15	16	17	18	19	20	21	22	23	24	25	26	27	28	29	30	31	32	33	34	35	36	37	38	39
30	I		I		I		I		I		I				O		/		⋏		I		I		I		I		I		I		I		⊖		/		⋏
28	I		I		I		I		I		I		O		/		⋏		I		I		I		I		I		I		I		⊖		/		⋏		I
26	I		I		I		I		I		O		/		⋏		I		I		I		I		I		I		I		⊖		/		⋏		I		I
24	I		I		I		I		O		/		⋏		I		I		I		I		I		I		I		⊖		/		⋏		I		I		I
22	I		I		I		O		/		⋏		I		I		I		I		I		I		⊖		/		⋏		I		I		I		I
20	I		⋏		\		O		I		I		I		I		I		I		I		⋏		\		⊖		I		I		I		I		I		I
18	I		I		⋏		\		O		I		I		I		I		I		I		I		⋏		\		⊖		I		I		I		I		I
16	I		I		I		⋏		\		O		I		I		I		I		I		I		I		⋏		\		⊖		I		I		I		I
14	I		I		I		I		⋏		\		O		I		I		I		I		I		I		I		⋏		\		⊖		I		I		I
12	I		I		I		I		I		⋏		\		O		I		I		I		I		I		I		I		⋏		\		⊖		I		I
10	I		I		I		I		I		I				O		/		⋏		I		I		I		I		I		I		I		⊖		/		⋏
8	I		I		I		I		I		I		O		/		⋏		I		I		I		I		I		I		I		⊖		/		⋏		I
6	I		I		I		I		I		O		/		⋏		I		I		I		I		I		I		I		⊖		/		⋏		I		I
4	I		I		I		I		O		/		⋏		I		I		I		I		I		I		I		⊖		/		⋏		I		I		I
2	I		I		I		O		/		⋏		I		I		I		I		I		I		⊖		/		⋏		I		I		I		I

NEEDLE DIAGRAM.

To initiate new stitches on the ribber bed, you can pick up the purl bar of an adjacent or opposite stitch, but be consistent in your choice since it affects the shape of the design's beginning. If you make new stitches from the opposite main-bed stitches, you'll have to take the purl bar from a stitch lying to the left or right of the empty ribber needle because the beds are in half-pitch. You can also pick up the purl bar from both opposite (half-pitch) needles on the main bed and hook them onto the same ribber needle. It will create a pointed or joined beginning for whatever shape you are knitting, but it will avoid slanting the first stitch from the right or left.

124. EMBOSSED TREES AND DIAMONDS.

Tree motif's branches were begun by P/U P bars from 2 adj RB STS, & ended by continuing direction of slant & tr them to appropriate opposite NDL. Inner-diamond motifs were begun by hanging 1 central P bar from opposite NDL on 2 NDLS to avoid a slanted beginning. They were ended by tr 2 STS to same opposite NDL.

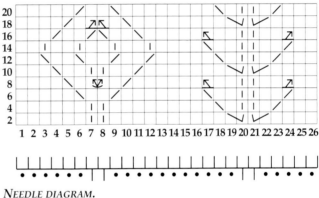

NEEDLE DIAGRAM.

IMITATING A STITCH ON RIBBER BED AND CONTROLLING ITS SLANT.

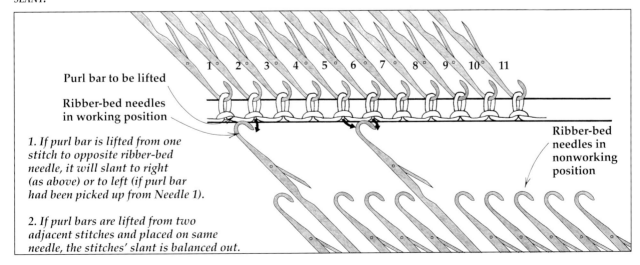

Purl bar to be lifted

Ribber-bed needles in working position

Ribber-bed needles in nonworking position

1. If purl bar is lifted from one stitch to opposite ribber-bed needle, it will slant to right (as above) or to left (if purl bar had been picked up from Needle 1).

2. If purl bars are lifted from two adjacent stitches and placed on same needle, the stitches' slant is balanced out.

125. DEBOSSED DIAMONDS.

Stockinette shapes are deeply reversed in FNR fabric. (Arrows on chart indicate where to tr STS from RB to MB & which P bars of MB STS are used to reestablish STS on RB.)

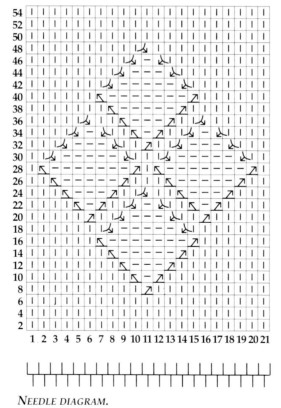

NEEDLE DIAGRAM.

You can terminate stitches on the ribber bed by transferring them to an adjacent ribber stitch or to an opposite main-bed needle. Stitches transferred to a main-bed needle will slant to the right or left of the ribber needle because the beds are in half-pitch. You can transfer a single stitch onto two opposite needles, which will eliminate the slant but widen the last stitch. Or you can terminate two stitches on the same needle to avoid the slanting effects and narrow the top of a shape.

Charts for double-bed embossed patterns show only the stitches on the ribber bed since it's understood that all the main-bed needles are working. Because the main bed is knitting a base stockinette fabric, the stitch size should be set as usual for stockinette. The stitch size on the ribber should be set several stitch sizes lower than on the main bed, but proportional to the number of needles in work. And whenever you plan to work crossed or twisted ribs, they should begin with an even number of nonworking needles between them, or you'll find that both ribs need to occupy the same needles simultaneously, when they should be crossing or twisting.

Debossed designs start as a totally ribbed fabric and then selectively eliminate stitches from the ribber bed to create a recessed design surface (swatches 125 and 126). Wherever the ribber stitches are eliminated, only the main-bed stitches knit, creating the pattern effect in reverse stockinette, surrounded by rib. Because the main carriage needs to knit pattern areas in stockinette, the main-bed stitch size should be suitable for stockinette. The ribber stitch size can be two numbers lower in most cases since it will always be knitting in rib.

Debossed fabrics require essentially the same technical handling as embossed fabrics. The beds are always in half-pitch, and pattern charts likewise show only the ribber stitches. However, stitches can be initiated and terminated on the main-bed needles as easily as on adjacent ribber needles. When adjacent stitches are used, the edges of shapes will be outlined by slanting stitches. Like their embossed counterparts, debossed fabrics tend to be thick and hence require some care in choosing yarns. Using an alternate-needle arrangement on the ribber bed will produce a lighter-weight fabric. If you use this setup, make sure the ribber's stitch size is larger than that of the main bed.

For single-knit, knit-purl fabrics, the two beds, as mentioned above, are in full pitch with working needles opposite nonworking needles. For elaborate patterning, having the needles in this complementary arrangement is time-consuming since you must pay careful attention to which bed every stitch knits on before knitting each row, transferring stitches back and forth between the beds. Although this setup produces a fabric that looks most like a hand-knit, it's really only practical with large patterns that do not change shape often, for example, alternating blocks of knits and purls. However, patterns of this type, with large, uninterrupted blocks of stockinette on the ribber, are often difficult for Japanese machines to knit. For smaller, busier patterns, I prefer working with a full complement of needles on the main bed and embossing the ribber stitches onto them (see pp. 224-229) or a combination method, as shown on p. 226.

A final variation on double-bed transfers involves transferring specific main-bed stitches to the ribber bed and holding them there for a number of rows before returning them to the main bed. The ribber bed does not knit; it is simply used as a stitch holder. The results of this maneuver are floats and other textures that can be automatically placed on the knit side of the fabric. This is a practical approach to patterns with lots of knit-side interest, like the butterfly stitch in Swatch 12 on p. 59 or the fish scales in Swatch 100 on p. 169.

To work these temporary transfers, the ribber must be in the first dropped position (because the ribber bed is not knitting, you can remove the ribber carriage). This method offers a good alternative to using multiple stitch holders or a hand-knitting needle when a lot of stitches must be removed from their needles. Use a bodkin or a pair of transfer tools to move the stitches back and forth from one bed to the other.

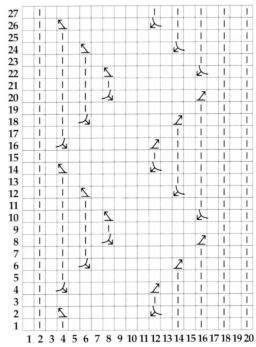

126. DEBOSSED ZIGZAG.

This EON ribbed arrangement produces a lighter-weight fabric than Swatch 125. Because there are stockinette areas K on MB alone, MB SS is larger than RB SS.

NEEDLE DIAGRAM.

CHAPTER 8

Cables

Cables are a perennial favorite in ready-to-wear sweaters and are probably the one knitted texture that nonknitters recognize instantly and can call by name. Knitters have always relied on cables for visual interest and as a challenge to their skills and powers of concentration. Whether you knit them by hand or by machine, cables are created by crossing two groups of stitches. In hand knitting, each cable is crossed as it interrupts the knitting of a row. In machine knitting, cables are crossed between rows.

The two groups of crossed stitches forming the cable are removed from their needles on a pair of transfer tools, crossed as they're returned to one another's needles, and then knitted as the carriage moves across the bed. Because all the cables in a single row are crossed and then knitted at the same time, it's quite easy to keep track of patterns, produce lots of cables quickly and combine cables with other effects.

The number of stitches crossed and the frequency and direction of the crossings are the three variable elements that define all cable designs. These variables can be expanded by applying some of the basic moves (see Chapter 2) or other techniques like twisting and lifting to the fundamental process of working a cable. The result, of course, is a variety of more complicated and decorative cables.

Cables can be produced vertically and diagonally (see Swatch 119 on p. 189), as horizontal insertions (see Swatch 91 on p. 162) or as allover patterns. You can add cables to ribs, mock ribs, yokes, seams and buttonhole bands; cross cables on the surface of wide cords; or rely on cabled texture to camouflage seams and joins.

Since many cable crossings involve stretching the stitches a little bit, wool is the easiest, most forgiving fiber to work with. Because cotton, linen and silk tend not to be as stretchy as wool, they are less suitable for beginners' cabling efforts. Acrylics and blends vary in their suitability, depending on their twist and actual fiber content.

Basic cable variables

Of the three basic variables in all cables—the number of stitches crossed, the number of rows knitted between crossings and the direction of the crossings—the number of stitches that can easily be crossed is generally considered the single greatest limitation to working cables on a knitting machine. However, by selectively enlarging stitches, almost any number of stitches can be crossed on a machine. Most knitting patterns show cables that cross two stitches over two stitches or three over three, but you can cross one stitch over two, one over three, two over three, three over four or any other combination that appeals to you or fits the number of stitches you have available (Swatch 127). (The number of stitches crossing in a cable is usually written as 1x2, 1x3, 2x3, and so on.) Although many samples in this chapter are 2x2 cables to simplify the presentation, most could easily be enlarged by adding more stitches to each group. Where pattern notes indicate groups of stitches, each group can include one or more additional stitches. The crossing directions remain the same, but the effect is enlarged when each group has four stitches, for example, instead of two.

Making and reading cable charts

CABLE SYMBOLS (SEE ALSO PP. 29-30).

Although some cables need verbal directions, most are easiest to understand by using charts. Generally, knitting charts indicate whether a particular stitch is a knit, purl, slip or tuck. Cable charts also show the direction in which the stitches cross and the order in which they're returned to their needles. Needle setups with brackets and labels or simple directional arrows can be used to describe cable activity, but more commonly you will find used the solid-line and broken-line charts created for hand knitting. Once you understand these charts, they are the simplest method for managing cables, and they eliminate the need for most verbal directions.

When reading the charts, remember that the broken lines represent the first stitches returned to the needles, those that show on the knit face of the fabric. The solid lines represent the last stitches placed on their needles, those that show on the purl side and actually name the twist of the cable.

When the first stitches returned to the needles are those on the tool in your left hand, the last stitches placed on their needles will slant upward from right to left and the cable will twist to the left. Think of this motion as "crossing left," which hand knitters call a front cross.

When the stitches on the tool in your right hand are replaced first and the last stitches placed on their needles slant upward from left to right, the cable will twist to the right. This "right crossing" is known to hand knitters as a back cross.

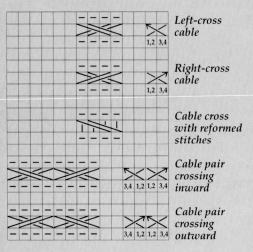

Left-cross cable

Right-cross cable

Cable cross with reformed stitches

Cable pair crossing inward

Cable pair crossing outward

The width of a cable is determined not only by the number of stitches crossed, but also by the number of rows knitted between crossings (Swatch 128). When crossings are closely spaced, the width of a cable is reduced. When they're spaced farther apart, the cable tends to spread and look wider. For general purposes, you can usually figure on knitting the same number of rows as stitches crossed or perhaps two more rows than stitches. In other words, if you're crossing 2x2 (four-stitch) cables, try knitting four to six rows between crossings. Also, the number of rows between crossings can be staggered or changed as part of a pattern

128. BOW-TIE CABLES.
Notice how much wider this cable looks when crossings are spaced 10 Rs apart, rather than EOR (as in Rs 2-8).

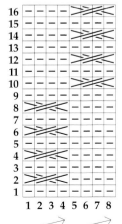

127. UNICORN CABLE.

This DB cable is K with half-pitch, modified-NDL setup. To begin, create 6 STS on RB by PU P bars of opposite MB STS. Cable's width is reduced by tr a RB ST to adj RB NDL & making a new ST on MB from P bar of adj MB ST.

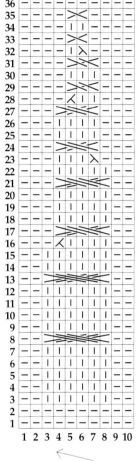

arrangement, from one vertical cable column to the next or on the same column. Generally, it's better to have fewer rather than too many rows between crossings, especially with some of the braids and woven cables in which having too many rows minimizes the interlaced effects.

Hand-knitting patterns call for crossing cables on right-side rows, usually with an even number of rows between crossings. On a machine, whether you're knitting an odd-numbered or even-numbered row, the wrong side of the fabric always faces you. However, having an odd number of rows between crossings alternately puts the carriage on the left or right side of the bed. If you deliberately incorporate odd numbers of rows between cables into your pattern, you can keep track of variations by crossing cables to the left when the carriage is on the left and crossing them to the right when it is on the right.

Simple patterns can be managed by keeping track of the row counter, but more elaborate patterns combining several different cables and assorted textures should be charted out row by row so that you know in advance exactly which cables you'll be crossing and which direction to cross them.

In addition to using the carriage side as a reminder of the direction in which cables cross, it's also a good way to keep track of two different motions. For example, when knitting diagonal cables, you can transfer the stitches when the carriage is on one side and cross them when it is on the other. You can also coordinate crossings with increases or decreases in your garment. When all the twists are the same—it doesn't really matter whether they're to the left or right—avoid any confusion by always crossing to the right if you're right-handed and to the left if you're left-handed.

The direction a cable crosses is the most crucial part of a cable design because one wrong crossing out of a hundred can stand out enough to destroy a pattern (see the

sidebar on pp. 202-203). When all of the crosses in a column are made in the same direction, the cable looks like twisted rope and is called a "closed" cable, with each twist disappearing behind the next. In closed cables, it usually doesn't matter whether the crossings turn left or right, but they must consistently turn in the same direction.

When the direction of the crosses alternates from one crossing to the next, the same stitches stay on the front of the fabric and the cable remains "open" and serpentine, rather than twisted. You can usually just look at the face of a fabric to figure out how each cable was crossed. Remember that the first stitches replaced on the needles are always the ones that show on the knit side of the fabric. Open and closed cables are used in combination to form many of the more elaborate decorative diagonal cables.

How to cross cables

The basic process of crossing a cable can be divided into three steps: removing the two groups of stitches from their needles, crossing and returning the first group of stitches to the second group of needles, and transferring the second group to the first group's needles.

As you remove the stitches on the two transfer tools, you'll find that they're easiest to manage when the fabric is well weighted. Use enough weight to help the stitches clear the latches and not split, but avoid using excessive weight or you'll never stop a dropped stitch before it ravels. I hold both tools together, side by side, using one in each hand for each group of stitches. I find that by extending my index fingers as I pull the needles forward (see the top photo on the facing page), I can keep the fabric back against the edge of the bed, where it belongs. To complete the removal, push back both tools (and the needles they're hooked onto) so that the stitches slip over the latches and onto the tools.

Once the stitches have been removed on the transfer tools, hold one of the tools off to the side while you cross and rehang the stitches from the other tool to the appropriate needles, as shown in the middle photo at right. For simple crossings, holding one tool off to the side is usually adequate to keep it out of the way. For larger, more difficult crossings, I temporarily hook the tool onto some needles at the side, as shown in the bottom photo at right. By using the extra needles as a third hand, I free up both hands to hang the first group of stitches on the appropriate needles. Using one hand to hold the stitches against the needles, I manipulate the tool with the other hand.

Because crossed stitches are under extra tension, you need to pay close attention when depositing them in their respective needles. Once the prongs of the transfer tool have connected with the needle hooks, pivot the tool until it's vertical and the stitches slip onto the needles. The larger the group of stitches, the farther each stitch is stretched and the trickier it becomes to slip the stitches from the tool to the needles. Don't be in a hurry to pull the transfer tool away until you're sure each stitch has been caught by a needle hook.

When I return the second group of stitches to the needles, I use the tool holding this group to pull these needles out to holding position, then I manually push the first groups out to holding position as well. This helps the cable knit more easily, with less chance of jamming the carriage, breaking the yarn or leaving some stitches unknitted. For cables that are under very little tension and hence cross and handle fairly easily, it's necessary to pull only half the needles (the last group replaced) out to hold. For tighter crossings, you'll need to bring all the needles involved in the

CROSSING CABLES WITH A PAIR OF TRANSFER TOOLS. Use two double-eyelet transfer tools to remove pairs of cable STS from their NDLS (top photo). When you're ready to pull NDLS forward to remove STS, extend your index fingers to keep fabric back against bed.

Hold L tool off to side & place RT pair of STS on L NDLS, as shown (middle photo). Then replace L STS on RT NDLS to complete cable crossing.

CROSSING 3x3 CABLES, WITH NEEDLES TEMPORARILY HOLDING TRANSFER TOOL TO FREE UP SECOND HAND.

crossing forward, and it helps to bring to hold even a few more on either side of these. For very tight cables, I find that upper working position offers even better relief from strained stitches and crossed needles, as shown in the photo below.

When crossing the stitches, if you've used the tool to pull the needles out to holding position, you must ease the needles back to upper working position. Doing this takes a little more time and effort than just leaving the needles in hold, but upper working position makes it much easier to move the carriage across the bed.

Enlarging stitches to ease cable crossings

There's seldom a problem crossing up to six stitches (3x3), but larger cables generally require extra ease to prevent broken, stretched or unknitted stitches and separations where stitches cross away from each other. You can add ease to a cable by using an out-of-work needle on each side of it; selectively adjusting the stitch-size dial; hand knitting stitches with a separate strand or the free yarn; or, on double-bed machines, using drop-stitch techniques (see also pp. 61-68).

It's not always necessary to enlarge all the stitches in a cable, and the background stitches never need to be enlarged. Generally speaking, however, the more stitches involved in a crossing, the likelier it is that stitches will need to be enlarged. But when increasing stitch size, try several sample swatches to see how the fabric looks when knit at different stitch sizes. Then enlarge stitches only as much as is really needed. If you add too much slack, the stitches will cross quite easily, but they will look large and sloppy on the face of the cable. Always enlarge the stitches in the row just before making the crossing, and knit all other rows as you normally would.

USING UPPER WORKING POSITION TO EASE STRAIN WHEN KNITTING TIGHT CABLE CROSSINGS.

Both of these pairs of extended NDLS hold 3x3 cables, but those at L will knit more easily because they're in UWP.

Fixing cable mistakes

When you discover that a cable crossed left when it should have crossed right, there are several things you can do to correct the mistake. If the work is still on the machine, you can rip back and recross the stitches. However, all of the cable crosses that followed the mistake must be un-crossed with transfer tools in order to rip back the rows.

If the error is only a few rows down, it might be simpler to drop the stitches from the needles that formed the cable and ravel them back. Use stitch holders and a latch tool to cross and then reform those stitches properly. Some mistakes are correctable even after many rows have been knitted by removing the work from the machine on scrap or a garter bar then dropping and reforming the individual stitches involved in the crossing.

Whether the work is on the machine or in your lap, drop each stitch to the row below the incorrect crossing, and hold the

If your plans for a cable include latching up a knit stitch at each side, dropping the stitches to be latched up just before you cross the cable may produce enough extra slack to ease the crossing. To prevent the dropped stitches from running too far, catch them on a stitch holder or knitting needle a few rows down, then latch them up after the cable has been crossed.

For most single-bed cables, my favorite method for enlarging stitches is to use holding position to interrupt the carriage so that individual groups of stitches can be knitted with customized stitch sizes (see pp. 49-53). However, this method is effective only for increasing the size of the cable stitches within the range offered by the stitch-size dial. For larger stitches, you can interrupt the carriage and manually knit the needles with the free yarn. The main advantage to interrupting the carriage is that you have no yarn ends to finish off later. But you also have no way to ease out the extra slack unless your design calls for large, oversized stitches. However, if the width of the cable (for example, 6x6) requires huge stitches just to make the crossing, you can hand knit those stitches to nonworking position, using a separate strand of yarn. This lets you remove the slack and adjust the stitch size after the knitting is complete.

stitches for each half of the cable on a separate holder. Cross the cable and then reform each stitch up to the next crossing or until it can be replaced on the appropriate needle.

If raveling the work is impractical, you can cut the yarn in the middle of an incorrect crossing and undo the cable stitches and several stitches on each side of them, leaving yarn tails long enough to work into the back of the fabric later. Hold the stitches on stitch holders or contrast yarn to keep them from raveling. Correct the cable cross or other stitch mistake and use a matching strand of yarn and even tension to graft the stitches back together.

Last but not least, you can use duplicate stitch to correct noncable mistakes, like stitches that tucked when they should have knitted or stitches formed at a flawed point in the yarns. Duplicate stitch, however, does not solve incorrect cable crosses (see p. 81).

CUTTING A CABLE TO REPAIR AN ERROR.

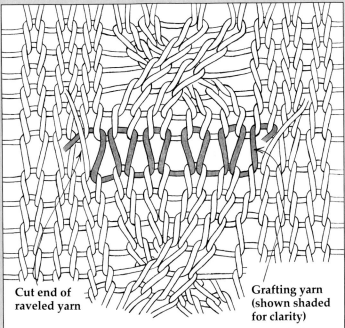

Cut end of raveled yarn

Grafting yarn (shown shaded for clarity)

1. When raveling a cable to repair an error is impractical, cut through cable row with mistake at center of cable and pull out incorrect stitches and enough stitches beyond to enable you to finish them off later.

2. Place stitches on holders to prevent raveling while you recross cable or fix stitch errors.

3. Then use a matching strand of yarn (as shown above) to graft cable stitches together.

129. ADDING SHORT-ROW EASE TO CABLES.

Wishbone cable at L has greater depth & definition than that at RT because, just before crossing, 2 extra Rs were K on 2 of the 4 STS that form each cable. The diagrams at RT below show how to add extra Rs for ropes & braids by using HP for SR.

To work: *COR. Hold all NDLS to L of NDL 6. K 1 R. Hold all NDLS to RT of NDL 7. Only NDLS 6 & 7 are working. K 1 R. COR. Place NDLS 5, 4 & 3 in UWP, & K 1 R to L. Place all NDLS except 3 & 4 into HP, & K 1 R. Ret all NDLS to L of NDL 3 to UWP, & K 1 R to L.* Rep from * to * before each cable crossing. With all cables of this type, be sure always to cross lengthened STS to front.

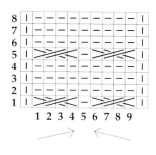

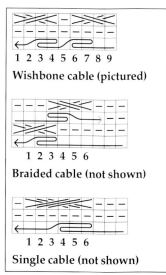

1 2 3 4 5 6 7 8 9

Wishbone cable (pictured)

1 2 3 4 5 6

Braided cable (not shown)

1 2 3 4 5 6

Single cable (not shown)

CARRIAGE MOVEMENT FOR ADDING TWO EXTRA ROWS OF EASE FOR CABLE CROSSING.

Drop stitch is the logical method to choose for enlarging stitches when working with both beds for wide ribs or purl stitches between cables, or when there are lots of main-bed stitches to be enlarged. Knitting and then dropping extra ribber needles (as indicated by X in the charts below) in the rows before cable crossings makes the cables cross more easily because it provides extra slack, which is absorbed by the main-bed stitches. I generally try to center or space the extra ribber stitches evenly opposite the needles to be used for the cable. Typically, I use one extra stitch in the middle of a six-stitch cable and two extra stitches for an eight-stitch cable (see pp. 65-67 for specifics of the method).

With the beds in half-pitch just prior to knitting the last row before the cable crossing, bring into working position on the ribber bed, opposite the cabling needles, those needles that will knit and drop. Knit the row and then drop the indicated stitches, either by manually moving each needle, or, if you want to drop all stitches from the ribber bed, by pushing the ribber carriage across the bed alone or using a ribber-release carriage. (Not all machines have a ribber-release carriage, but they're excellent for drop stitch. As you move the carriage across the bed from left to right, the needles all slip forward to holding position. When you

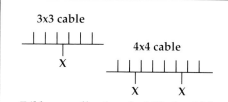

3x3 cable

X

4x4 cable

X   X

Ribber needles (marked X) should be brought to working position prior to knitting last row before crossing cable. Stitches formed on these needles should then be dropped to add ease for crossing.

NEEDLE DIAGRAMS FOR CABLES, SHOWING RIBBER STITCHES TO DROP FOR EASE.

move the carriage across the bed from right to left, the needles are pushed back to working position. Because this carriage carries no yarn, the second motion drops all the stitches.) Finally, return the empty needles to nonworking position, cross the cables and continue knitting.

Holding position can also be used to stop knitting background stitches while you knit extra rows across the needles holding the cable stitches. The extra rows add ease to the crossing and extra dimension to the cable surface, as shown in Swatches 129 and 130 (see also p. 58).

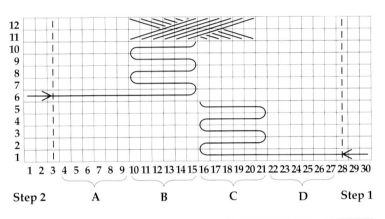

130. *SHORT ROWING TO EASE A GIANT 6X6 CABLE.*

To work: *K 12 Rs. COR. Hold NDLS in groups A & B. K 1 R. COL. Hold NDLS in Group D. K 4 Rs on Group C. Cut yarn. Hold Group C & move COL to rep (in reverse) from L side, holding groups A, C & D to K Group B. Cut yarn. Cross cable. P/U 2 or 3 STS from selvage edge of strip that crosses behind cable & hang them on NDLS that hold front group of STS (see the drawing at RT) to prevent a gap at center of cable.* Rep from * to *. Darn in & hide all yarn tails along P STS at edge.

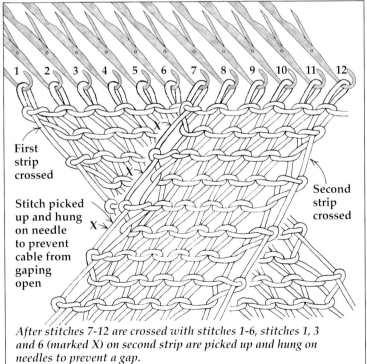

After stitches 7-12 are crossed with stitches 1-6, stitches 1, 3 and 6 (marked X) on second strip are picked up and hung on needles to prevent a gap.

GIANT 6X6 CABLE CROSSING.

A glossary of cables

Once you understand the basic cable crossings, you'll be able to create endless cable variations. You can combine or contrast complex crossings with background and surrounding textures, lace eyelets or colors effects.

The background texture of a cable can be plain stockinette, but usually the stitches at each side of a cable are worked to help

define the cable to make it stand out from the surrounding stitches. These adjacent stitches may also be used to ease the crossing. Leaving a needle out of work creates a ladder that helps define the edges of the cable and may also add some ease. However, ladders are often unsightly in the finished fabric unless the yarn, like cotton, tends to shrink and close them up when the sweater is washed.

A better solution than ladders for defining the edge of a cable is to drop the adjoining stitches just before crossing the cable and latch them back up after the crossing is complete. This method creates a contrast

131 AND 132. SINGLE, PARALLEL AND OPPOSING CABLE ROPES (THIS PAGE) AND SINGLE, PARALLEL AND OPPOSING SERPENTINE CABLES (FACING PAGE).

Comparing these swatches & charts, you'll see that single rope always crosses to RT, while single serpent alt crosses RT, then L. Opposing pairs of ropes form wishbone cables, while opposing pairs of serpents form ring & honeycomb cables.

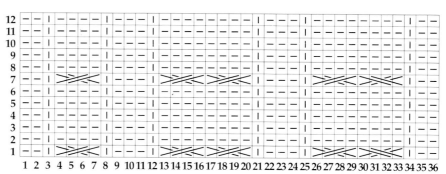

1. Single rope cable   **2. Parallel ropes**   **3. Opposing ropes**

stitch at each side of the cable. These stitches can be reformed as knits or tucks. Latching up tuck stitches creates a more open effect than simply reforming a purl as a knit stitch. This method also allows the fabric more lateral ease. Purl stitches can be knitted automatically if you want to work with a double-bed arrangement. However, unless there are a lot of purl accent stitches or ribs to be knitted, the second bed is often more of a hindrance than a help.

It's also possible to produce stockinette cable stitches against a textured background, which is manually reformed or punchcard-controlled. The manual patterns can also be used to add a nice touch inside cable shapes. The cable stitches, however, are usually knitted in stockinette when the background stitches are textured.

Parallel and opposing pairs of cables

More elaborate designs can be formed by applying the basic variables to pairs of cables (swatches 131 and 132). When cables parallel each other, they twist to the right or left at the same time. Opposing cables cross toward or away from each other, twisting in or out in relation to an

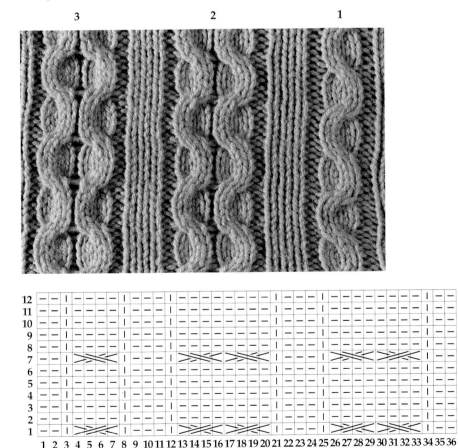

1. Single serpentine cable

2. Parallel serpents

3. Opposing serpents

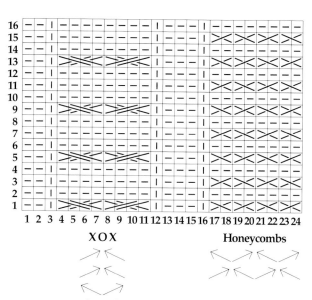

133. OPPOSING SERPENTINE CABLES AND HONEYCOMB PANEL.

Opposing pairs of 1x1 serpentine cables cross easily to form honeycomb panel on L. Vertical XOX pat on RT is formed by a pair of opposing cables that are hybrid rope/serpents, alt crossing twice in each direction (out, out, in, in, out, out, etc.).

134. CABLES WITH AN ODD NUMBER OF STITCHES.

The opposing 1x2 cables on L cross out from center tuck ST; same cables on RT cross in, towards plain center ST. Two center cables are roped 1x3 variations. In all examples, a single stitch lies on front of cable cross, producing very little strain on STS. These cables are good choice for beading (see p. 74).

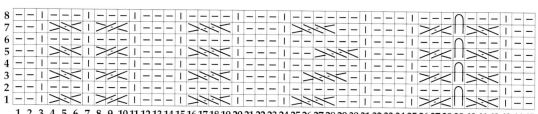

(imaginary) center point (Swatch 133). Sometimes a single noncabled stitch is included in the center of a cable pair to help relieve the strain and separation when cables oppose. This extra stitch can also add vertical contrast to the diagonal slant of the cabled stitches.

Progressive, braided and woven cables

You can achieve the look of a wide cable, without straining stitches or making special adjustments, by crossing three adjacent groups of stitches in progressive order. All twists are made in the same direction so that Group A crosses B, then B crosses C. Having fewer rows than stitches between crossings helps to create the wide, roped effect in Swatch 135. When the center group (B) always crosses first (or last), the cable becomes a braided cable instead. In other words, Group B crosses

A, then B crosses C, as in Swatch 136 on p. 210 and Swatch 137 on p. 211. In short, progressive cables are made with parallel crossings from one row to the next, while braided cables require opposing crossings from row to row.

Woven cables are formed by alternating the direction of the crossings from one row (of crossings) to the next, with all of the crosses in a single row made in the same direction. Woven cables also require splitting pairs, which means that every other cable row has one less crossing than the previous or following rows do, as in Swatch 138 on p. 211. When the pairs are split from one crossing row to the next, but the direction of the crossings remains the same, the effect is one of an overlaid grid, rather than a woven cable. It is, in fact, just a very wide progressive cable, as in Swatch 139 on p. 212.

2   1

135. PROGRESSIVE CABLES.

In both examples, same 3 groups of STS were crossed, but direction of crossings varied to create either progressive cable on RT or braided cable on L.

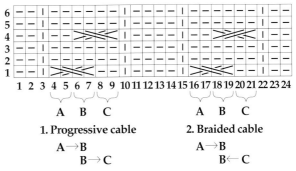

1. Progressive cable
A→B
B→C

2. Braided cable
A→B
B←C

136. BASIC AND COMPLEX PROGRESSIVE AND BRAIDED WIDE CABLES.

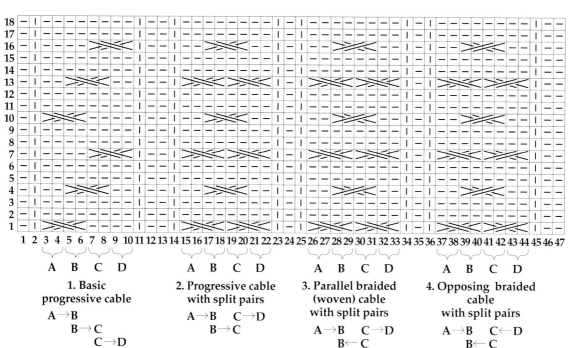

1. Basic progressive cable

A→B
 B→C
  C→D

2. Progressive cable with split pairs

A→B   C→D
 B→C

3. Parallel braided (woven) cable with split pairs

A→B   C→D
 B← C

4. Opposing braided cable with split pairs

A→B   C←D
 B← C

3 2 1

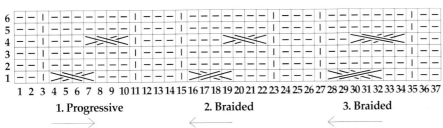

1. Progressive   2. Braided   3. Braided

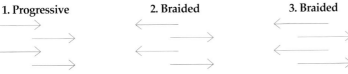

*137. PROGRESSIVE
AND BRAIDED CABLES
WORKED ON ODD
NUMBER OF STITCHES.*

*Progressive and
braided cables
formed on odd
numbers of STS
often have a softer,
more rounded edge
where STS overlap
from 1 group to next.*

138. 2x2 BASKETWEAVE CABLES.

*Because crossing direction alt with each R,
this is an excellent pat to K with odd number
of Rs between crossings. When carr is on RT,
cross to RT; when it is on L, cross to L.
1x1 basketweave is easiest to K, 2x2 can
be very tight, & 3x3 is impossible
without enlarging STS.*

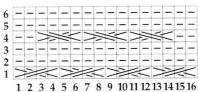

139. DECORATED DIAMONDS.

Cables that outline diamond shapes & those that form basketweave & grids within them are crossed on alt Rs to reduce confusion.

Weaving 1x1 cables is easy to do, but, with so many adjacent cables crosses pulling away from each other, the strain is considerable when working 2x2 basketweave cables. By modifying the structure with the addition of two plain stitches between each cable crossing, the fabric is easier to knit and actually has a softer appearance (Swatch 140). Both the basketweave and the grid overlay can be done with pairs of multiple transfer tools that cross several cables at once. (See also embossed/crossed ribs on pp. 190-193.)

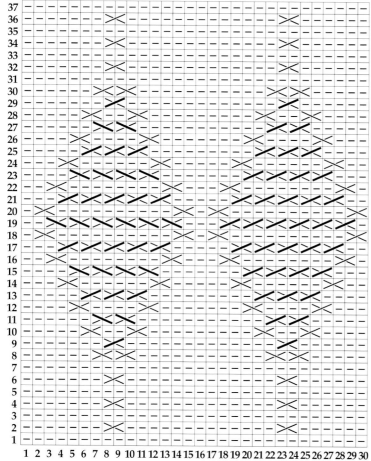

Basketweave   Overlay grid

140. SOFTLY WOVEN BASKETWEAVE.
This modified basketweave has a softer drape than the standard version in Swatch 138.

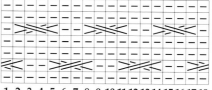

Crossing several cables at once

You can cross several cables simultaneously with either a pair of multi-pronged transfer tools or a garter bar. (In the photo at right, I am using a pair of multiple-eyelet tools with prongs arranged to handle alternating pairs of stitches.) When you work the crossing with a pair of transfer tools, the order in which you use the tools to remove the stitches from their needles is important. The last stitches removed must be the first ones replaced, and these stitches will lie on the face of the cables. The first group of stitches removed will be replaced last and lie on the back of the cable. You'll be able to cross 1x1 and 2x2 cables with these tools, but 3x3 cables will cause too much strain.

To make multiple 2x2 right crosses, remove the first two stitches on the left and every alternate pair of stitches on one tool and hold this tool to the left (in the photo, this is the lower tool held in my left hand). Remove the alternate pairs of stitches on the second tool and place them on the first set of needles that were emptied to their left. Replace the second set of stitches on the remaining empty needles.

To make multiple left crosses, begin with the first two stitches on the right, reversing the process above. To cross 1x1 cables, use a pair of tools arranged for every other needle.

The garter bar too can be used to cross several cables at once. The late Fred Stafford, a trailblazing knitter, is credited with having worked out a method for using the garter bar in this way. These directions are based on his method.

Do not attempt to cross garter-bar cables without allowing at least two plain stitches between them. In addition, empty one needle at each side of every cable by transferring the stitch to an adjacent needle. Leave the empty needles in working position. There will be at least four noncable needles between each group of four cable needles (two that are empty and nonworking, plus some plain

stitches between them). The cable needles are numbered (from the left) 1, 2, 3 and 4, etc.

Knit four rows and then, to ease the crossings, drop the stitches from the previously emptied needles at the sides of each cable. Remove all of the stitches on the garter bar and return them to their needles according to the following directions for left and right crosses. Even though all of the stitches are on the garter bar, the cables are crossed one at a time as you work your way across the row. You can combine crosses in a single row, but it isn't easy. This method is best for a lot of cables that all cross the same way. After the cables are crossed, knit four more rows, making sure that the empty needles are in working position so they can cast on and knit; their stitches are dropped before crossing the cables. Periodically latch up the stitches on each side of the cables and hold them on stitch holders so you can continue to drop stitches formed on their needles.

To work a left cross, start at the left end of the bed and work toward the right. Replace plain stitches on their original needles. Make the first cable crossing by shifting the garter bar two positions to the right or left. First, shift to the right to place stitches 1 and 2 on needles 3 and 4. Then shift the bar back to the left to place stitches 3 and 4 on needles 1 and 2.

To work a right cross, start at the right end of the bed and work toward the left. First place stitches 3 and 4 on needles 1 and 2. Then place stitches 1 and 2 on needles 3 and 4.

CROSSING MULTIPLE CABLES SIMULTANEOUSLY.

Using pairs of multiple-eyelet tools to cross several cables at once, 1st 2 STS at L & alt pairs of STS are removed on 1st tool (in L hand) & held to L. Rem pairs of STS are removed on 2nd tool (in RT hand) & shifted 2 NDLS to L to begin cable crossing. First STS removed are then ret 2 NDLS to RT to complete crossing.

Textured cables

Although cables themselves create texture, you can piggyback other textures on the surface of a cable (Swatch 141). Large cables can split into smaller ones (Swatch 142) or stitches can be twisted before they're replaced on the needles (Swatch 143). Popcorns (see pp. 135-142) and beading (see p. 74) can also be used in, on and around cables. While a little short rowing will add subtle depth to a cable, additional short rowing provides extra ease for crossing giant cables (see Swatch 129 on p. 204 and Swatch 130 on p. 205). Short rowing can also be used to create exaggerated textures on a cable surface (Swatch 144 on p. 216).

In addition to reforming stitches on the surface of a cable, you can also add purl stitches in the middle of a cable to add depth and definition (Swatch 145 on p. 217). Lots of purl detail should be handled with the ribber bed, but for isolated stitches, reforming is easier and frees you from having to work blind in a double-bed setup.

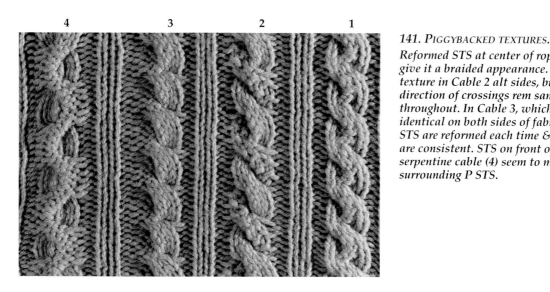

                4   3   2   1

141. PIGGYBACKED TEXTURES.
Reformed STS at center of roped Cable 1 give it a braided appearance. Seed-ST texture in Cable 2 alt sides, but direction of crossings rem same throughout. In Cable 3, which is identical on both sides of fabric, same STS are reformed each time & crosses are consistent. STS on front of serpentine cable (4) seem to melt into surrounding P STS.

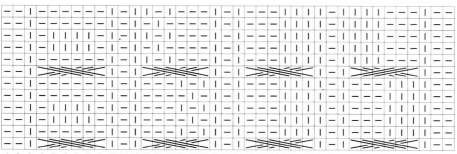

1 2 3 4 5 6 7 8 9 10 11 12 13 14 15 16 17 18 19 20 21 22 23 24 25 26 27 28 29 30 31 32 33 34 35 36 37 38 39

1. Reformed rope   2. Seed-stitch rope   3. Reversible cable   4. Caged serpent cable

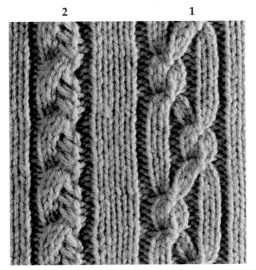

2　　　　　**1**

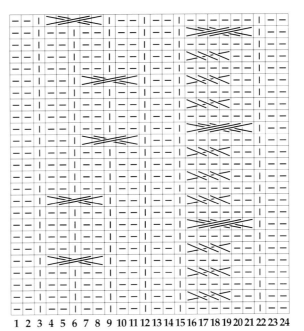

142. SPLITTING AND REGROUPING STITCHES.

In Cable 1, split pairs form a smocked pat.
Cable crosses are 2x2 over 5 STS, behind a ST
that rem on center NDL, giving a tied look to
each cross. Cable 2 splits from 3x3 to 1x3.

1 2 3 4 5 6 7 8 9 10 11 12 13 14 15 16 17 18 19 20 21 22 23 24

1. Smocked cable　　　**2. Gull-stitch rope**

143. RUFFLED CABLE.

This cable combines reformed STS,
twisted STS & cabling. P side of fabric
is RT side.

To work: *K 5 Rs & reform STS 3, 4
& 5. Remove reformed STS on 1 tr tool
& hold aside. Remove STS 6, 7 & 8 (the
3 P STS) on another tool. Replace STS
6, 7 & 8 on NDLS 3, 4 & 5. Use 2nd
(now empty) tr tool to twist STS 3, 4 &
5, & then complete cable cross by
depositing them on NDLS 6, 7 & 8. K 6
Rs, reform STS indicated.* Rep steps *
to *, reversing the direction of the
crossing and the group of STS
reformed (see also p. 89 for two-tool
twisting method). (Pattern courtesy of
Nihon Vogue.)

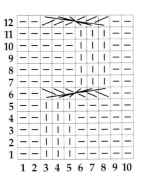

1 2 3 4 5 6 7 8 9 10

2   1

144. STEGOSAURUS CABLE.

Short-row triangles are K 6 STS wide in R before crossing 3x3 cables (see Swatch 70 on p. 142 for same basic method). When this texture is piggybacked on serpentine cable, it alt slants L & RT. RT cross produces L-slanting texture; L cross produces RT-slanting texture. When texture is added to roped cable, direction of crossing can be used to control slant.

To work: K 3 Rs, *ending COR. Hold all NDLS to L of 1st cable. K 1 R across 1st bridge & 1st cable group. Hold bridge NDLS. 6 NDLS working. COL. Wrap. (K 1 R, then bring 1 NDL to HP on carr side) 5x. 1 NDL rem working. K 2 Rs, ending with COR. (Ret 1 NDL to UWP on carr side & K 1 R)5x until 1 NDL rem in HP at RT edge of cable. Ret this last NDL, next bridge & cable group on L to UWP & K 1 R. Cross cable NDLS and bridge just knitted to HP.* Rep from * to * for next cable. K 3 Rs, reform K STS & rep entire sequence.

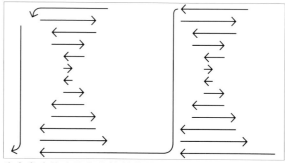

1 2 3 4 5 6 7 8 9 10 11 12 13 14 15 16 17 18 19 20 21 22 23 24

STEGOSAURUS CABLE SHORT-ROW SHAPING FOR SETUP ROW BEFORE CROSSING CABLE (ROWS 4, 8, 12, ETC.).

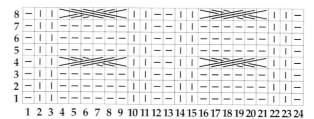

1 2 3 4 5 6 7 8 9 10 11 12 13 14 15 16 17 18 19 20 21 22 23 24

1. Stegosaurus cable (serpentine)　**2. Roped cable**

Cables and lace

Cable and lace patterns are knitted either by simple combinations of independently formed eyelets and cables (Swatch 146 on p. 218) or by cable crossings that form lace eyelets simultaneously by replacing two stitches on the same needle (Swatch 147 on p. 219 and swatches 148 and 149 on p. 220).

Whether the eyelets are formed by manual transfers (see pp. 174-178) or with an automatic lace carriage, the cables are still crossed by hand. If you're adding cables to an automatic (lace-carriage) pattern, make sure the pattern provides enough plain rows and stitches between the eyelets and cable crossings. Otherwise, you may find that the lace is swallowed up by the twist of the cable. You can also adapt regular lace punchcards by taping over some of the holes to create larger areas of stockinette with which to work.

To produce cables and lace simultaneously, replace the first and then the second group of stitches so that one (or more) of those stitches is placed on a needle already holding a stitch, leaving another needle empty. The empty needle remains in working position, where it casts on with the next pass of the carriage and forms an eyelet. This kind of a crossing can also be

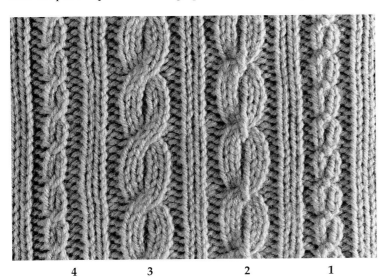

4   3   2   1

145. *Reformed center stitches.*

In cables 1 & 2, single center ST (marked X) rem on its NDL & cable crosses behind it, producing a sort of `tied' look. To work with DB arrangement, center ST has to be tr from RB to MB just before crossing cable & then ret to RB immediately afterward.

In cables 3 & 4, just before crossing cable, drop & latch center ST, holding it on latch tool until cable has been crossed & ret to its NDL. Reformed ST lies behind cable, on back of fabric & does not show on face of fabric. In DB arrangement, center ST rem on RB throughout & requires no special attention.

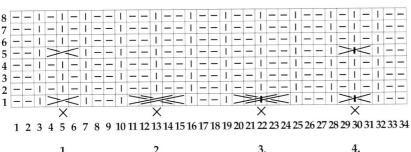

1 2 3 4 5 6 7 8 9 10 11 12 13 14 15 16 17 18 19 20 21 22 23 24 25 26 27 28 29 30 31 32 33 34

1.   2.   3.   4.

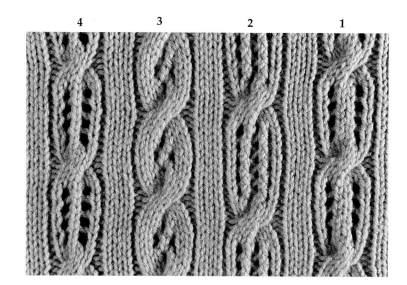

146. EYELET CABLES.

Notice that each eyelet pat is followed by 4 plain Rs before crossing cables, but that lace appears to be perfectly centered between cables on fabric. Pats 1 & 2 use an even number of STS; pats 3 & 4 use an odd number of STS. While Pat 4 uses an odd crossing (3x2), Pat 3 removes center ST from its NDL & replaces it after crossing cable.

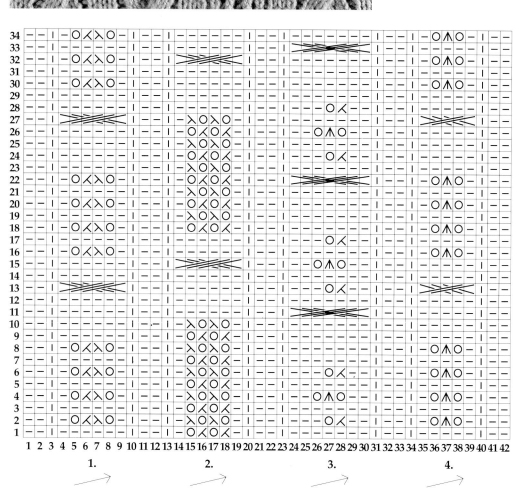

applied to raglan decreasing. But, in that case, the empty needle is placed in nonworking position, where it cannot cast on again. The doubled stitch lies on the back of each cable and becomes the decrease, which shapes the garment piece.

Ladders alongside cables produce vertical lace effects, as in Swatch 150 on p. 221. And entire rows of drop stitch (see p. 66) provide huge stitches to cross for rows of lacy, open cables.

Cables can also be combined with other automatic pattern stitches like tuck and Fair Isle by designing pattern cards that include blocks of stockinette or stripes of solid-color stitches to cross. Depending on the repeat capabilities of your machine and how often you want to introduce a cable, you may prefer to override the carriage by bringing specific needles to holding position before every row is knitted. This enables the needles to knit stockinette (in the case of one-color, textured stitches) or the second color alone (in the case of two-color work). When choosing or designing a Fair Isle punchcard to combine with cabling, you'll avoid excessively long floats if you lean toward smaller patterns. Otherwise, cage the floats to the back of the fabric with vertical weaving (see p. 109).

2   **1**

147. BRAIDED AND WOVEN LACE.
STS 3 & 4 in both pats always move 1st & out from center. 2x2 woven lace is wider version of braid that's easier to K than plain basketweave because STS do not move as far.

To work both pats:
Step 1. Cross STS 1 & 2 with 3 & 4 so that STS 3 & 4 are on NDLS 1 & 2, & STS 1& 2 are on NDLS 2 & 3. NDL 4 is empty in WP. K 3 Rs.
Step 2: Cross STS 3 & 4 with STS 5 & 6 so that STS 3 & 4 are on NDLS 5 & 6, & STS 5 & 6 are on NDLS 4 & 5. NDL 3 is empty in WP. K 3 Rs.

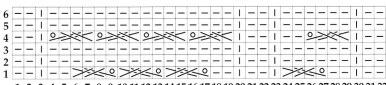

1. Woven lace   **2. Braided lace**

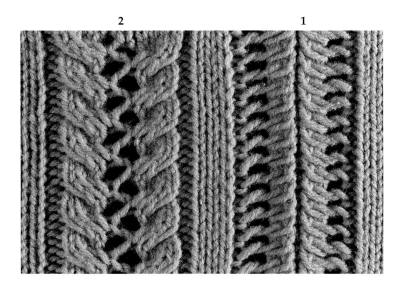

2   1

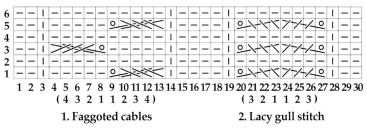

```
6  — —  I   — — — — —   I        I  — — — —   I   — — — — —   I  — —
5  — —  I   — —   o ⤬⤬⤬   I        I  o ⤢⤢⤢⤢⤢ o   I   — — — —   I  — —
4  — —  I   — — — — —   I        I  — — — —   I   — — — — —   I  — —
3  — —  I   ⤬⤬⤬ o — — — — —   I        I  o ⤢⤢⤢⤢⤢ o   I   — —
2  — —  I   — — — — —   I        I  — — — —   I   — — — — —   I  — —
1  — —  I   — — o ⤬⤬⤬   I        I  o ⤢⤢⤢⤢⤢ o   I   — — — —   I  — —
```

```
1 2  3  4  5  6  7  8  9 10 11 12 13 14 15 16 17 18 19 20 21 22 23 24 25 26 27 28 29 30
   ( 4  3  2  1  1  2  3  4 )           ( 3  2  1  1  2  3 )
```

1. Faggoted cables   **2. Lacy gull stitch**

148. LACY GULL STITCH AND FAGGOTED CABLES.

To work lacy gull stitch:
Remove STS 1, 2 & 3 on triple-eyelet tool & ST 4 on single tool. Replace ST 4 on NDL 1. Place STS 1, 2 & 3 back on NDLS 1, 2 & 3. (NDL 4 is empty in WP & NDL 1 holds 2 STS.) K 2 Rs. Rep from * to *.

To work faggoted cables: *Remove STS 1 & 2, & STS 3, 4 & 5 on separate tr tools. Replace STS 1 & 2 on NDLS 4 & 5; replace STS 3, 4 & 5 on NDLS 2, 3 & 4 (NDL 4 holds 2 STS, & NDL 1 is empty in WP). K 2 Rs.* Rep from * to *, alternating sides, as shown on chart. This faggoting also looks good with 1x3 cables.

149. INTERWOVEN CABLES.

In this cable, eyelets are formed inside the cable crossing. Effect is more textural than lacy, with eyelets providing ease for crossings.

To work: *Tr ST 1 to NDL 2, & remove both on single-eyelet tr tool. Remove ST 3 on tr tool. Cross STS so that NDL 3 holds STS 1 & 2, & NDL 1 holds ST 3. NDL 2 is empty in WP. K 2 Rs.* Rep from * to *, alt ST & direction. Doubled ST should always lie on front of crossings.

```
4  — —  I   — — — — — — — — — — — — — — — — — — —   I   — —
3  — —  I   — — — ⤬•⤬ — — — — ⤬•⤬ — — — — ⤬•⤬ — —   I   — —
2  — —  I   — — — — — — — — — — — — — — — — — — —   I   — —
1  — —  I   — ⤬•⤬ — — — — ⤬•⤬ — — — — ⤬•⤬ — — — —   I   — —
```

```
1  2  3  4  5  6  7  8  9 10 11 12 13 14 15 16 17 18 19 20 21 22 23 24
```

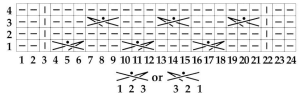

⤬•⤬ or ⤬•⤬
1 2 3   3 2 1

150. CABLED LADDERS.

*This combination of ladders, tuck STS &
cables produces lace with no eyelet trs (only
trs are made in 1st R to create ladders).*

To work: Note that NDL at L or RT edge
of each cable group goes into HP
immediately after cable has been crossed &
before R (Rs 4 & 8 in chart) is K. Single ST alt
L & RT, & because this is 3-R pat, it can easily
be coordinated to carr side. For even softer,
more open fabric, allow empty NDL to C/O
& K, then drop ST before crossing cables.
You can also leave 2 empty NDLS
between each cable. (Pattern courtesy
of Nihon Vogue.)

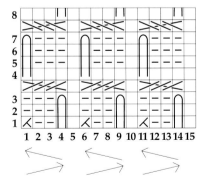

Diagonal, two-colored and multicolored cables

Diagonal cables are knitted by moving the
same group of stitches over, usually by one
needle, every other row (see Swatch 119 on
p. 189). The stitches in the group lie at a
definite angle to the rest of the stitches in
the fabric so that when the cable is crossed,
it, too, lies at an angle. A somewhat
diagonal effect can also be achieved by
staggering regular vertical cables in
successive rows so that they always cross
one needle farther to the right (or left) and
by knitting fewer rows between crossings
so that one cable seems to connect to the
next. (See also p. 224 for information on
double-bed diagonal cables.)

Two-color cables can be created in various
ways, ranging from mock cables (Swatch
163 on p. 229) and contrasting cords laced
through plain cables (Swatch 151) to using

*LACING CORDS
FOR MOCK TWO-
COLOR CABLE.*

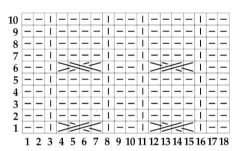

Serpent   **Rope**

**151. MOCK TWO-
COLOR CABLES.**

*Knitted cords or
silky ribbons can be
laced through roped
& serpentine cables
to create very easy
2-color 'cables.'*

152. TWO-COLOR CABLE.

To work: Set carr to K NDLS in HP & set cam lever to slip. Thread MC in L mast, & CC in RT. If you're manually changing colors, start MC from L & CC from RT. With a color changer, both colors should start from side on which color changer is mounted to KM. Wrap on steps 1 & 2 where colors join except in Rs just before cable crossings. Depending on yarn, you may be able to rep each step 4x, which eliminates half the color changes. But it may also create a more noticeable zigzag line where colors join. (Charts below & at RT show relationship of color sections throughout working of cable.)

Step 1. COL. Using MC, (bring all NDLS in Section A to HP & knit 1 R) 2x. Change colors & move empty carr to RT.

Step 2. COR. Using CC, (bring all NDLS in Section B to HP & K 1 R) 2x. Change colors & move empty carr to L. Rep steps 1 & 2 twice more before crossing cable. Once cable is crossed, sections 1 & 2 are interrupted by contrasting STS that changed place as cable was crossed.

Step 3. Same as Step 1, but there are now 2 sections numbered A, the main section & smaller section that shifted with cable crossing. Be sure to bring both groups of STS out to HP. Yarn will float behind Section B STS.

Step 4. Same as Step 2, but with STS in Section B split into 2 groups. Yarn will float behind Section A STS. Rep steps 3 & 4 twice more before crossing cable. This 2nd (& every alt crossing) will return cable STS to their own side. Rep steps 1-4.

To work 3-color version of this cable: Follow directions for Swatch 152 , (using 3 colors & knitting 2 Rs per color) 3x, & then cross cables. To keep yarns from tangling, begin with CC1 on L, & CC2 & CC3 on RT. K 2 Rs with CC1 & leave yarn on L. K 2 Rs with CC2, & leave yarn on L. K 2 Rs with CC3, & return it & CC2 to RT. See charts at RT below.

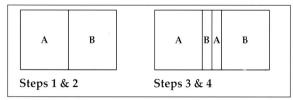

FOR TWO-COLOR CABLE

153. FANCY TWO-COLOR CABLES.

In this more elaborate version of Swatch 152, each color K several stripes. Each step is rep to K a total 6Rs per color, with cables crossing 3x3. Do not wrap where colors join.

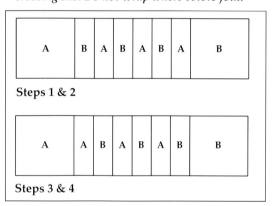

FOR FANCY TWO-COLOR CABLE

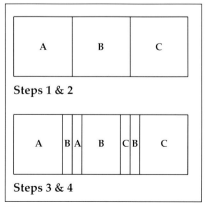

FOR THREE-COLOR CABLE

154. INTARSIA WOVEN CABLE.

This large woven cable is made up of 3x3 cables crossed every 5/Rs, as shown in charted drawing, which indicates paths 4 colors travel as cables are crossed. The basic fabric is actually a stripe design, knitted with an intarsia carriage/cam setting. Short floats are produced on back as each color shifts position, but they are of minor concern & certainly less problematic than cutting yarns & starting them over every 5/Rs.

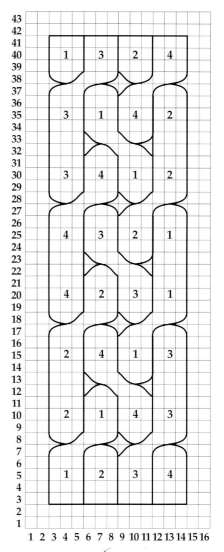

CHART INDICATES *ST* AND *R* NUMBERS AS WELL AS THE PATH EACH COLOR TRAVELS AS THE CABLES ARE CROSSED.

155. *SOLID-COLOR CABLE WORKED ON STRIPED BACKGROUND.*

To work: To K solid-colored cables on K face of striped fabric, K 2 Rs per color, with carr set to slip NDLS in WP & K NDLS in HP. SS is inc to K cable STS to offset fact that they only K 2 of every 4 Rs.

Step 1. COR. Using MC (cable color), *push to HP all NDLS that should K up to, but not including cable NDLS, & K 1 R. Ret carr to RT side, change to largest SS, bring cable NDLS to HP, & K 1 R. Ret carr to RT side & ret to original SS to K next bridge section by bringing those NDLS to HP. Continue changing SS to K each section until all sections have K once. COL.* Rep from * to *, working from L to RT.

Step 2. Using CC, (bring all NDLS to HP except cable NDLS & K 1 R), 2x. For 2-color cable at L, one-half of cable K with each color, & color not in use floats behind other color knitting other half of cable.

To work a DB variation on this cable that embosses cable on P side of striped fabric: K 2 Rs per color, with MB carr K, E/R. RB carr K 2 Rs, then slips 2 Rs. RB SS should be as large as possible to compensate for fact that half as many Rs are being K. Although this 2x2 cable crosses every 4/R, background has knitted 8 Rs on MB. You can easily incorporate diagonal moves with this method.

Double-bed cables

Double-bed arrangements are most commonly used to knit single purl stitches automatically alongside cables or groups of ribbed stitches between them. Practically speaking, when half the stitches on a single bed need to be latched up, you should be working double-bed. The ribber should also be used for cable patterns that rely on wide rib arrangements (swatches 156 and 157) or knit-purl contrast between stitches that are too time-consuming to latch up.

Although you can work with the beds in full pitch so that working needles are directly opposite empty needles, gaps usually form between knits and purls where the yarn stretches across the beds. The full-pitch arrangement is most useful for simple rib patterns or when you want a little more garment ease , because full-pitch ribs are less elastic than half-pitch ribs. Most double-bed cable work, however, especially where stitches make lateral transfers, is done with the beds in half-pitch.

Vertical designs are knitted on needle arrangements that do not change on either the ribber or the main bed. However, with diagonal designs, the needle arrangements change from row to row. When a stitch changes position on one of the beds, a stitch must also be shifted on the other bed in order to maintain the correct relationship between working and nonworking needles. These double transfers make it possible to achieve Aran and other intricate hand-knit patterns on a machine. And, like anything else, they cease to be difficult with practice. This is challenging, interesting knitting for experienced knitters, definitely not beginner territory (swatches 158 and 159 on p. 226 and Swatch 160 on p. 227).

Individual preferences and your machine's capabilities will determine on which bed you knit the cables. I prefer to cross my cables on ribber stitches because I find it easier to keep track of pattern variations. Because the crossing motion is upside-down, however, many people find it easier to cross cables on the main bed as usual.

Double-bed cables can be knitted on either of two half-pitch needle arrangements. Assuming that the cables will be knitted on the ribber bed, only specific needles (following a chart) will be working on the ribber. With all the needles knitting on the main bed, the cables appear as embossed knit stitches on the purl surface of the main-bed fabric. Where ribber needles are working, the fabric knits as a full-needle rib. Where there are no ribber needles working, plain stockinette is produced on the main bed. This is the fastest way to produce double-bed cables, but they tend to look rather flat—especially by hand-knit standards.

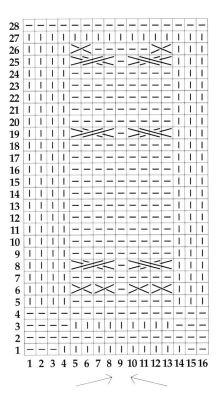

156. OWL CABLES.

There are several hand-knit versions of these owls. I've added a center ST to eliminate strain where cables cross away from each other.

To work: Reform STS in RS 1 & 3 manually, then before R 5, tr appropriate STS to RB (STS 1-4, 14-20, 30-32, etc.). There are no lateral trs necessary, but beds are still in half-pitch. Make 1 extra MB ST at 1 end of groups transferred in order to retain half-pitch NDL arrangement. These cables are crossed on MB. This pat can also be K on SB, reforming all K STS in Rs 5-27 after R 27.

157. CROSSED RIBS.

Center 2 STS in each group rem same, but edge STS alt beds from 1 NDL arrangement to other, every 6/R.

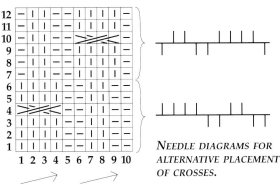

NEEDLE DIAGRAMS FOR ALTERNATIVE PLACEMENT OF CROSSES.

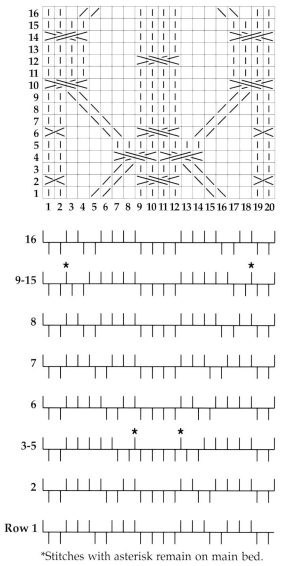

*Stitches with asterisk remain on main bed.

NEEDLE DIAGRAM FOR BOTH BEDS
(IN HALF-PITCH).

158 AND 159. BARBARA WALKER'S SIX-RIB KNOT CABLE II.

To work: Swatch 158 (top) was K with all MB NDLS working so that wherever MB & RB NDLS are working tog, fabric is K in FNR. Chart is read for RB STS, & no MB STS are tr at all. This embossed cable is fast, but rather flat.

Swatch 159 (above) follows same chart, but with modified NDL arrangement so that no MB NDLS work opposite vertical column of rib STS (on NDLS 1, 2, 9, 10, 11, 12, 19 & 20). MB STS on other NDLS must shift as diagonal moves are made on RB to retain half-pitch NDL arrangement and prevent gaps. R-by-R diagram expands chart to indicate working MB NDLS. This effect is more sculpted than Swatch 158 & looks more hand knit.

When there are two or more adjacent needles working on the ribber, main-bed needles are required only at the edges of the group, not behind the entire group. This modified needle arrangement does require lateral stitch transfers on both beds, but it produces a more sculpted cable. For example, when a ribber-bed stitch is decreased on the right of a group, a main-bed stitch must shift to the left to prevent a gap. You may have to decrease stitches or initiate new stitches from time to time, and these beginnings and endings will be less noticeable when done on adjacent, rather than opposite, needles. In some situations you can leave an extra stitch on the main bed without getting an embossed look. I've suggested doing this in rows 3 to 5 and rows 9 to 15 of Swatch 159, where you would no sooner eliminate the center stitch (indicated on the chart by an asterisk) than you would have to initiate a new one in its place because the design shifts back and forth.

Half-pitch needle arrangements not only prevent gaps but also produce a knit-purl fabric that can often pass for hand-knit. Whether cables or plain stitches are formed on one of the beds, there will always be an odd or even complement of needles for each group, from one bed to the other. An odd number of working needles is always opposite an even number of nonworking needles; an even number of working needles is always opposite an odd number of nonworking needles.

When cables are knitted on the ribber, the charts are read in reverse so that solid lines represent the first stitches placed on the needles and the broken lines represent the last. As was noted where diagonal, traveling stitches are described (see p. 189), there should be an even number of nonworking needles between stitches that travel towards each other to intersect or cross. In addition, cables can be crossed from one bed to the other to contrast knit and purl textures. And, if all stitches on the ribber are traveling the same number of needles in the same direction, the swing (racking) method can be used to advance the stitches before crossing them.

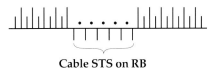

Cable STS on RB

NEEDLE DIAGRAM.

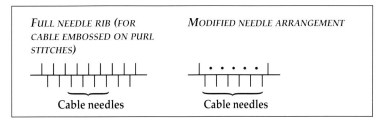

FULL NEEDLE RIB (FOR CABLE EMBOSSED ON PURL STITCHES)	MODIFIED NEEDLE ARRANGEMENT
Cable needles	Cable needles

ALTERNATIVE NEEDLE DIAGRAMS FOR WORKING CABLES ON RIBBER BED.

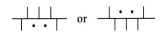

When there is an odd number of working needles on one bed, there will be an even number of nonworking needles on opposite bed, and vice versa.

HALF-PITCH NEEDLE DIAGRAMS TO PRODUCE KNIT-PURL FABRIC.

160. DIAGONAL CABLE.

To work: 6 STS on RB that form cable are shifted 1 NDL to RT A/R, & cable is braided every 3/Rs. When cable must shift & braid on same R, make shift 1st. Pat should be K with beds in half-pitch, & there will be 5 empty MB NDLS opposite 6 cable NDLS. Each time you shift cable STS 1 NDL to RT, also dec 1 ST on MB opposite RT edge of cable NDLS. Opposite L edge of cable NDLS, inc 1 ST on MB by making ST from adj P bar.

2   1

161. CABLED ENGLISH (1x1) RIBS.

To work: NDL Diagram 1 is suitable only for cable that runs length of fabric because K-P alternation of background STS has to be altered to accommodate cable's even number of STS. NDL Diagram 2 can be used anywhere because cable's odd number of STS makes it possible to beg & end blocks of plain STS without affecting background STS. In this case, cables are crossed on MB, which is set to K. All tucking is done on RB.

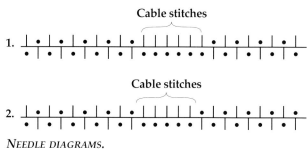

NEEDLE DIAGRAMS.

162. SMOCKED FALSE CABLE.

Susanna Lewis adapted this clever cable from a European hand-knitting magazine. It is worked by K a ribbed fabric (or stockinette with reformed STS) & using a strand of same yarn to sew through ribs, as shown in the drawing. Pull ends of yarn to draw up STS, magically turning plain fabric into cables. Leave enough slack to retain vertical stretch of fabric.

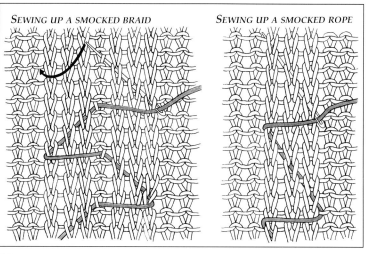

MAKING A SMOCKED CABLE.

Rib patterns are useful for creating smocked fabrics based on 1x1 ribbing. Cables can be crossed on either bed, with pairs split on every alternate row. You can also smock 2x2 ribs, but unless the stitches are very large, there will be more strain and the rows will be harder to knit. And, of course, you can always knit a ribbed fabric to smock by hand later on. A 1x3 rib is a common choice for this. It isn't practical to bead cable smocking, however, as was done with stitches pulled through stitches (see Swatch 49 on p. 117) because you would first have to bead the specific stitches and then cross them.

If you want to combine cables with double-bed tuck stitches, confine the cables to the nontucking bed. The cables should cross on single-knit, stockinette stitches that face empty, nonworking needles on the opposite bed. English ribs (fisherman ribs) and allover tuck patterns are especially suitable for this (Swatch 161).

Mock cables

Mock cables are stitches or techniques that give a cabled effect with less work and strain on the stitches than genuine cables. Some versions are worked right on the machine, while others are completed when the fabric is finished. Closed-eyelet patterns (see p. 183), slip stitch and tuck stitch can all be used to create textured effects that look like cable twists. You can preknit strips or cords and braid them together to sew them to the surface of a fabric, or lace them through the stitches, through eyelets or through other cables. Duplicate stitch, worked in large scale, can also mimic a cable (swatches 162 and 163).

CHART FOR MAKING CABLE STRIPS.

163. MOCK CABLES.

To work: Mock cable on RT is 5-ST cord sewn in duplicate-stitch fashion through a series of eyelets. Other 2 cables are constructed by K 2 strips of fabric with evenly spaced eyelets. Strips are laced through each other & form more even, permanent spiral than simply twisting them tog. Finished pieces can be sewn on, used for horizontal insertion or seamed to another fabric as you K it. Small cable (shown in the drawings) uses 5-ST strips with eyelets every 10/Rs, while larger one uses 10-ST strips (with eyelets spaced every 20/Rs). Assemble cable by alt 2 steps illustrated, with RT sides facing you.

Step 1. Strip B passes down through 1st eyelet on RT edge of Strip A & out to L.

Step 2: Strip A passes around Strip B & up through L edge.

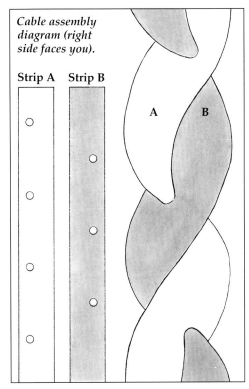

Cable assembly diagram (right side faces you).

Strip A   Strip B

A   B

Appendix: Planning Garments

The collection of fabrics and techniques presented in this book will enable you to produce wonderful sweaters, but unless you plan your garment carefully, you're apt to be disappointed with its fit. All hand-manipulated textures affect the gauge of the knitting, some more than others. Because hand-manipulated techniques tend to be slower than electronic or punchcard patterning, knitters are often tempted to skimp or to guess when it comes to swatching. However, the only entirely reliable way to calculate guage is to knit and measure a large swatch that includes the texture you plan to use for your garment, in the proportion you plan to use it.

If it's impractical to make a swatch (for whatever reason), you can work from the following rules of thumb: For simple, unfitted garments in which exact ease is not an issue, knit the entire garment with one stitch size larger than you would normally use for the yarn with which you're working. If the stitch size cannot be altered, knit the entire garment according to the directions for the next largest size. The texture should absorb the extra ease so that the garment is not, in fact, knit in the larger size.

When the fabric contains a number of cables, add one plain stitch (at the edges of each cable or between them) for every four cable stitches. Count the total number of cable stitches in the garment, then divide by four for the total number of stitches to be added, distributing them evenly throughout the garment sections.

Generally speaking, the more elaborate the texture, the simpler the garment shape should be. This is especially true when the texture distorts the fabric. One solution to working with these fabrics is cut-and-sew construction, using sandwich bands and bindings and basic sewing methods to cover the cut edges. Another solution is panel construction—knitting several strips or sections that are seamed together to form the garment pieces. This construction method is the easiest way to keep track of a variety of textures in a single garment and also to make allowances for differences in gauge, yarns or stitch take-up. The seams can be hidden by adjacent textures.

Elaborate combinations of patterns and textures should be charted so that you know in advance exactly what needs to be done in a given row. You can work with graph paper, in which each square equals one stitch and one row, or two stitches and two rows. If you're working with a charting attachment, do a run-through with no yarn and watch the paper move through the unit. Make notes and draw lines on the paper to indicate where each pattern begins and ends. Pay attention to where the texture will conform to your body when the garment is worn, making adjustments to keep the placement flattering. Make sure that repeats are not left dangling at the neckline or cut off at the armhole. When spacing cables, for example, try to avoid crossings in the first or last rows. If there are six rows between crossings, you should begin and end with three or four plain rows.

Glossary

Adjacent needles
See Needle positions.

Alternate needles
See Needle positions.

Back bed
See Beds, machine.

Beds, machine
Knitting machines have either one or two beds housing the needles, and they are usually designated accordingly as single-bed or double-bed machines. Japanese machines are sold as single-bed machines to which a second bed is added to produce ribbing and double-bed stitches. European machines are routinely available as double-bed units.

Beyond any differences in capabilities from one brand to another, the major distinction between an added ribber bed and a true double-bed machine is that the added ribber cannot knit alone but instead is designed to work in tandem with the knitter bed. By contrast, each bed of a true double-bed machine can be used alone.

When you're working on two beds, the bed clamped to the table and located farther from you is referred to as the back bed, or knitter bed. The bed closer to you is called the front bed, or ribber bed. Additionally, the term *main bed* is generally used to refer to the bed with automatic needle selection or the bed able to knit alone. For all machines except Passap, the back bed is the main bed.

Bias
The diagonal grain of a fabric.

Bind off
Methods of securing stitches as they're removed from the machine to prevent them from raveling. This term can also refer to decreasing. (See Chapter 2 for specific bind-off methods).

Bridge
By placing needles in holding position and interrupting the carriage, it's possible in one row to make selected needles knit plain stitches while others knit patterned, textured or different-sized stitches. (It may take several passes of the carriage to complete a particular texture.) The bridge is the group of plain stitches knitted up to or between the groups of patterning stitches (see p. 58).

Cage
To secure or trap separate or contrast yarn floats to the back of a fabric by vertical weaving (see pp. 104-108).

Cams
The moving metal or plastic parts that make up the needle pathways on the underside of the carriage. The cams can be shifted by the cam lever on the top of the carriage to alter the pathways' configuration and hence change the needles' function and patterning. The cams additionally control stitch size. (Instead of cams, the Bond uses a set of interchangeable fixed keyplates that alter stitch size and enable the machine to form knit stitches.)

Carriage
The carriage contains the cams and also carries the yarn, laying it into the needle hooks while moving across the bed. A single-bed machine has one carriage; a double-bed has a carriage for each bed. The carriage is called "the lock" by Passap, and Japanese manuals may refer to the K or R carriage (knitter or ribber carriage). Some machines additionally have available lace, transfer and intarsia carriages. (Also, some books use the term *cam* or *cambox* to refer to the carriage.)

Cast on
Various methods of initiating stitches on empty needles. Some cast-ons are automatically knitted by the carriage; other must be formed by hand. A cast-on edge will either be "closed" and unable to ravel, or "open" and require further treatment to secure the live stitches. The term *cast-on* may also refer to increasing, that is, initiating new stitches in a piece already in progress on the machine. (See pp. 35-41 for cast-on methods.)

Close rib
See Rib.

Contrast color
A second color or pattern color. Multiple contrasts are referred to as CC1, CC2 and so on.

Cross-bed transfer
Removing a stitch from a needle on one bed and placing it on a needle on the opposite bed. This transfer can be done with hand tools or a special transfer carriage (see pp. 190-195 for specifics).

Decrease
Methods of knitting two or more stitches together to reduce the total number of stitches on the machine and the width of the fabric. (See Chapter 2 for specific decrease methods.)

Eyelet
The hole, or opening, formed by making a decrease and leaving the empty needle in working position so that it casts on in the next row knitted. Eyelets are one of the basic elements of lace knitting.

Fair Isle
Derived from the hand-knit patterns of Fair Isle in Scotland, the name is generically applied in machine knitting to two-color, slip-stitch patterns in which each color knits specific needles while the other color slips and is carried along the back of the work as floats. Patterns can be hand pulled or controlled by a punchcard or electronic system. Some manuals refer to Fair Isle as "knit in."

Float
Yarn carried across the surface of the knitting from one specific stitch to another without knitting the stitch or stitches in between. Floats are typically formed in Fair Isle where two colors knit in the same row, one floating while the other knits.

Free pass
A free pass is produced when the cam setting or release lever allows the carriage to be moved across needles in working position without knitting them. Needles in holding position and upper working position, however, will still be affected by the setting of the return levers.

Free yarn
The yarn between the carriage yarn feeder and the needle hooks.

Front bed
See Beds, machine.

Full-fashioned transfer
Methods of increasing, decreasing and transferring that maintain the same edge stitch by working the increases, decreases or transfers two or more stitches in from that edge.

Full pitch
See Pitch.

Full-needle rib
See Rib.

Gauge
Describes the number of stitches or rows per inch or centimeter in a knitted fabric. Knitting machines are referred to as standard gauge or bulky (or chunky) gauge, according to the needle spacing. Standard-gauge needles are set 4.5mm or 5mm apart. Bulky-gauge needles are set 8mm or 9mm apart (see the chart below).

Hand knit
To form stitches on the machine by manually guiding each needle through the various phases of stitch formation.

Hand pull
To bring needles manually into patterning position, that is, into upper working or holding position, with or without an automatic patterning system.

Half-pitch
See Pitch.

Heel
See Purl loop.

Holding position
See Needle positions.

Increase
Methods for adding new stitches and increasing the width of the knitting (see pp. 34-41).

Knit stitch
See Stitches.

Knit weave
A supplementary yarn, carried in front of the carriage or manually laced through needles in holding position, which weaves through the stitches formed by the main yarn. The effect is that of floats and close interlacements and is seen on the purl face of the fabric, unless you manually place this effect on the knit side.

KNITTING-MACHINE GAUGES.

Gauge	Machine Brand							
	Bond	**Brother**	**Knitking**	**Singer**	**Studio**	**Toyota**	**Passap**	**White**
Bulky/Chunky	8mm	9mm	9mm	9mm	9mm	9mm	—	9mm
Standard	—	4.5mm	4.5mm	4.5mm	4.5mm	4.5mm	5mm	5mm

Notes: 8mm = bulky gauge. 9mm = chunky gauge. 5mm = European standard gauge. 4.5mm = Japanese standard gauge.
Older machines may not conform to this chart. Mid-gauge (6.5mm and 7mm) basic machines are recent additions to the market.

Ladder
A column of enlarged sinker loops formed by the yarn that floats across the space between two working needles when there are one or more nonworking needles between them.

Latch up
To use a tappet, or latch, tool to reform either a dropped stitch or the floats of a ladder (see pp. 69-81).

Lateral transfer
Moving a stitch to a needle on the same bed (see Chapter 7).

Live stitches
Stitches removed from the machine without being bound off and which will run unless they're secured on some type of stitch holder or waste knitting.

Main color
When two colors are used, the main color is generally the background color.

Main yarn
Yarn used for the main knitting, as opposed to scrap yarn, supplementary yarn or contrast yarn, which is used for decorative effects like knit weaving or wrapping.

Make a stitch
To prevent an empty needle from casting on and forming an eyelet, a stitch is made by picking up the purl bar of an adjacent or opposite stitch and hanging it on the empty needle.

Needle numbers
All machines have numbered beds for easy reference. Zero is the central point on the bed, with the numbers increasing on each side of it. There are times when pattern instructions refer to needles and/or stitches by their bed number, for example, Needle 3 left or right. At other times, Needle 3 refers to the third needle in a specific group.

Needle positions
Referring to the chart below, you can see that there are four specific needle positions, each with its own function: nonworking, working, upper working and holding positions.

In nonworking position, the needle butts are all the way back in their channels, and the needles do not knit. This position is the resting place for empty needles, but it can also be used as a holding position for needles with stitches.

DESIGNATIONS FOR NEEDLE POSITIONS.

Needle Position	Machine Brand							
	Bond	**Brother**	**Knitking**	**Singer**	**Studio**	**Toyota**	**Passap**	**White**
Nonworking (NWP)	NWP	A	A	A	A	A	RP (reset position)	0
Working (WP)	WP	B	B	B	B	B	WP	1
Upper working (UWP)	1/2 knit or yellow card	D	D	C	C	C	NDLS WP/ Pushers WP	2
Holding (HP)	HP	E	E	D	D	E	NDLS WP/ Pushers WP	3

In working position, the needle butts are aligned mid-bed, where they can be channeled through the cams as the carriage moves across. The hooks of the needles are even with the bed's front edge.

In upper working position, the needle butts are roughly halfway between working position and the front edge of the bed. On Brother, Knitking and Toyota machines, this is the patterning position. For all other machines (except Passap), this is simply an advanced working position. This is the position used for manually returning specific needles from holding position to working position on all machines (except Passap).

In holding position, needles are pushed all the way forward on the bed with the appropriate levers set to prevent them from knitting. White and all Japanese machines have levers that can be set to leave needles in this position or shunt them back to working position. The Bond has no levers to set, and needles can be returned only by manually placing them in upper working position. (On the Passap, needles are designated as holding while they physically remain in working position. The carriage is set for BX with pushers in rest. Needles are returned to work by placing pushers into working position below them.)

Needles are spoken of not only in terms of bed position but in relation to other needles. That is, a needle may be adjacent, alternate or opposite. Adjacent needles are the needles on a single-bed machine immediately to the left or right of a given needle (see the top diagram at left). On double-bed machines, adjacent needles are located on the opposite bed, one needle to the left or right of a given needle.

Alternate needles are every other needle, that is, the first, third and fifth needles, or second, fourth and sixth needles, and so on. If directions call for knitting on every other needle and then specify manipulating alternate needles in some way, this refers to every fourth needle—those marked X in the middle diagram at left.

Opposite needles are found in double-bed needle arrangements, as shown in the bottom diagram at left. If the machine is in full pitch, the needles of both beds are exactly aligned and the needles on one bed are directly opposite those on the

NEEDLE DIAGRAM: ADJACENT NEEDLES.

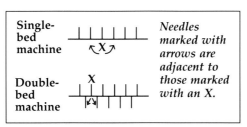

Single-bed machine / Double-bed machine — Needles marked with arrows are adjacent to those marked with an X.

NEEDLE DIAGRAM: ALTERNATE NEEDLES.

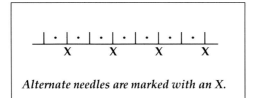

Alternate needles are marked with an X.

NEEDLE DIAGRAM: OPPOSITE NEEDLES.

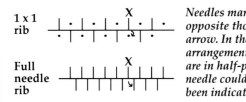

1 x 1 rib / Full needle rib — Needles marked with an X are opposite those marked with an arrow. In the full-needle rib arrangement, because the beds are in half-pitch, the opposite needle could alternatively have been indicated to the left.

other bed. With the beds in half-pitch, the opposite needles are shifted to the left or right of one another by half a needle space.

Nonworking position
See Needle positions.

Opposite needle
See Needle positions.

Pitch
Refers to the alignment of two beds in double-bed knitting. The beds can be in either full pitch or half-pitch.

When a machine is in full pitch, the beds are directly opposite, with all working needles opposite nonworking needles (if working needles were opposite other working needles, the carriages would jam). Pitch is generally indicated in pattern directions by the abbreviation P (though Passap directions call for "Handle Up"). In this book, however, pattern directions always spell out the word pitch, reserving the abbreviation P for "purl stitch."

When a machine is in half-pitch, the working needles on both beds alternate so that opposite needles can be used on both beds without jamming the carriages. Directions call for the beds to be in half-pitch with the abbreviation H (or, for Passap, "Handle Down").

Purl stitch
See Stitches.

Purl loop
The characteristic horizontal bar formed at the neck of all purl stitches. Also called the "heel of the stitch."

Reform
To repair or restructure a stitch that has been accidentally or deliberately dropped.

Rib
Double-bed fabrics and the needle arrangements that produce them, in which working needles alternate beds. Full-needle rib (also called "close rib") uses all the needles on both beds with the beds in half-pitch (see Needle diagram 3 on p. 21), producing a double-knit fabric with moderate stretch. It is generally used for garments rather than welts, or ribs. A 1x1 rib uses every other needle on both beds, so that working needles are opposite nonworking needles, producing an elastic fabric suitable for welts (see Needle diagram 2 on p. 21). A 2x2 rib alternates pairs of needles, while wide ribs alternate larger groups of working needles. Other rib arrangements may call for an irregular setup of needles from one bed to the other. Generally speaking, for all ribs, the wider the rib, the less elastic it tends to be.

Ribber bed
See Beds, machine.

Right side
The knit face of a fabric and the side that lies against the bed of the machine, not facing you, as you knit.

Row count
The number of passes of the carriage as counted by the row counter on the machine. The row count can differ from the actual number of knitted rows if those rows are patterned rather than worked in stockinette, and there are empty passes of the carriage required to produce the pattern effects.

Scrap off

To end the knitting with eight to ten rows of waste knitting, dropping the work from the machine without binding off. The waste knitting serves as a stitch holder and is later removed after the live stitches of the main fabric have been seamed or otherwise secured.

Selection system

The method a machine uses to differentiate needle functions in each row, that is, to produce knit stitches on some needles, for example, while others tuck or slip. There are two basic types of selection systems, manual and automatic. In a manual system, the knitter selects needles by hand before knitting each row. In an automatic system, either a punchcard or an electronic mechanism with light-sensitive and/or magnetic-sensitive scanners selects the needles required for patterning in a given row.

Punchcard systems can automatically select 12-stitch, 24-stitch, 30-stitch or 40-stitch patterns or multiples of these numbers. Electronic systems can usually handle any number of stitches up to 60 without regard to even multiples. Several new knitting machines can perform full-bed (180-stitch or 200-stitch) patterning.

SPLITTING PAIRS.

(XXXX) (XXXX)

Two groups of stitches

XX (XXXX) XX

Same two groups split into pairs for next repeat of pattern

Short-row knitting

Also called "partial knitting," short-row knitting uses holding position to prevent specific needles from knitting with the rest of the needles on the bed. In addition to serving to shape shoulders, darts and hemlines, short-rowing is also used for intarsia designs and sculptural knitting. (Passap refers to this procedure as knitting graduations. Because the needles do not have a holding position on this machine, the effect is worked with pushers and the BX setting.)

Sinker loop

The yarn that extends from and connects one stitch to the next.

Sinker posts

The parts of the bed that separate each needle from the next. They are also called "gate posts" or "pegs" on older Japanese machines, and "flow combs" on European machines.

Slip stitch

See Stitches.

Splitting pairs

A method for dividing stitches from one even-numbered repeat to the next, in which half the stitches from one group are combined with half from an adjacent group. The new group contains the same number of stitches as each of the original groups, but there will be a half-group left over at each end of the row and one less group in the row. The remaining half-groups at the ends of the row may not be large enough to be cabled, twisted or otherwise manipulated and would then knit as plain stitches.

Stitches

Knitting machines form three kinds of stitches: knit, tuck and slip. All other stitches are made by combining, varying or hand-manipulating these basic stitches.

The knit stitch is the basic stitch that all knitting machines are capable of producing. A knit is formed as the needle moves forward and back in its channel, taking on new yarn and pulling the old stitch through the new one (see also p. 6). The front (knit) side of the fabric is smooth and is characterized by vertical columns of V-shapes. The back (purl) side of the fabric is characterized by slight horizontal ridges, as shown in the top drawing at right. A fabric made solely of knit stitches is generally referred to as stockinette or plain knitting.

A tuck stitch is formed as a needle reaches forward just far enough on the bed to take on a new loop of yarn, but not far enough to knit off the stitch it already holds (see also p. 7). Tuck-stitch fabrics are generally textured because of the accumulated loops that knit together (as shown in the middle drawing at right), and·very often either side can be used as the right side.

A slip stitch is formed when a needle does not move forward to take on more yarn. The yarn simply passes the needle by and forms a float on the purl side of the fabric. The stitch that was in the hook of the needle before the row was knitted remains there with the new float below, as shown in the bottom drawing at right. (See also p. 8).

Stockinette

See Stitches.

Take-up

The amount of vertical or horizontal shrinkage caused by the structure of a particular stitch. For example, because tuck stitches cause more vertical take-up than stockinette, a tuck fabric will always be shorter than an equal number of rows knitted in stockinette.

Tuck stitch

See Stitches.

Upper working position

See Needle positions.

Waste yarn or knitting

Waste knitting, worked with waste, or scrap, yarn, provides rows for hanging weights when casting on or dividing sections of a fabric. When used to begin or end knitting with live stitches, it functions as a stitch holder. (*See also* Scrap off.)

Working position

See Needle positions.

Wrapping a needle

When knitting short rows, a hole forms unless the yarn is wrapped around the last needle placed in holding position before the carriage returns to the opposite side. Wrapping can be done manually or automatically. Although needles can also be wrapped for decorative purposes or for casting on stitches, the term *wrap*, when used in knitting directions, always means to prevent a hole from forming in short-row knitting.

Wrong side

The purl face of the fabric, or the side that faces you as you knit at the machine.

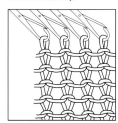

KNIT STITCH (PURL SIDE FACING).

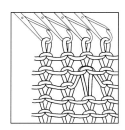

TUCK STITCH (PURL SIDE FACING).

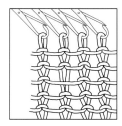

SLIP STITCH (PURL SIDE FACING).

Bibliography

Books

Crosby, Doris. *Aran Knits for the Machine Knitter*. Self-published, 1989. (available from Maple Crest Knits, Maple Crest Rd., E. Parsonfield, Maine 04028).

Davis, Johanna. *Machine Knitting to Suit Your Mood*. London: Pelham Books, 1982.

Emery, Irene. *The Primary Structure of Fabrics*. Washington, D.C.: The Textile Museum, 1966.

Hutchinson, Alles, compiler. *The Garter Bar*. Self-published, 1983. (available from Alles Knitting Publications, P.O. Box 27287, Pittsburgh, Pa. 15235).

Kinder, Kathleen. *Handtooling for the Chunky Knitting Machine*, Volumes I and II. Settle, Yorks, England: The Dalesknit Center, 1987.

Lewis, Susanna. *A Machine Knitter's Guide to Creating Fabrics*. Asheville, N.C.: Lark Books, 1986.

Norman, Mary Louise. *Nicely Knit Cable Classics*. Self-published, 1984. (available from the author at 1310 Clermont St., Denver, Colo. 80220).

Petersen, Grete and Elsie Svennas. *Handbook of Stitches*. New York: Van Nostrand Reinhold Company, 1970.

Peterson, Juanita and Joan Sohlstrom. *Cables and Decreases*. Self-published, 1986. (available from Joan's Custom Knits, Rt. 5, St. Cloud, Minn. 56301).

Walker, Barbara. *Charted Knitting Designs*. New York: Charles Scribner's Sons, 1972.

Periodicals

Knitter's magazine, 68 Middleton St. Watsonia, Victoria 3087, Australia.

Knitting Machine Digest, Hazel Ratcliffe, 142 Frant Rd., Thornton Heath, Surrey CR4 7JU, England.

Knitting Machine News and Views, Alles Hutchinson, P.O. Box 27287, Pittsburgh, Pa. 15235.

Nihon Vogue and *ZaZa*, Yo's Needlecraft, 940 E. Dominguez, Carson, Calif. 90746.

Western Knitting Machine Guide (WKMG), P. O. Box 1527, Vashon, Wash. 98070.

The following periodical publications are available from local knitting-machine dealers or mail-order catalogs. Although each of them is published by a specific knitting-machine manufacturer, the information can usually be applied to other machines as well.

Brother Fashion, Brother International Corp., 8 Corporate Pl., Piscataway, N. J. 08854.

Keyplate News, P.O. Box 450, Stockton, N. J. 08559.

Knitking Magazine, 1128 Crenshaw Blvd., Los Angeles, Calif. 90019.

Passap Modelbooks, Passap Knitting Machines, Inc. USA, 271 West 2950 South, Salt Lake City, Utah 84115.

The following magazines, available in many yarn shops and libraries, occasionally feature articles related to machine knitting.

Cast On, Knitting Guild of America, P.O. Box 1606, Knoxville, Tenn. 37901.

Fashion Knitting, All American Crafts, 70 Sparta Rd., Sparta, N. J. 07871.

Fiberarts, 50 College St., Asheville, N. C. 28801.

Knitters, Golden Fleece Publications, 126 S. Phillips, Sioux Falls, S. D. 57102.

Schaffhauser, published in Europe and available only at yarn shops.

Simplicity Knitting, Simplicity Pattern Company, 200 Madison Ave., New York, N. Y. 10016.

Threads magazine, The Taunton Press, 63 S. Main St., Box 5506, Newtown, Conn. 06470-5506.

Vogue Knitting, 161 Avenue of the Americas, New York, N. Y. 10013.

Sources of Supply

In addition to the small accessories and tools available from knitting-machine companies, you should be aware of the following machine-knitting suppliers:

DanNa Enterprises
10025 S.W. 122nd Pl.
Vashon, Wash. 98070
(206) 567-4137
MT transfer tools (6-prong and every-other-needle) and Stitch Tenders (12-prong).

Hallandall, Inc.
Box 91, Dept. SG
Rembrandt, Iowa 50576
(712) 286-KNIT
Jolie Unicorn, transparent design graphs.

Knit-O-Rama
2630 Eaton Rapids Rd.
Lansing, Mich. 48911
(517) 887-0060
Capped stitch holders for Japanese standard and bulky machines.

Kruh Knits Corporation
P.O. Box 1587
Avon, Conn. 06001
(203) 674-1043
Catalog of books, accessories and tools, including Easy Bob yarn bobbins. Catalog fee is $3.00.

Needle Nuts
22 Jefferson St.
Brookville, Ohio 45309
(513) 833-5490
Double latch tools, combination tools.

The Netcraft Company
2800 Tremainsville Rd.
Toledo, Ohio 43613
(419) 472-9826
Plastic netting shuttles.

WKMG The Machine Knitters Source
P.O. Box 1527
Vashon, Wash. 98070
(206) 463-2088
Books, *WKMG* Magazine and miscellaneous small accessories.

Yo's Needlecraft
940 E. Dominguez, Suite Q
Carson, Calif. 90746
(213) 515-6473
Japanese knitting magazines, including *Nihon Vogue* books; Bunka brushes; "bird" clips; and miscellaneous hand-knitting, crochet and finishing tools.

The following distributors represent the major brands of knitting machines sold in the United States. They sell their machines and accessories through local dealers and usually try to direct any inquiries to these dealers as well.

Brother International Corp.
200 Cottontail Lane
Somerset, N.J. 08875
(800) 284-2844

Elna, Inc.
(Knitcraft knitting machines)
7642 Washington Ave. South
Minneapolis, Minn. 55344

Kimberley Mkt. Corp.
Bond knitting machines
P.O. Box 450
Stockton, N.J. 08559
(800) 548-2663

Knitking Corporation
1128 Crenshaw Blvd.
Los Angeles, Calif. 90019
(213) 938-2077

Passap Knitting Machines, Inc. USA
271 West 2950 South
Salt Lake City, Utah 84115
(800) PAS-KNIT

Singer Company
135 Raritan Center Pkwy.
Edison, N.J. 08837
(201) 632-6700

Toyota Knitting Machines
Newton's Knits, Inc.
2100 Howell, 209
Anaheim, Calif. 92806
(714) 634-9116

VWS, Inc.
(Studio and White knitting machines)
11760 Berea Rd.
Cleveland, Ohio 44111
(800) 367-0518

Index

Editor: Christine Timmons
Designer: Deborah Fillion
Copy/production editor: Ruth Dobsevage
Art/production manager: Robert Olah
Layout artist: Connie Huebner
Illustrator: Lee Hov
Editorial assistant: Maria Angione
Art assistants: Jodie A. Delohery, Iliana Koehler
Computer-applications specialist: Margot Knorr
Computer graphics: Jeanne Criscola, Andrea DiFranza
Print production manager: Peggy Dutton
Indexer: Harriet Hodges

Typeface: Palatino
Paper: Warren LOE Dull, 70 lb., neutral pH
Printer and binder: Arcata Graphics/Kingsport, Kingsport, Tennessee